JOURNALS AND LETTERS

OF

STEPHEN MACKENNA

Stephen MacKenna at forty. From an oil painting by Amy Drucker.

JOURNALS AND LETTERS OF STEPHEN MACKENNA

EDITED WITH A MEMOIR BY

E. R. DODDS

AND A PREFACE BY

PADRAIC COLUM

CORACLE PRESS

San Rafael, Ca

Second, Facsimile edition,
Coracle Press, 2007
First edition, William Morrow & Company, N.D.

For information, address:
Coracle Press, P.O. Box 151011
San Rafael, California 94915, USA

ISBN 978-1-59731-318-6 (pbk.: alk. paper)
ISBN 978-1-59731-330-8 (pbk.: alk. paper)

TO

ALL THOSE FRIENDS OF STEPHEN MACKENNA WHO HAVE SPENT TIME AND TROUBLE IN PROVIDING MATERIAL FOR THIS BOOK; AND IN PARTICULAR TO TWO PERSONS WITHOUT WHOSE HELP ITS PREPARATION WOULD HAVE BEEN IMPOSSIBLE

MARGARET NUNN

AND

SIR ERNEST DEBENHAM

CONTENTS

LIST OF ILLUSTRATIONS

PREFACE

BY PADRAIC COLUM

THE first time I saw Stephen MacKenna was in the office of the *Freeman's Journal*, in one of the shabby dens in which a leader-writer confined himself between 11 p.m. and 2 a.m. He entered the den and was startled to see me waiting there ; he did not know who I was, and it seemed that I bore a striking resemblance to a friend of his who was dead—to Lionel Johnson. He got over his surprise, and I told him my name and mentioned that Arthur Griffith had told me I ought to step in to see him when I happened to be in the *Freeman* office at night : Stephen MacKenna had only recently come back to Dublin, and I was then doing an occasional literary article for the *Freeman*.

As I walked home after my talk with him I felt that Stephen MacKenna was one of the most extraordinary persons I had ever met—extraordinary, but winning. The trait that mainly impressed me was his eloquence. I don't mean to say that he had burst into oratory or had declaimed anything. But his was a speech that was ready and apt, original and witty ; his mind was like a violin string, his voice vivacious and many-cadenced, often taking on the mounting enunciation of the Gaelic speaker. Yet this was not a public man : he was diffident, with a courtesy that respected the personality of others. I suppose he was about forty at the time, with blue-black hair, an odd face that showed marked cheek-bones, an open mouth covered with a moustache, and quickly-moving dark eyes—a face that had rapid changes of expression. I thought that perhaps he was an aloof and fitful man who, because he was so natively Irish, could be—as indeed he was—gay and companionable.

After that first meeting I used often to see him at night in the office. He wrote leaders, as I have said—not on political matters but on "off" subjects. He would have liked to treat these "off" subjects with wit and erudition : his ideal was the free personal comment of the Parisian journalist. But needless to say he got little opportunity to write thus in a journal that was given its tone by the Archbishop of Dublin. Often at two o'clock in the morning when we had written our leaders (for I began to do an occasional one) we would walk to Donnybrook together through the deserted streets. I said to him once, "It is worth while being out at this time to hear the curlews that are flying over the city." He looked up in amazement. "I thought the curlew was purely literary —invented by Yeats : 'O Curlew, cry no more into the air!' Do you mean to say that these are curlews I have been hearing?" This gave me the notion that Stephen MacKenna paid little attention to the sights and sounds of nature.

He had come back to Dublin from America, Greece, Paris. He had had a short but very successful career as a special correspondent under Pulitzer. But before that success he had been in low water in New York. I recall an encounter with a member of an oath-bound society whose affiliation in America was with the Clan-na-Gael. He told me how once at a meeting of the organisation he had got into conversation with a remarkable stranger. After the meeting they walked along a couple of streets together, and my informant invited the other to have a glass of beer and a sandwich in a café. When they had done that the stranger said, "I don't mind telling you now that this is the first bite I've had in two days." His name was Stephen MacKenna.

Stephen lived in New York amongst a Greek population —florists, waiters and the like—and his experience at this time deepened his Hellenism. The Greek which he had learned at school hadn't meant very much to him. But in the Greco-Turkish war he had come to know and love the Greek vernacular—it was his chief gain from a disappointing adventure. I asked him once about the excitements of warfare (for in those days war was still romantic). He said, " It was like waiting for a train at Mullingar."

It was with Arthur Griffith and Seumas O'Sullivan that I first went to the MacKenna house, 5 Seaview Terrace, Donnybrook. Saturday was their at-home evening : Stephen did not have to write his leader that night. Of course he stayed up as late as if he had been in the office ; and next morning he would be roused earlier than his wont by his Irish-speaking boy knocking at his door and announcing " *Aifreann Dé*," so he would have to get up to attend ten o'clock mass. That first evening, I remember, Mrs. MacKenna played for us : she was an accomplished pianist, and for her the drawback to living in Dublin was the infrequency of concerts there. She played some of MacDowell's pieces ; it was the first time I had heard anything of this American composer's. The talk that night was mainly about Gaelic League activities. For the MacKenna house in those days was the headquarters of a branch of the Gaelic League, actually if not literally. There the enthusiasts of the movement met on a regular afternoon—Thursday, I think : urban and world affairs were discussed in Gaelic ; words were discovered or made up ; if one came short of a word one was permitted to use a French or a German one, but English was under *geis*. Mrs. MacKenna, American-born and French-educated, was absorbed no less than MacKenna himself in these revival activities.

This is perhaps the place to say something about Marie MacKenna. Slender, sallow-faced, with a wide mouth and dark eyes, dressed in bright colours, with an odd spontaneity in speech and movement, she stood out in any group of Dublin women. At that time she went about with a huge hound, a Great Dane that she had given a Gaelic name to—" Lochlannach." One evening I sat beside her at a concert and we began our conversation, as was the fashion, in elementary Gaelic. Suddenly she burst into tears, saying something in a whisper that seemed to me to be out of a saga. And no wonder it seemed that, for what she said was the very words of a saga—" Lochlannach is dead."

Stephen had always been a strong Irish nationalist. With a great deal of diffidence, as one admitting a dark secret, he once spoke of his father who had been an officer in the British Army and wrote adventure stories which had been popular. But like many of the old Catholic and propertied families, his had kept contacts with the services of the European states. Was it an uncle or a grand-uncle of his who had been the Austrian governor of an Italian city and had forgotten his English? It must have been a grand-uncle. I remember Stephen describing for Marie the speech of this old military gentleman. Stephen had joined the remnants of the old Fenian organization and had hoped to have a part in an insurrection. At this period his nationalism was concentrated round the work of the Gaelic League. He and Mrs. MacKenna, a newly married pair, had sat together of nights on the benches of a county council school in London learning Gaelic. Now, back in Dublin, he was saddened to find that the intellectual leaders—men like W. B. Yeats and Arthur Griffith—took only a perfunctory interest in the language revival. To him the language movement meant the whole of Irish nationalism: that some day there would be no response to a Gaelic sentence, that the name Cuchulain would awaken no echo in any breast—this was to him the most dire of possibilities. He regarded every other movement in Ireland as irrelevant beside the language one: Home Rule, Women's Franchise—what use would they be if Gaeldom ceased to live? He became mournful when he spoke of that peril, and his intimates were ashamed that they had any other interest except the language one.

At MacKenna's evenings I would meet "A. E.," occasionally Arthur Griffith, occasionally John Eglinton, occasionally Arthur Lynch, in the early days John Synge who had been a comrade of Stephen's in Paris, Joseph Hone, Rudmose Brown, Osborn Bergin, Thomas Bodkin. The talk was the best that could be heard anywhere—but how difficult it is to get down the suggestion of good talk ! Stephen shrank from personalities or anything approaching gossip, so there was never anything malicious or petty tossed about on those evenings. He had also a scholarly fastidiousness that made him turn away from what in the realm of ideas was wide of the mark. He was, although he could commit himself to action, essentially a scholar, a man who could become absorbed in a subject as remote, say, as the problem of Aryan words in cuneiform inscriptions ; and this scholar's discipline and knowledge gave substance to what he said. But he was incapable of saying it pedantically or dully : there was passion, wit and grace in everything he said. Reflectiveness and activism seemed to be in conflict in him : there were his remote interests—the abiding one being Plotinus—and there were the swift images that came one after the other in his sentences.

I remember one evening in which there was much gay laughter from Stephen. John Eglinton maliciously quoted a few things Goethe had said against Catholicism and Irish Nationalism. " An Olympian mind ! ": I was misled into committing myself to the legend of the Goethean wisdom on every subject. Marie MacKenna had no doubts about the profundity of the sage who had talked with Eckermann. She became very solemn, very receptive, as Stephen took down the *Conversations* and opened it at random. The page yielded something very much like the uplift written by some fashionable prophet for an American magazine. Marie MacKenna and I were greatly distressed and insisted he should turn to the middle pages. He did, and produced something hopelessly banal. We took the book from him and began our search for the passages of shining wisdom. Stephen made us read out our selections, and he would laugh and ask us, " Isn't that just what we do our best to prevent ourselves from saying?" We had to admit it was, after we had gone through a hundred pages, each page bespelled so that nothing came to our eyes save what might go into the last paragraph of a *Freeman* "off" leader. The "Olympianness" of Goethe was distasteful to Stephen: he had an uneasy feeling that sometime he himself might begin to pontificate.

He would speak of what his heart was set on doing, but in an impersonal way. Talking about Plotinus he would wonder how much of the obscurity in the *Enneads* was due to the subtlety of the thought and how much to the general human idiocy from which philosophers were not immune. What passage in his talk do I best remember? One, I think, that brought over to me something of the nobility that is in Pindar's odes. He was working on a Gaelic version of certain of these, hoping that with the help of some Gaelic speaker who had knowledge of traditional poetry he might recreate the Greek in Gaelic. He showed how the conventionalized passages that are nonsensical in English could go magnificently into such a conventionalized Gaelic as we find in the "runs" in the longer folk-tales. "The best of all things is water"—how real and how significant that might become in Gaelic! He went on to talk of contrasts in the genius of languages, and gave lists of place-names to illustrate them. I remember now only one contrasted pair, Verona and Enniskerry: both beautiful names, but one like a rich fabric and the other, he said, like a coloured rag caught on a hedge—for a coloured rag on a hedge is beautiful. Then he talked about the Greek and Gaelic words for the moon: both meant "the Shiner" and could be contrasted with the English or French names which are expressive of glamour and beaminess. He could speak memorably upon such themes.

This was a period in Dublin when intellectual contacts were easily and happily made. It closed abruptly: Home

Rule and Carsonism came into the foreground ; the Gaelic League branches turned themselves into volunteer corps and began to arm and drill. Stephen MacKenna, to the grief and distraction of his wife, began to have fits of dangerous illness. He rallied. But the mood of Dublin had now changed, and his with it : more and more, though a sick man, he became an activist. The illuminating, exciting, delightful evenings in 5 Seaview Terrace went amongst the Remembrances of Things Past. Everything changed—even Stephen MacKenna's theological beliefs which seemed so well-founded. Yet one thing remained : his dream of somehow uniting his Hellenism and his Gaelicism. On the opening page of his Plotinus appears a sentence in Gaelic. It reproduces the most noble of all dedications, that of *The Annals of the Four Masters :* TO THE GLORY OF GOD AND THE HONOUR OF IRELAND.

MEMOIR

Prefatory Note.

Stephen MacKenna's working life was divided among three countries, and was further broken by two complete changes of occupation and by continual changes of residence. When he died, he left behind him no wife, child or lifelong friend ; no near relative, save two brothers[1] *in Australia who since childhood had seen him only at rare intervals ; and with the exception of the 1907-9* Journal *no papers of any considerable biographical value. He left instead a legend. In the Memoir which follows I have endeavoured to recover and present the facts underlying the legend. But while I believe that up to a point I have succeeded in this aim, I am conscious of certain unfilled gaps, particularly in the early part of MacKenna's life, for which relatively little documentary evidence was discoverable ; and it would be too much to hope, the individual memory being so fallible, that in combining material drawn from the memories of a great diversity of people I have admitted no error of fact, date or emphasis.*

[1] One of these, Robert MacKenna, died a few weeks later.

MEMOIR

" Le bonheur n'est pas chose aisée : il est très difficile de le trouver en nous et impossible de le trouver ailleurs." CHAMFORT.

I

" I DON'T know anything about the MacKennas, and frankly I care less : I abhor all that sort of thing : one of the very few things in the Ireland of to-day that really pleases me is that cobblers and ploughers are at the top and that no one talks, as far as I know, of any social glory or birth-ban." So wrote Stephen MacKenna to a sister-in-law in 1924. His pedigree is nevertheless of some interest. His father, Captain Stephen Joseph MacKenna, had in him the blood of three long-established Irish Catholic families—the MacKennas, lords of Truagh in the county of Monaghan and alleged descendants of " blameless " Enna Ceinnsealach, a fifth-century Irish king ; the Taaffes of Smarmore Castle, Co. Louth ; and the Aliaga Kellys, a dynasty of Dublin merchants who could trace their descent through 30 generations from an ancestor who fought at Clontarf. He inherited a tradition of Ascendancy politics. The captain's father, Theobald MacKenna, Q.C., had been Assistant Under-Secretary for Ireland, and his brother John was at the time of his death secretary to the then Lord-Lieutenant. Among his forebears was that Theobald MacKenna who published in 1793 " An Essay on Parliamentary Reform, and on the Evils likely to ensue from a Republican Constitution in Ireland," and in 1799 "Constitutional Objections to the Government of Ireland by a separate Legislature." [1]

[1] Stephen MacKenna had a distaste for this ancestor of his ; but it should be mentioned to his credit that he founded a society " for the purpose of promoting unanimity among Irishmen, and removing religious prejudices."

Captain MacKenna appears to have had qualities not wholly explained by this decorous ancestry. Exceptionally tall and very goodlooking, with a shock of red hair and a voice of singular charm, he was by all accounts a man of violent temper, fantastic humour, and volcanic changes of mind. As an officer of the 28th Infantry, known as the Kinegad Slashers, he displayed such gaiety of spirit that on more than one occasion disaster was averted only through the exercise of his father's political influence. After seeing service in India he finally, upon a sudden resolution, took French leave from his regiment and offered his sword to Garibaldi. Italy furnished him with many adventures, military and other : these he recorded in a singularly candid diary which startled his family after his death but is now unhappily lost. Returning about 1869 to England he married Elizabeth Mary Deane, a girl of mixed English and Irish descent, and set about perpetuating his name. But his world had changed: the mid-Victorian age of respectability had set in ; his father was dead, and his mother, a woman of notable piety, had stopped his allowance and cut him out of her will. Upon the advice of his friend T. P. O'Connor, the ex-Slasher had recourse for a livelihood to journalism and the composition of romantic fiction for the young—tales of military adventure in which the narrator is usually a gallant but unlucky soldier of fortune, heir to a great estate from whose enjoyment his youthful escapades have unwarrantably excluded him. So it came about that the younger Stephen's earliest memories were of rejected manuscripts plumping through the letter-box of the small suburban house in Liverpool where his father endeavoured to discipline and feed an increasing mob of children.

In the year 1883, the number of his offspring having reached ten—eight boys and two girls—Captain MacKenna suddenly died from an attack of the malaria which he had contracted in India. Since the ten were almost wholly without financial provision, two unmarried sisters of the Captain, Miss Katie and Miss Lizzie MacKenna, who lived at Ramsgate, undertook the upbringing of two of the older boys—Stephen, who had been born on the 15th of January, 1872, and Robert, who was by a year or two his junior. They were entrusted at first to " an old humbug of a private tutor " ; later Stephen was sent to Ratcliffe College, a small Catholic boarding-school in Leicestershire, and Robert to St. Joseph's, Mill Hill.

The young Stephen is described by a schoolfellow as " a quiet, retiring boy with a round, plump baby-face of olive hue that was saved from commonplaceness by beautiful brown eyes." He was frail and unathletic : " I never played any game, was perhaps foolishly dispensed as too delicate or at least too pulseless (I have the slowest pulse in the world) ; and this means," he wrote near the close of his life, " that I have no escape now from thinking or brooding." [1] Physical enterprises were apt to end disastrously : he went swimming in the river Wreak, had a seizure, and was all but drowned ; he took up gymnastics, broke an ankle in falling from a trapeze, and limped for the rest of his schooldays. In compensation he developed a precocious interest in literature and politics. He spent his pocket-money on books, in which he had the sort of taste that his contemporaries found " queer ": one of them remembers him surreptitiously reading Boswell's *Life of Johnson* night after night throughout prep. His politics too were " queer ": in the school debating-society which he helped to found he argued passionately that the complete independence of Ireland must and would be brought to pass within his lifetime—an idea as foreign to English Catholic thought in the 'eighties as it was to the family tradition of the MacKennas. Such a boy could hardly be very popular, even if he had not added to his offence by a manner that was " reserved and somewhat haughty "; but he made one or two friends, and his combination of moral courage with a ready and

[1] Letter to Robert MacKenna, January 27, 1931.

devastating wit appears to have extorted from the rest of his schoolfellows a measure of respect—there is at any rate no record of his having been subjected to more than the normal brutalities of a Victorian boarding-school. In the class-room he showed linguistic and literary gifts which impressed his contemporaries : one of them recalls with delight after forty-five years his *viva voce* renderings of the *Georgics* and the *Antigone* into a crisp and shapely English. In mathematics and science he had no interest and made no headway : algebra, in particular, he found " not only loathsome but even, in principle, unintelligible." [1]

It was decided that he should take a classical degree at London University. He matriculated in 1889, but remained at Ratcliffe for another year to read for his " Intermediate," nominally the first university examination, but one which was often taken before leaving school. What happened next may appear odd to those unfamiliar with the practical working of the British examination system. At this very ordinary pass test the candidate who was later to be described by Sir John Squire as " one of the greatest prose writers of our time " [2] failed to satisfy the examiners in English, which had been his best subject at school. The grounds for their dissatisfaction are not known. It seems possible that the admirer of Dr. Johnson said what he thought about English literature and not what his text-books advised him to think. Be that as it may, the decision of these examiners was unfortunate : almost certainly classical scholarship is to-day the poorer for it ; quite certainly it robbed the young MacKenna of a training in method whose absence he felt cruelly in later life.

For he declined, or was not permitted, to knock a second time at the gate of academic learning. Instead, he followed the example of a school friend and the persuasion of his aunts, and entered a religious order. His novitiate was of brief duration. Within a few months his friend

[1] *Journal*, February 1908. [2] *London Mercury*, May 1934.

received a letter from him. " Dear Charles," it ran, " I have left W——.[1] It was the damn ' discipline ' did it : we had to take the beastly thing every morning : I couldn't stand it. It wasn't the pain, of course—I didn't mind that. It was the absurdity of the thing, the coddology of the thing—whacking oneself as if one were a lazy old donkey ! " So ended the first phase of Stephen MacKenna's religious experience.

It may be supposed that by this time Aunt Lizzie and Aunt Katie felt considerable disappointment and some twinges of anxiety. Their nephew would not, it seemed, become a man of God ; he could not, it appeared, become a man of learning : he must become something quickly, and if possible something safe. The family was consulted. From his mother's people, who had hereditary connections with Irish banking, there came an eminently safe suggestion. It was accepted. A place was found for him in the Munster and Leinster Bank, and for the next five or six years he occupied a stool in the Dublin branch of that institution. It is improbable that he made a good clerk : I have never known any man more impatient of routine, more careless of everyday detail, or more completely innocent in all financial matters than Stephen MacKenna. But Irish banks are tolerant.

For the boy himself they were years of angry discontent. He imagined a bitter little epitaph :

HERE LIES STEPHEN MACKENNA

God made him a Man but he died a Bank Clerk.

The Irish Sea cut him off from brothers and school friends : his home was the small house in Rathmines where his aunts, " two little Dresden china ladies " now verging on middle age, lived henceforth in a genteel seclusion. They loved their disappointing nephew, and they had his affection to the end of their days : he admired not only the old-fashioned prettiness of their

[1] The place of novitiate.

manners but the essential goodness of their hearts: a letter describes one of them in later years making tea for a couple of beggars—" she stands behind her lace-curtains looking down on them and in spirit drinking their tea with them as they sit on a dustbin which seems to be kept there in the front garden for that only purpose."[1] But if there were kind hearts behind the lace curtains there was no play of life there, nor any stir of ideas.

Nevertheless these years confirmed for MacKenna the importance of two discoveries which he had already made in his schooldays—his Irish nationality, and his gift as a translator. He formed the habit of spending Sundays at the house of his father's cousins, the Aliaga Kellys; and there he met for the first time people to whom Ireland was not a comic appanage of England but a spiritual entity in bondage to alien ideas. His response was quick and passionate: it was in his nature to feel an immediate sympathy for underdogs and for revolutionary policies. " There is deep down in me something lawless," he wrote later in his journal[2]: " always, whether my mind wills it or not, I find myself on the side not of the weeder but of the weeds. . . . I like wild growth in gardens, and am not angry when in nations there is tumult and even crime." Fenianism was such a wild growth, and for all his English schooling the young Stephen welcomed it. But while his mind was fertilised by these strange seeds it was also incubating others, whose original implanters were perhaps the Rosminian Fathers at Ratcliffe College. Their earliest fruit was an English version of the *Imitatio Christi*, which was published by a Dublin bookseller in 1896. Of this piece of work he wrote long afterwards, " Dipping into it here and there, I see that I made it less subtly true to the original and less emotionally rich than I had thought: I was only a schoolboy when I did it: I still remember the fervour of exultation in which I spent

[1] To Mrs. A. F. Dodds, September 12, 1923. Cf. letter 33.

[2] June 27, 1907.

the ten pounds it brought me."[1] The volume does not bear the translator's name, which could not, it appears, "go into a base layman's rendering of a book so semi-sacred."

It is proper to add that not all of the young man's evenings were spent in study, meditation, or the society of his aunts. In Dublin, as later in London and Paris, his exercise and pleasure was to roam the humbler streets, listening to the talk of children on the doorstep of a tenement house or mingling with a Saturday-night shopping crowd, merging himself in their life and occasionally striking friendship with a man or woman who attracted him. One typical story of such an encounter seems to belong to this first Dublin period. He had made acquaintance with a prostitute by the canal bank, and the two were walking homeward together when they passed the open door of a Catholic church. MacKenna inconsequently[2] suggested that they should drop in and say a Hail Mary. "Is it me?" said the girl, "— me to go into that place? Sure the candles that stand and burn there before the Blessed Virgin would go black out if the likes of me was in it." Her companion went home enraged against the Irish puritanism which infected the Church with the social taboos of the drawing-room and built so dark a mental barrier between sinner and intercessor.

It was in 1895 or 1896 that Stephen MacKenna decided to give his epitaph the lie. His eldest brother, Theobald MacKenna, who on his father's death had started life at thirteen as a printer's devil, was now a journalist on the staff of the *Daily Chronicle* working hard to pay for the schooling of the two youngest brothers, Octavian and Myles, and to maintain a home in Brixton for them and his mother. The rest of the family were by this time either

[1] Letter to E. R. Debenham, 1913 or 1914.

[2] MacKenna was not at this time, or at any time, addicted to "slumming." He cultivated the society of the poor because he liked it, not with the intention of conferring spiritual benefits.

dead or dispersed in various parts of the world. With Theobald's help Stephen obtained a reporter's job on a London newspaper, and he joined the struggling household in Brixton. For a year he wrote up fires and street accidents and visited the scenes of murders. When not thus employed, he spent his time in the picture galleries, in the British Museum, among the book-stalls in the Farringdon market, or in long rambles eastward through the foreign quarters. Much of his earnings went on books: he would eat nothing all day and return home late at night, exhausted but triumphant, his arms laden with books and books bulging from every pocket. He joined the Irish Literary Society and the revolutionary association called Young Ireland, and began to be known as a speaker at Fenian gatherings. His schoolboy brother Octavian—naturally a harsh critic—thought poorly of his oratory ; but he had, or imagined he had, the compensating glory of attracting the notice of the police—the house in Brixton was said to be watched, and for a time he went about in the thrilling expectation of arrest.

He was not arrested ; and he found he did not care for reporting.[1] In the winter of 1896-7 he was offered a small post as Paris correspondent of an English Catholic journal and embraced the chance with joy. His friend Richard Best (now Chief Librarian of the Irish National Library), whom he had met first at the Irish Literary Society, was already established in Paris, and the two young men occupied adjacent *appartements* in the rue d'Assas. Through Best and through the branch of Young Ireland which Maud Gonne had created, MacKenna soon became intimate with the small Irish colony. It was an interesting group of writers, journalists and conspirators : besides Maud Gonne herself, it included the old Fenian, John O'Leary, " that flaming, ineffective lover of Ireland and of Irish freedom,"[2] Arthur Lynch (then Paris corre-

[1] Cf. *Journal*, September 27, 1907.

[2] MacKenna in *Irish Statesman*, November 3, 1928.

spondent of the *Daily Mail*) and his wife, and J. M. Synge.[1]

With Synge and with the Lynches the newcomer established a fast friendship. Lynch and MacKenna were men of oddly similar stamp : each was a journalist with the interests and the gifts of a scholar and the temperament of a mediaeval knight errant ; Lynch was presently to fight for the freedom of the Boers, as MacKenna for the freedom of the Greeks ; they were to die within a few days of each other, both of them voluntary exiles from the country they loved best, and neither was to leave on the world a mark proportionate to his ability. Synge and MacKenna on the other hand made, in appearance, a strange pair, the one shy, silent and morose, the other a born talker ; but they had in common an ironic humour, a passionate interest in the problem of style, and an unresting curiosity about the secrets of religious experience. Of their alliance Lynch wrote many years later,[2] " The man who knew Synge best was Stephen MacKenna, and Synge's first book bears evident marks of MacKenna's influence, or, as I should say perhaps, MacKenna's active help. Stephen MacKenna had himself pushed modesty and diffidence to a higher extreme than Synge, and we have but the scattered fragments of one capable of achieving enduring fame. Little of his imagination and delicate spirit remains except the recollection in a few minds of conversation, the richest, the most charming, at times the most wonderful, I have ever heard."

MacKenna himself repudiated the suggestion that he had given Synge " active help." " We were the most intimate of comrades," he wrote,[3] " and talked days and nights through, and mainly on literature and the technique of it ; but except for *The Aran Isles* and his critical

[1] An account of this group and its doings will be found in Bourgeois' *John Millington Synge and the Irish Theatre*, p. 20 ff. Cf. also Arthur Lynch, *The Story of my Life*, p. 144 ff.

[2] *Irish Statesman*, October 20, 1928 (abbreviated here).

[3] *ibid.*, November 3, 1928.

work for some London journal—*The Speaker*, I think—I never knew what he had on the loom. He often read me an isolated sentence from the sheet on his Blick—often an entire day's work—but I never knew where the sentence fitted. I did know, curiously, a good deal about his unpublished work ; I imagine because he never intended it for publication. He gave me once an immense wad of his verse to read and return ; we never spoke of it ; I have wondered what he did with it." In a private letter to Lynch of about the same date he remarks, " Synge used to get, I remember, very angry when I disliked something which he liked ; I think, however, he often accepted the adverse judgement, tacitly."

Both Synge and MacKenna were distressingly hard up. " How do those two young men live ? " said an inquisitive person. " Oh, Synge lives on what MacKenna lends him, and MacKenna lives on what Synge pays him back." Synge in fact lived on an annuity of some £40 a year, which he endeavoured with little success to supplement by free-lance journalism. MacKenna's " Paris Letter " brought him fifteen shillings a week ; and to this he presently added a " Rome Letter " which he compiled in the rue d'Assas out of newspaper cuttings and a fertile imagination. It was not enough. Synge is reported as looking " ghastly " at this time from under-nourishment, and MacKenna used to say that he owed to Lynch (who would ask the two to supper as often as he decently could) " his almost weekly rescue from starvation." It seems likely that both men laid in these years the foundations of future ill-health.

But, poor as he was, MacKenna was not too poor to help the destitute. Prowling one night on the Seine embankment he fell into talk with one of the homeless men who sleep on the benches there. His new acquaintance proved to be an Armenian doctor, by name Elmassian, whose socialist activities had made him a refugee. MacKenna loved men who preferred their conscience to their comfort : he took the Armenian home, gave him bed and board, and assisted him to pursue his studies at the Pasteur Institute. The refugee became in the end a distinguished bacteriologist ; he became also a fast friend both of MacKenna and of Synge, and contributed some interesting material to Bourgeois' life of the latter. He died in 1913 as director of the Bacteriological Institute of Paraguay.

In the spring of 1897 war broke out between Greece and Turkey. The sympathies of the world were strongly on the side of the Greeks. One evening in April, MacKenna came with Synge to the Café Harcourt to dine with the Lynches, Maud Gonne, and some other Irish folk. The party were sitting out of doors with their glasses, engaged in *conspuer les Turcs*, when a mob of students, similarly engaged, swept past them down the Boulevard St. Michel, closely followed by the police, who were laying about them with their batons. To escape their blows the Irish party jumped on chairs and tables and pressed tight against the plate-glass windows of the café. Synge, less agile or more obstinate than the rest, received a heavy stroke on the head ; but with characteristic reticence he let fall no word on the matter, and it was only when MacKenna had taken him home that he was discovered to be bleeding profusely.[1]

It seems likely that MacKenna's philhellenism was intensified, however illogically, by this happening. Was not the Holy Land of all humanists being overrun by the barbarian, just as Synge had been bludgeoned by a Paris policeman ? And was not he, Stephen MacKenna, the son of that Slasher who had fought for Garibaldi ? When he learned that Garibaldi's son had raised a new legion of red-shirts to serve the sacred cause on Greek soil, he knew that he must do as his father had done. A day or two after the café incident he appeared in Best's flat and

[1] Mrs. Lynch is my authority for this incident, of which Bourgeois gives a rather different account.

announced his immediate departure for Athens as a member of a privately organised company of volunteers.[1] His adventures in Greece, and on the journey back to Paris, are the subject of a number of pleasing but mutually contradictory stories. What follows may be taken as at least relatively accurate. It is based on an account which MacKenna contributed to an Irish paper soon after his return,[2] supplemented here and there by the recollections of Mr. J. A. O'Sullivan, who was a fellow-volunteer though in a different company, and of Dr. Best, who heard his story when he came back to Paris.

MacKenna's company was composed of Frenchmen, Greeks from America, Greeks of Crete, Smyrna, Constantinople, Arabia, several Armenians, a Roumanian, two Russians, and an Irishman. "We volunteers were not exactly the cream of Europe, in fact I imagine that on the whole scum would be the truer word—but we were rare good fellows in regard to each other." Report says that MacKenna had barely landed when he lost the whole of his meagre resources by having his pocket picked. If so it did not impair his admiration for the Greeks. "I found them splendid fellows—courteous, generous, high-spirited, proud of their race and traditions, singularly well acquainted with their history, full of a passionate love of country, and above all deeply penetrated with respect and hospitality towards strangers." Their talk had the dramatic quality which characterised his own. "It is a land of speeches and you need never be afraid of delivering richly coloured orations which would make you ridiculous in these colder-blooded countries. . . . Almost every plunge which you make in the realms of the ridiculous brings you closer and closer into the core of their

[1] The legend which attributes MacKenna's action to a romantic passion for a Greek girl (whom on his return he found wedded to another !) is probably due to confusion with a later episode : see below p. 22.

[2] *Weekly Freeman*, October 9, 1897. Passages in inverted commas are quotations from this article, whose discovery I owe to the kindness of Mr. O'Sullivan and Mr. T. P. O'Donoghue.

hearts." From this time dates the interest which for many years MacKenna took in the literature of the modern Greek vernacular.[1]

When the company set out northward from Athens, Thessaly was already in the enemy's hands and the Greek army was in full retreat. Near Thermopylae they made contact with the Légion Philhellène (of which they were not officially part), and for some days they were encamped within three miles of the Turkish lines. But they saw no real fighting. This was probably fortunate for MacKenna, who had never handled a weapon. Posted for the first time on sentry-duty, he explained the fact politely to an astonished Greek officer : " I do not understand, monsieur, the etiquette of this situation." He had to be taught there and then how to salute, how to challenge, how to hold his rifle. A further legend, perhaps apocryphal, relates that he was once involved in a bayonet charge. He hesitated in bewilderment, then, as a fat Turk sped past him, gently prodded the flying figure with the butt end of his weapon. It seemed an unmannerly act ; and the next moment the amateur man of blood, forgetting once more the etiquette of the situation, murmured instinctively, " Pardon, monsieur ! " The Greeks are a humorous race, and the utterance is said to have earned for MacKenna the affection of his companions in arms.

The young man's memories of the brief campaign were principally of long marches, often executed on empty stomachs, and of bivouacs round the camp-fire. " Sometimes we marched for days on only a couple of army biscuits, hard as nails and about as digestible ; at other times, when we fell into a ' lamb country,' we slaughtered them by the score with our bayonets and roasted them on great poles, which we turned *chacun à son tour*, over roaring fires." At night there was story-telling and dancing under the stars—the traditional dances of the Levant, Greek,

[1] Cf. *Journal*, February 22, 1907 ; and letter 69.

Turkish, Armenian, "all accompanied with strange croonings or wild prolonged howls in a high key, with a curious periodical wavering that somehow or other gave the whole thing a suggestion of nightmare. . . . Simply to sit quiet for hours, watching and listening, was a perpetual delight; and then one would fall asleep just as one lay on the ground." MacKenna's closest comrade was a young Roumanian, a vagabond student from the university of Bucharest, who would sing to him in a low voice the songs of his people as they lay side by side, watching the others dancing or making merry in the firelight.

The war was over too soon for his liking. According to O'Sullivan's recollection he was one of those who agreed, when his company was disbanded, to take service with a captain of comitadji, known as Black Michael, and make a dash in a transport for Crete, where the insurgents under Venizelos were still making head against the Turks. But the plot was discovered before it could be carried out. Instead, MacKenna found himself, with a number of others, bound for Marseilles, "huddled on board a small Greek trading vessel, and thrown entirely on the hospitality of the sailors. All but absolutely penniless, we had no resource but to share their biscuit and pilaf, sitting in a circle on deck round the common pannikin and fishing out more or less nauseating morsels with a kind of chopsticks improvised by the carpenter." The sailors were kindly, and one of them, by name Panagiotes Kapetanaki, insisted on sharing nightly with MacKenna his one luxury —a tiny pot of Turkish coffee, a drink, as MacKenna rightly calls it, "of rare potency and excellence." One night, perceiving that the pot held scarcely enough coffee for one, the Irishman declined the proffered hospitality. "Then," cried the Greek, "the churi[1] shall enjoy it," and before anyone could stop him he emptied the pot into the sea. There were loud cries of protest. "Nay," he retorted, "it shall never be said that Panagiotes

[1] A kind of small fish.

Kapetanaki drank coffee when the stranger who fought for his country had none." The two became friends; they knocked about Marseilles together while MacKenna waited for money from home to take him to Paris, and they continued to correspond later.

When the money came, MacKenna decided that he must share it with another new acquaintance, an American Greek named Constantine, who was stranded in Marseilles without any means of reaching Paris (where he hoped to procure help from a compatriot). Two could not travel on one ticket, so the pair set out to walk the 800 kilometres which separated them from the capital. It was an eventful journey. Their funds were exhausted long before they arrived at their goal, and they had to depend on such hospitality as they could get by telling their story. The country folk as a rule treated them well. "Often the proprietor of some little café would invite us to come 'chez moi un peu, messieurs,' and he would spend half a day making heroes of us. . . . This was good for M. le Propriétaire and good for us: he would fill his café with customers; we had at our disposal unlimited supplies of the *vin du pays*." But often too they had to doss in barns or outhouses, sometimes in odd company. "On one occasion when seeking such shelter we saw a faint light twinkling through a chink in the wall of a dismantled cabin standing a little off the high road. Pushing towards it, we were astonished to see the light go out suddenly, while two men dashed out of the door full into our arms. The shock of our encounter gave the fellows time to see for themselves what manner of men we were, and they pulled themselves together, rather shamefaced, and informed us that they had thought we might be the police, and they were not *en règle*. I explained that we were in the same plight, and we were hailed as brothers in misfortune. The candle was lit, wine was broached, and we spent the whole night long in mild carousal conversing on the iniquities of the police of France, the unequal conditions of life, the sustaining powers of good wine, and so forth." Another time they had difficulty in resisting the invitation of a fellow-tramp to join him in a raid on a chicken farm, " pour faire la soupe."

Lacking both identification papers and visible means of subsistence, they were frequently in trouble with the police. At one place MacKenna was mistaken for a notorious murderer then at large in the district, and spent the night in the vault of the village church, which was the only available lock-up. At another, two itinerant gendarmes found the Greek and the Irishman asleep under a railway bridge, and demanded their papers. " We could give no satisfaction, and to all our explanations the only answer was ' yes, that may be so.' For three hours the two mounted guard over us, talking very pleasantly about all sorts of things, but refusing to allow us to go on our way. At dawn we were marched into the village, two wretched bedraggled objects, stared at with sleepy eyes by the early peasant setting forth to toil. We were examined as usual, and kept waiting as usual for the inspection by the chief; but they gave us each a welcome bowl of steaming, fragrant coffee, and drinking this we blessed and forgave them." The police of Lyons were less amiable. There was a strike in progress, and the town was in a hubbub. " The principal streets were thronged with rioting crowds, and myself and my companion, with the luck which had never deserted us throughout our expedition, were soon being beaten and hustled about in the thick of the scuffle. The police made finally a desperate charge, and in the tumult I was thrown down, and so separated from my friend. I soon met him, however, at the police office—he and I charged, in the company of some half dozen others, with being concerned in a breach of the peace." But here too they succeeded in establishing their innocence; and at length the hour came when they passed the Paris *octroi*. Best, returning late one night to the rue d'Assas, found a battered Greek asleep in MacKenna's bed and a battered MacKenna stretched beside him on the floor.

While these adventures were befalling the outward Stephen MacKenna, the interior man appears to have been occupied with adventures of his own, equally romantic and perhaps more dangerous. MacKenna talked of them even less than of those others ; but a Commonplace-Book [1] which he began to keep on December 1, 1897, gives some hint of what they were. It opens with a series of detached paragraphs in which he sets forth a theory about human nature :

" Behind and above the thinking and feeling and willing soul, or souls, is the real Man—the unalloyed soul, which studies and judges the others. It does not so much feel as see that the inferior souls of him, the outer husk of the spirit, feels. This is the calm lonely thing, really untroubled by the vagaries of life, which presides over all. . . . Its pronouncement is immutable : it is all that the Man will ever see of truth ; it is the unquestionable fruit of his individuality ; it is his entire draft upon the ' All Knowledge.' . . . It is the Dweller on the threshold, looking before and after, seeing things material and things spiritual in their whole nature and tendency—but always by its own light. . . . Here is the ground of the Equality of Man—and of a certain equality in all nature. . . . The criminal is often a moral idiot, essentially undefiled : often one feels in dealing with those whose conduct one most abhors that it is only the outer husk of one's own soul that is disgusted and repelled, and only by the outer husk of their soul. It is why we may often love a person without caring to say we respect him."

Such a conception of Man involves a corresponding view of Art, which MacKenna briefly states on another page :

" The art of expression in poetry and in philosophy is

[1] Now in the possession of Mr. F. A. Turk, who was good enough to place it at my disposal.

the art of descent : it is limiting and cabining the wide vision of the Spirit : it is telling a truth so as to be understood, not so as to be true : it is materialising the spiritual and losing much in the decanting."

These thoughts were far from new in 1897. But there is something in the young MacKenna's statement of them which suggests that for him they were not so much the fruit of reading as the expression of a temperament and of an inner experience. And for many years afterwards they kept such a place at the core of his thinking as borrowed thoughts cannot long maintain. In 1907, having just thrown up a comfortable career for a point of honour, he notes with surprise that " nothing in him really cares, nothing in him is even occupied by the crisis," and asks himself whether it is childishness or wisdom, or perhaps both, " because the two are one." [1] A year later he predicts that " If men cease to pray to God they will all the more, and all the more imploringly, consult their own Highest, which is but God more nearly seen "; [2] and in 1915 he propounds in an unpublished essay on " Experimental Ethics " the notion of living " by and in and for my own sense of the Highest " as the only adequate basis for a rational system of morals. Through all his later changes of outward creed this Protestant and antinomian mysticism lay, one may guess, as a secret source of strength at the heart of MacKenna's dealings with the world : its last transformation is the " desupernaturalised Yoga " which at the end of his life he recommended to Margaret Nunn.[3]

The remainder of the 1897 notebook consists of extracts from MacKenna's reading. Almost all of them relate to one or other of two topics—the problem of style and the problem of conducting one's life. On style, he quotes the advice of Anatole France, of Flaubert, of Rémy de Gourmont, of Buffon. On the conduct of life he cites Whitman, Schopenhauer, Nietzsche (very copiously excerpted),

[1] *Journal*, April 11, 1907. [2] *ibid.*, February 11, 1908. [3] Letter 80.

Thoreau and Emerson, Plato and Marcus Aurelius, Pater, Lafcadio Hearn, and a motley assortment of other persons, including Ouida and Arthur Lynch. Such a Board of spiritual directors would scarcely have been approved by the good Rosminian Fathers at Ratcliffe College. Explicit references to Christianity are very few ; but having copied out several pages of Diotima's discourse from the *Symposium* of Plato he appends a note " Surely no man or god ever wrote more nobly! That Christianity instead of Platonism became the religion of the later ages is the eternal proof of the imbecility of man."

II

For the next six or seven years MacKenna was fighting for a livelihood as a journalist. He seldom spoke of these years, and little record of them remains. He seems to have left Paris for London in the late autumn of 1897. In 1898 he was in Dublin, sharing rooms in Kildare Street with the late D. J. O'Donoghue ; in 1899 he was in New York, where tradition says that for a time he earned his living by sweeping out a restaurant. To this period belongs the encounter described in Mr. Colum's preface. Fortune intervened, and MacKenna exchanged his broom for a hardly more congenial employment as assistant editor of " a pseudo-literary freak production "[1] called the *Criterion.* It may be supposed that his conscience revolted, or that he confessed too candidly his opinion of the *Criterion* : at any rate before the end of 1899 he was back in Paris, doing night work for Gribayedeff.

The little *appartement* in the rue d'Assas which he had shared with Elmassian was now tenanted by Synge ; MacKenna found rooms in the rue Boissonade. He was at first desperately poor, and was often living on credit ; luckily the tradesmen of the Quartier liked and trusted

[1] Letter to Debenham, 1917.

him. Gradually the young man with the burning eyes and the wild black hair began to be known in the world of journalism. Gribayedeff introduced him to Henri Dumay and to the eccentric Gordon Bennett, who in those days edited the *New York Herald* by cable from his house in Paris. Bennett gave him employment as an interviewer. For this work he had the qualification, at that time somewhat uncommon, of being a gentleman. Hating publicity himself, he did his best to protect his victims from the more blatant forms of it, and thereby gained their confidence and not infrequently their friendship. It was thus that he won the heart of J. D. Rockefeller when he was sent to interview him in his retirement at Chantilly : he liked to tell how the millionaire took him into the village shop and bought him, after interminable haggling, a two-franc walking-stick as a memorial of the occasion. So, too, a business correspondence with Rodin led to MacKenna's becoming a frequent visitor at the famous house in Meudon ; at a later date the sculptor presented to Mrs. MacKenna his well-known bronze The Centauress—a work which Stephen disliked, declaring himself ready to pawn it " for a pint of creamy porter." [1]

In 1902 there occurred a crisis in MacKenna's personal life. In a letter of January 21, 1902, Mrs. Synge (J. M. Synge's mother) writes, evidently from information supplied by her son : " MacKenna is the only friend he [J. M. Synge] had left in Paris, and he is leaving for good as he is going to marry a Greek girl." [2] MacKenna did not marry the Greek girl. Soon after Mrs. Synge's letter was written he met, in the studio of his friend Spicer Simson, a young American named Mary Bray,[3] who had been Hans Pfitzner's pupil and was now being trained as a concert pianist at the Conservatoire. She was de-

[1] Letter to Bodkin, December 22, 1913. Cf. letter 27.

[2] The reason appears inadequate. Possibly MacKenna contemplated settling in Greece, but the facts are not now ascertainable.

[3] She later adopted the French spelling " Marie."

scended on her father's side from an old County Wicklow family ; her face could light up with " a glorious flash of urgent intelligence and quick emotion "[1]; she loved Ireland, music, and the cause of justice. MacKenna demanded to meet her again. A supper party was arranged, and when the party was over the two young people transferred themselves to a café to finish their talk. The café closed ; they found another, and then another. When all the cafés were closed, the Bois de Boulogne received them, and here they walked till breakfast time. They were married in London in January 1903.[2] It was a mixed marriage, but Mrs. MacKenna shortly afterwards became a Catholic, and in later years her frightened piety was one of the influences which deterred her husband from making an open breach with Catholicism.

Not long after his marriage MacKenna suddenly achieved financial prosperity. His work for Gordon Bennett's *New York Herald* had attracted the notice of Bennett's rival, the Americanised Hungarian, Joseph Pulitzer, " the founder of so-called yellow journalism," [3] who was just then engaged in thrusting the *New York World* into the front rank of American daily papers. Pulitzer was a man quick to recognise new talent and quick to make a pre-emptive bid for it. He appointed MacKenna first as a special correspondent and later as continental representative of the *World*, with a staff of assistants, a central office in Paris, and a salary that in those days was considered princely. Between 1903 and 1907 MacKenna had his first and last taste of what is called success.

His headquarters at this period was a flat overlooking the Luxembourg Gardens, a flat full of books, grand pianos, and old French furniture ; he had also a week-end cottage at Clamart. But at first he had little time to enjoy

[1] Letter 6.

[2] The date depends on Lynch's statement that the news of Lynch's condemnation to death for high treason reached MacKenna just as he started on his honeymoon.

[3] R. D. Blumenfeld, *The Press in my Time*, p. 41.

these novel luxuries. In the autumn of 1903 he was sent as special correspondent to Berlin, and in the following year to London. In the winter of 1904-5 the abortive " first revolution " shook the fabric of the Russian Empire, and MacKenna was despatched to investigate it. He interviewed high officials like the formidable Trépof, Governor-General of St. Petersburg, and Kachanov, the man responsible for the Odessa massacre ; liberal leaders like Prince Paul Dolgorouki and Count Hayden ; intellectuals like Tolstoi and Baron von Meyendorf (who told him to come again in ten years, " when perhaps I shall have invented a better system "). He penetrated to the garrets of revolutionary students in St. Petersburg, was one of the two or three foreign representatives admitted to the historic Zemstvo Congress at Moscow, and ferreted out in Odessa the tangled and pitiful facts of the *Potemkin* mutiny and its terrible consequences.

With MacKenna's first visit to Tolstoi there is associated a curious little tale, which provoked a correspondence many years later. I give it in MacKenna's own words :[1]

" One winter in the early years of this century, Michael Davitt and myself went to Yasnia Polyana, saw the Count Tolstoi, looking eminently County, walking his woods, knocked for long at his door, and were at last let in by the Moujik Tolstoi, as Moujiky as in any of the current photographs, to be seated at a table covered, peasant-fashion, with a cloth foul with stains of eggs and coffee—and never, either of us, I think, felt quite easy again about the doctrine trumpeted forth from that stagy shrine. Of course, one tries to believe that, somehow, the man's soul was nobler than his practice ; certainly his death—with yet again a touch of the stage ?—was moving."

MacKenna refrained from regaling the American public with this quaint example of inverted snobbery ; but the story got about among his friends, was eventually quoted,

[1] Letter to *Irish Statesman*, October 1, 1927.

long after Tolstoi's death, by " A. E." in the *Irish Statesman*, and excited the indignation of Tolstoi's English admirers. It was fathered at first on MacKenna's namesake the novelist :[1] see letters 54 to 58.

MacKenna was strongly moved by the events which he witnessed in Russia, and he felt that they had a profound significance for the development of western civilisation. " Japan and Russia," he wrote in July 1905, " appear now to hold much of the secret of the world's future, and Russia more of it than Japan. . . . Russia's awakening is the great interesting fact of our day. . . . There will be a new force set to work in the world, and there will be in the universal intelligence an answering change, both direct and by reaction, similar to that set up by the great liberating movements of a hundred years ago." Like most daily journalism, MacKenna's despatches from Russia bear some marks of hasty composition ; but their vivid portraiture of leading personalities, their psychological acumen, and their essential humanity make them interesting reading even to-day. For the purposes of this memoir they have little documentary value, since for the most part they are studiously impersonal and bare of autobiographical detail ; but I shall allow myself to quote the paragraphs in which he described the reception in St. Petersburg of the news of the assassination of the Grand Duke Sergius, who was believed to be the Czar's evil genius and the real ruler of Russia. The passage, which I print as it was originally drafted by MacKenna,[2] throws some light both on its writer's manner of life at this time and on the attitude which he was later to adopt in face of events not altogether dissimilar in a country closer to his heart than Russia.

" It is ghastly all the same. One perfectly understands

[1] The two men were constantly confused : see letters 51 and 95.

[2] The original drafts of a number of MacKenna's despatches (which often reached the American public in a garbled form) were preserved among his papers.

it : to a certain degree one sympathises perhaps : assuredly one is interested, for it is a sudden revelation of the secrets of hearts, the leaping up of light on the whole mystery of the common mind of Russia. But it is ghastly all the same.

" We are at lunch together—a band of cosmopolitan correspondents, an attaché of an embassy, a booted officer returned wounded from the front, two Petersburgian journalists. All over the room from innumerable tables laughter, the popping of corks, the sounds of friendly discussion ; everywhere the uniforms of soldiers, police-officials, functionaries, the gay toilettes of smiling women.

" A waiter willows a rapid way through the cheerful groups to our table.

" ' You know ? '

" ' What ? '

" ' They have killed him ! '

" ' Trépof ? ' we all cry.

" ' No : Sergei ! '

" There is a rapid shoving back of chairs, a flinging down of serviettes, glass crashes, the correspondents make rapid exit, calling for their couriers, yelling for sleighs : they are off to embassies, ministries, newspaper offices, to secret centres of information : in a quarter of an hour there will be fifty men besieging the Moscow Telephone Company's servants, striving with each other to get from their carefully prepared sources the answer to the question, ' Is it one man's work or was it a mob ? Is it the revolution ? ' But even as we fly I hear the officer's gruff voice in one word, ' Svinaia ': it is his comment, his requiem over the dead, and it means—well, to translate discreetly, it means ' Brute ! ' He will not say that, probably, before his brother officers at the caserne, where he does the routine work permitted by his convalescence and whither he now hastens as fast as two horses can whirl his sleigh through the mud : the news spreading through the city may stir slumbering passion to sudden flame, and in these days every officer flies to barracks on the lightest word of possible disturbance. He will not say ‘ Svinaia ’ at the caserne : but it was a true speech none the less, an authentic expression of feeling before discretion came into play.

“ In an hour or two most of us are satisfied that there is nothing to be done for the moment : one man made Moscow famous, there is no general movement : let Moscow gather up the fragments. Back in the restaurant, the scene is unchanged : some few guests have slipped out, others have come in : everyone knows that Duke Serge is in pieces. From every table there comes the sound of cheerful talk, of laughter of men and women ; there is a popping of corks. As you pass by table after table you hear the word Sergei or Alexandrovitch or Nicholas or Zemsky Sobor : but there is not a cloud on any face ; only here and there rarely is there any sign of earnest talk, of any feeling. At our table a brilliant London writer tells the Russian journalists laboriously the tale of Punch's timid curate wrestling with a bad egg at his Bishop's breakfast table : ‘ Dear me, Mr. Golightly,’ says the Bishop, ‘ I am afraid your egg is bad.’ ‘ No, your Grace . . . that is . . . it is quite good in bits.’ This is the prologue : the application is ghoulish : ‘ So I have imagined the Grand Duchess mourning her doubtful husband : “ He is quite good in bits.” ’ There is an uproarious laugh ; the thing hits admirably the situation, if there be truth in the legend that the gentle and good wife had long since come to loathe her husband. From the next table there is an application for a translation into Russian of the story that must be so funny : from French the whole thing goes into Russian, by the agency of the attaché ; and our Russian neighbours, who include an ex- ‘ Maid of Honour ’ of the Imperial Court, laugh consumedly. I find it ghastly.

“ It is the mood of the evening. A French visitor does not like a sauce they have served with his fish. He calls the maître d'hôtel and with great gravity begs for the assassination of the chef. The waiter, as Russian as kwass or bortch, replies ' But the chef is not a Grand Duke,' and again from all the environment there is laughter.

" I ask a man who passes for so very moderate a liberal as to be almost a reactionary what he thinks : the answer is startling, ' Bah ! do I think at all of the skin of a dog ? '

" Surely never man died so execrated ; never was a hideous death so flippantly or so ghoulishly handled ; never was an assassination treated with such simple good faith, as the natural exit for that particular victim.

" ' It was only a question of putting a date on the thing,' said a rich merchant of the Nievsky, ' everyone knew it must come some day : everyone is glad now that it has come—even the Csar.'

" In fact it is extremely probable that Nicholas is glad to be rid of his evil genius, the Heliogabalus of Moscow —I borrow the word from an officer once in Sergius' suite—whose brutal will power had mastered the master of all the Russias and withered—with a sneering tongue, they say—the Csar's inborn spirit of peace and goodwill.

" The hotel reeked with ugly stories of the monster while his pitiful fragments, we were told, had not yet been gathered up. This dead man no one spared, and no one said, of many whom I heard and questioned, one good word for him ; not one good trait recorded, no single pleasant anecdote. The air was infected. Some of us went out late at night, partly for relief, partly because conceivably there might be trouble. I veritably believe the people were for the moment too glad to be dangerous. The Nievsky was a cheerful promenade even in the slush of the sudden thaw : no sign, even, of that grave preoccupation that the circumstances surely warranted, however the duke deserved his doom : people were gay in an entirely simple acceptance of a piece of good news. I doubt if to anyone in Petersburg there was present any thought that after all this thing belonged, roughly speaking and pending a thoughtful justification, to the category of crime. I don't think the notion of crime existed in Petersburg, even to be rapidly dismissed as inapplicable. The thing was envisaged only in its relief, and a little in its consequences, as what the law calls an Act of God. It was remarkable that no curiosity was expressed as to the person or motives or associations of the man that threw the bomb : he did not count : only the relief counted—and that shone in every face, seemed almost to show in the cheerier gait of every promenader.

" I find this ghastly : all said and done, it indicates a wide demoralisation, not to be blamed perhaps, but to be deplored ; and what a light is here on the state of the public mind of Russian society, on the grave possibilities of the future."

In the autumn of 1905, when the Russian upheaval had subsided, MacKenna was sent to Stockholm, and thence to Budapest to study the constitutional crisis in Hungary. This too subsided, and he returned to Paris. He had enjoyed his work as a special correspondent ; his duties as head of the Paris office proved much less to his taste. The society of newspaper men was not congenial to him : " I am dazed and saddened," he wrote in his journal, " by their many-sided knowledge, taking in all the world of active life so beyond my grip ; and I am wearied by the talk of these men, so shy of general ideas and so disdainful, placidly, of all that they conceive to be poetic or artistic." But there was worse than this. In the absence of political sensations he was expected to disinter, or cause others to disinter, the less savoury scandals of Paris society for the delight of a coprophagous public. To a man of MacKenna's sensitive conscience such duties were a torment. " I cannot go on with this work," he told his cousin Ambrose Kelly about 1906 : " I am a journalist, not a muck-raker." Though in his journal he tries more than once to reassure himself with the thought that in daily work " it is foolish to hope to be always handling noble themes," this interlude of prosperity seemed to him " an ugly idleness." " It is certain that to handle the daily fact for the daily press is neither work to my heart nor freedom to any man : it is for those who have stifled the innermost self—for the unhappy, then, or for the fallen."

This growing dissatisfaction was accompanied and intensified by a revival of earlier interests. In 1897 he had of ancient Greek, by his own account, " but a few words remembered from schooldays." [1] At what date he resumed his study of it is not clear ; but in 1902 he began working on a translation of Marcus Aurelius, which he never completed, and a version of the *Menexenus*, found among his papers after his death, may belong to the same period. A little later he embarked on an interesting attempt to render Pindar, his favourite Greek poet, into equivalent English metres, but did not persevere with it. These early experiments seem to have brought home to him the inadequacy of his equipment as a scholar : his note-books show him toiling at Greek irregular verbs and working through Goodwin's *Moods and Tenses* as he rushed about Europe to interview this and that political notability. His interest in the *Enneads* appears to have been born amid the gunfire of the 1905 revolution ; in that year he bought in St. Petersburg Creuzer's Oxford Plotinus, and in Moscow the Didot edition. By the beginning of 1907 he was definitely contemplating the vast task of translating the whole of Plotinus for the first time into English.[2] " It seems to me," he wrote later in that year, " that I must be born for him, and that somehow someday I must have nobly translated him." [3]

On his thirty-fifth birthday MacKenna experienced " a great moral upheaval—35 and nothing done, and almost certainly nothing ever to be done." He resolved on an

[1] *Weekly Freeman*, October 9, 1897. But the Commonplace-Book shows a continued interest in the classics.

[2] *Journal*, March 29, 1907.

[3] *ibid.*, December 5, 1907.

earnest effort of self-improvement: μὴ παύσῃ τεκταίνων τὸ σὸν ἄγαλμα, "cease not to be the sculptor of thine own image," he quotes to himself from Plotinus. The journal for 1907-9 reflects a persistent conflict between his tormented conscience and that fatalistic indolence which is an element in the temper of nearly every Irishman. "To have no set purpose in one's life," he tells himself, "is the harlotry of the will." "It seems to me that it is quite useless and silly to live unless one is either very intelligent or very good." But again, "why need we be ceaselessly examining our consciences: 'what am I doing with my life?' . . . The forces outside humanity that put us here or leave us here and will one day take us away, will do their will with us, if they have a will about us: if they have no will about us, why should we try to give them one?" He could neither escape this fatalism nor rest in it: "I am like the princes of Greece round Penelope, a ten-years' wooer; I am always in my mind waiting for some bell to ring that never rings." Such a man, he wrote, "is footsore early, because his walking is nowhither and because his heart is always fighting with his feet." "I feel a great need," he says in October 1908, "of having on the work-table some piece of writing, serious and linked, which every day I might bring nearer to an end firmly set for some gravely formed purpose." For the next twenty years Plotinus was to satisfy that need.

A man who felt like this was evidently ill-fitted to preside over the Paris office of the *New York World*. But his final breach with American journalism was brought about by a trivial personal incident in the spring of 1907. Joseph Pulitzer, owner and editor of the *World*, visited Paris and demanded that MacKenna should attend upon him as a sort of courier. MacKenna consented, but with reluctance, and relations became somewhat strained as he trailed round shops and cabarets in the wake of his exacting employer. At last the newspaper king departed to his yacht on the Riviera. The respite was brief: a few hours later Pulitzer wired MacKenna to buy six chickens and six ducklings, take them to the Gare de Lyon, and there deliver them to a valet for conveyance to the yacht. It was the last straw: was an Irish gentleman to do the work of a personal servant—to "buttle," as he expressed it—for any man? MacKenna wired back, in words which were for years afterwards proverbial among Paris journalists, "Refuse de vous acheter six poulets et six canetons: ceci est ma résignation." On the fourth of May he handed over to his friend Colonel Lynch both his duties and the admirable flat beside the Luxembourg, and retired to the cottage at Clamart to consider his future. In July he moved to lodgings in London, and in the following summer to Dublin, which was to be, with one interval, his home for the next sixteen years.

This affair of the chickens merely precipitated a decision which was already, as the journal shows, prepared in MacKenna's inward growth. But it is characteristic of the man. While in his dealings with his fellows he normally practised the most scrupulous courtesy, he had inherited from his father a liability to sudden accesses of rage which discharged themselves in impulsive action and sometimes in actual physical violence. The occasion when he forcibly ejected from his house a well-known Dublin professor is still remembered with joy or embarrassment by those who had the good or bad fortune to be present. Such incidents were infrequent, but they sometimes had inconvenient consequences. One day during his last Paris period, Célestine, the MacKennas' faithful *bonne*, presented herself in a state of extreme agitation at the studio of the Spicer Simsons: Monsieur had been arrested; with her own eyes she had seen from the balcony of the flat the dreadful spectacle of Monsieur being marched down the street between two *gendarmes*. Mrs. Simson hastened to the police station. There she learned that MacKenna had entered a barber's shop to have his hair cut. Confronted with the great lock of raven hair which in those days hung over MacKenna's eyes or floated behind him on the wind, the barber demanded permission to prune it. MacKenna was reading Plotinus in the tonsorial chair. "Laissez ça," he said, and went on reading. The barber expostulated tactlessly: "mais ça a l'air vraiment ridicule," he observed with a simper. The next moment his client leapt from his chair and brought down Plotinus with all his force on the critic's head. There was a fracas. The barber and his assistant fled from the shop, adroitly locking their berserk customer inside, and returned presently with two *gendarmes*. MacKenna was haled before the *juge de paix*, and in due course paid twenty francs for the privilege of chastising insolence.

His resignation from the *New York World* was followed by a period of hesitancy and experiment. He could not afford to abandon journalism altogether. His wife had a life interest in certain monies which down to the time of the war—when dividends dropped heavily—yielded an income sufficient for her personal needs. But MacKenna did not propose to live on his wife. He continued to write for the *Freeman's Journal* (then the leading Irish nationalist daily), to which he had long been an occasional contributor, and meanwhile he prepared himself for more serious work. He tried his hand for a time at writing short stories, but with little success. Critics have found in his Plotinus "a mind and a style which might have produced fine original poetry or prose";[1] but MacKenna lacked that patient devotion to concrete detail which Edwardian literary fashion demanded. "I have no power," he notes, "over the fact bound in time and place"—a curious admission on the part of a journalist. His temperament revolted against the surface realism and the tight, rather mechanical construction

[1] Sir John Squire in *The Observer*, January 4, 1931.

which most people admired in 1907 : in his journal for that year he predicts a day when "plot will go by the board and real life will be taboo . . . the matter of books will be delicately critical, piercingly 'psychological,' or wholly fantastic : we shall have the novel of the other-world and of the deeper man." Had he been born a quarter of a century later he might, I think, have been a novelist.[1] Edwardian literature he found to be, with few exceptions, "almost whining-weak, or else strong with sordidness." He turned from it with relief to the old authors, and especially to the Elizabethans. It is worth recording that among modern poets he had an especial fondness for Hopkins, in whom he recognised the same passionate twofold search for spiritual unity and for the freshly significant word by which he himself was tormented. He read, and read aloud to his friends, all he could discover of Hopkins' work before the edition of 1918 ; as early as 1913 he was urging the publication of certain poems of Hopkins which existed in MS. in Ireland ;[2] and later we find him copying out the sestet of *The Windhover* on a postcard and sending it to Bodkin to whet his appetite. For the rest, to the end he approached his younger contemporaries in literature, as he approached the classics, with humility ; but he was not to be suggested into fashionable appreciations : thus he confessed himself unable to get through *Ulysses*, though he judged that Wyndham Lewis's attack on Joyce was only half justified.[3]

MacKenna's years of daily journalism had not, in his own view, taught him to write English : "I read nowhere, outside of the very sorriest reporter-work, any prose less like prose than mine is."[4] As a journalist he

[1] Some of D. H. Lawrence's characteristic ideas are oddly anticipated in the *Journal* : see especially the entry of June 23, 1908.

[2] In a letter to Bodkin, December 22, 1913.

[3] Letter to W. K. Magee, March 23, 1927.

[4] *Journal*, June 27, 1908.

had been content to "defy all the sanctities if only I might anyhow please myself with a yell and a flare and a fit of ribald glee: now only I begin to know that it is not 'the Phrase' that counts to any good; it is 'la Phrase'—the Sentence, the orderly, suave and gracious setting of the true word in the clear meaning."[1] In 1907 he set himself to learn to write, by the laborious—and to most judgements unpromising—method of constructing for himself a thesaurus of classical English word-usage.[2] It was found among his papers after his death, and contains many thousands of entries, alphabetically arranged. Among the authors whom he read, in entirety or in part, for this purpose between May 1907 and September 1908 are Chaucer, Maundeville, Sidney, Spenser, Chapman, Marlowe, Greene, Fletcher, Massinger, Ben Jonson, Nicholas Breton, Puttenham, William Webbe, Milton, Herrick, Crashaw, George Herbert, Otway, Whetstone, Sedley, Congreve, Pope, Wordsworth, Hazlitt, Browning, Tennyson, Meredith and Walt Whitman, besides a good deal of the Authorised Version. He recognised that such labour stands to style "only as scourging and fasting to holiness." But by September 1907 he notes that although he does not yet write well he is already writing better than ever before.

While he toiled thus to forge for himself an English style he pondered long and earnestly on the use which he should make of it and of his life. Two dreams contended for the mastery of his will: should he consecrate to Plotinus whatever leisure he could spare from journalism? or should he settle in Dublin, throw himself into nationalist politics, and work through the Gaelic League (now an increasingly influential force) "at putting the new soul into Ireland"? His friends at home, notably Fionán MacColuim, strongly pressed the latter course.

[1] *ibid.*

[2] He later made himself similar, though less complete, thesauruses for Greek and Irish.

Either seemed to him "worth a life."[1] For some years he attempted to do both things. He got ready a specimen of the Plotinus translation—the essay on Beauty, *Ennead* I. vi.—and Synge promised to sound Irish publishers for him. "It would be a mistake," wrote Synge, "to send your MS. to Yeats and AE, as what one likes the other hates—that is sad but true, '*tantane* something in celestial minds,' Virgil."[2] Eventually, towards the end of 1908, the slender treatise was published as a separate booklet, by Bullen. Reading it in proof, MacKenna judged it "a very pleasant piece of English,"[3] though he condemned it later.[4] The original limited edition of 300 copies was sold out, and it was twice reprinted, but the translator's total receipts from it were between four and five pounds.

Meanwhile he had made up his mind to return to his own country. He had thoughts of more formally repairing the gaps in his early education, and in 1908 he actually started reading for the Matriculation Examination of the Royal (now National) University of Ireland. In February of that year the late head of the Paris office of the *New York World* notes in his journal with modest pride that he now really understands and enjoys elementary geometry "and even algebra." Geometry he finds "a rare searcher of the brain": "looking in this mirror one knows what manner of man one is." He looks forward also to mastering "the principles of machines": "schoolboys," he exclaims, "are given these pearls too soon, or at least I was." But it proved impossible to combine academic studies with daily journalism. In November 1908 MacKenna obtained permanent employment as a leader-writer for the *Freeman's Journal*, and the notion of taking

[1] *Journal*, January 15, 1908.

[2] This and some other letters of Synge to MacKenna are preserved in the National Library of Ireland. They have unfortunately at some time been so shockingly mutilated, in an attempt to excise libellous and blasphemous matter, as to render them almost worthless.

[3] *Journal*, August 28, 1908.

[4] See letter 4.

a degree was dropped : in the army of scholarship he was destined to fight to the end as an irregular.

In compensation he embarked on a serious attempt to learn Irish. In his years of wandering he had already dabbled in it for odd half-hours ; in London he had attended the evening classes organised by the Gaelic League ; and now that he was settled in Dublin he began to work for the Diploma of the College of Irish. He also did administrative work for the League, as a member of the committee which organised its annual assembly, the *Oireachtas* ; and he was full of ideas for the further development of its activities. He raged against those who thought of Irish as a patois for peasants, " who in grotesque ignorance or in lying malice assert that the Irish of so much poetry is fit only for discussing the feeding of pigs and the promise of cows." [1] " A man could do anything in Irish," he wrote to a friend in 1914, " say and express anything, and do it with an exquisite beauty of sound." For himself he lamented that he had come to the language too late to make it his medium of expression. " I consider it the flaw and sin of my life," he says in the same letter, " that I didn't twenty years ago give myself body and soul to the Gaelic to become a writer in it, as some—God forgive me—some Conrad in English or some Flem flammanding in French, and help to make the literature which would re-root the language." As it was, he could only read and criticise the work of others. The contemporary fiction and poetry which was beginning to be written in Irish was narrow in range, tenuous in substance, and too often childishly sentimental ; but the few educated critics who were able to read it refrained from saying so, either from patriotic motives or for fear of making enemies. MacKenna, measuring these things by European standards, demanded something better, and in later years did not hesitate to state his view of them in print : " those pretty wee comfits," he called them, " very

[1] *Memories of the Dead*, p. 13.

sweet and delicate, but not equal in a bagful to one solid, sticky, jaw-exercising chunk of toffee." [1]

In this and other ways MacKenna's function in Dublin was to be a missionary of Europeanism. Ireland's geographical position has exposed her through the centuries to two alternative perils, Anglicisation and Balkanisation —to become a cultural dependency of England or to exist as an isolated and therefore stagnant community on the fringe of civilisation, a moribund limb dangling unheeded over the Atlantic from the extremity of the European tree. Most of MacKenna's fellow-workers in the Gaelic movement realised only the first danger ; MacKenna realised both. His ideal was an Ireland Irish in speech, in culture, in institutions, but not an Ireland cut off from the fertilising waters of the great European tradition.[2] He has often been called an extremist ; but he had only ridicule for the "formulistic side-taking," as he once termed it, of Irish political discussions ; and he was ready to leap to the defence not only of Synge, who was a personal friend, but of men like W. B. Yeats and Hugh Lane when they were denounced as heretics or "anglicisers" by clerical bigotry and the zealots of Sinn Fein. When Yeats' *Collected Works* appeared in the winter of 1908-9, Brayden, the editor of the *Freeman's Journal*, wanted to arrange for a hostile review : "he would have given it," wrote MacKenna long afterwards to "A. E.," "to a good fellow who, I don't know why, honestly thought W. B. raised up by the devil to corrupt and humiliate Holy Ireland, and himself raised up by God and I think the Blessed Virgin to save and protect her." MacKenna insisted on doing the review, and wrote, in defiance of his editor, a long and eloquent defence of Yeats' poetry against the then current charges that it was "obscure," "affected," and "un-Irish." The review evoked a letter of praise from the dying Synge, who found in it "a sure-

[1] *New Ireland*, December 15, 1917.

[2] Cf. *Journal*, February 18, 1908.

ness of touch and an entirely successful vehemence that delighted me."

Of Synge's own failure to satisfy the canons of nationalist orthodoxy, MacKenna wrote later: "I judged S. intensely, though not practically, national. He couldn't endure the lies that gathered round all the political movement, flamed or rather turned a filthy yellow with rage over them, gently hated Miss Gonne for those she launched or tolerated, loathed the Gaelic League for ever on the score of one pamphlet in which someone, speaking really a half truth, had urged the youth of Ireland to learn modern Irish because it would give them access to the grand old Saga literature; I have never forgotten the bale in his eyes when he read this and told me 'That's a Bloody lie; long after they know modern Irish, which they'll never know, they'll still be miles and years from any power over the Saga.' I have never known a man with so passionate, so pedantic a value for truth as S. He didn't so much judge the lie intellectually or morally as simply hate it—as one hates a bad smell or a filthy taste. This alone would put him off any public movement whatever."[1]

The MacKennas' home from 1908 to 1913 was a quiet old house where Trollope had once lived: it lies on the outer skirt of the city at the end of a little cul-de-sac, looking across green fields to the sea. Here every Saturday evening they entertained their friends. Dublin hospitality was very simple in those days; innumerable pots of strong tea were consumed, but at most houses little else—"a cup of coffee and a stale biscuit, with I hope fresh talk," MacKenna offers in one letter of invitation. Dubliners, like the Athenians whom St. Paul knew, have a peculiar passion for fresh talk; and MacKenna quickly gathered round him an interesting group of young men—among them Thomas Bodkin, later Director of the National Gallery of Ireland, the Celtic scholar Bergin, the

[1] Letter to Lynch, autumn 1928.

critic J. M. Hone, Edmund Curtis, afterwards Professor of History at Trinity College, and four young poets, Padraic Colum, Thomas MacDonagh, " Seumas O'Sullivan " and James Stephens. " A. E." was also a fairly frequent visitor, but I think that he and MacKenna were never wholly at ease in each other's company, or even perhaps in their correspondence—on the second point the reader of this book can judge for himself. It is true that in later years, at any rate, each respected the other's achievement. MacKenna honoured the man who " taught us to make butter and to defend our national soul and potentialities in the name of the Soul and the powers behind " ;[1] " A. E." could appreciate the " exquisite labour " of MacKenna's workmanship in the Plotinus, with its long sentences that " keep their upward flight like great slow-moving birds." [2] And each prized the other's good opinion.[3] But the " Papist Celt " in MacKenna found " A. E." insensitive to many things which he himself valued in religion and in literature,[4] while the northerner in " A. E." suspected, I fancy, some taint of insincerity in MacKenna's alternating moods of exaltation, despair, and flippant irony.

MacKenna was by this time at the height of his conversational powers. " I am not a man of the pen," he wrote in 1913 to " A. E.": " I can say more in five minutes with my little tongue than with the longest fountain-pen in the world." And most of those who knew him well will agree that he talked, at his best, better than he ever wrote. In the period immediately before the war, and for some years after, there was as good conversation to be heard in Dublin as in any capital city in Europe ; but even Dublin critics found in MacKenna's talk the quality of genius. Unfortunately, like all really spontaneous expression, it loses its flavour in the cold storage of print : it depended for its perfection upon tone and gesture, the

[1] Letter 15. [2] " A. E." in *The Irish Statesman*, December 6, 1924.

[3] Cf. letters 1A, 37, 48. [4] Cf. letter 15.

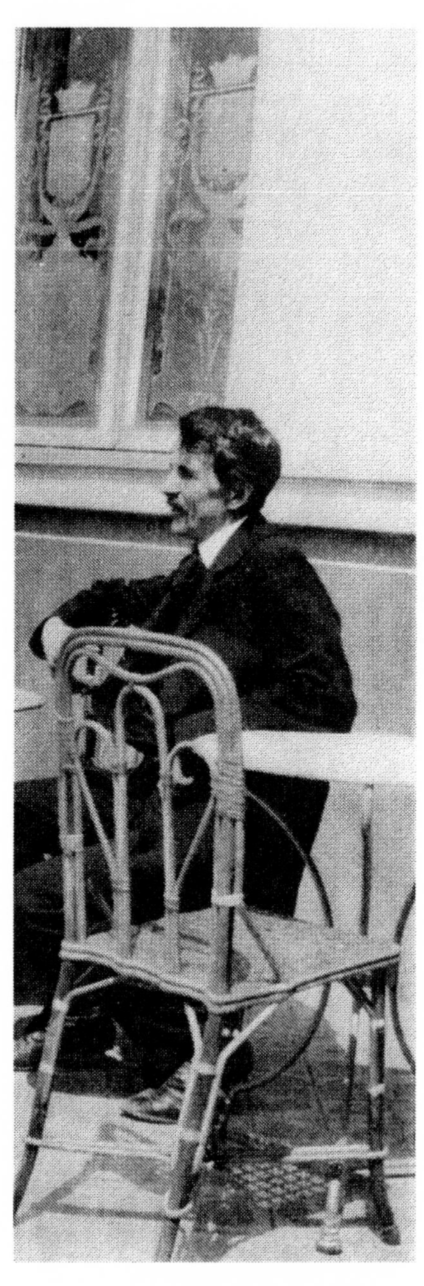

Stephen MacKenna talking in a Paris café.
From a photograph.

by-play of an eyelid, the instinctive emphasis of a pair of mobile hands. Its emotional range was amazing : it would soar passionately, without effort or affectation, then of a sudden swoop to earth on a note of mockery, like a chorus in Aristophanes. When he was moved by anger or awe or pity, MacKenna's speech had such dignity and imaginative splendour as was achieved by no Irishman of his time save W. B. Yeats ; when his spirit was gay, it sprang delightedly into that world of comic phantasy whose other inhabitant was James Stephens. A good many aging Dubliners still treasure the recollection of a particular occasion during the war when MacKenna after a long disappearance turned up unexpectedly at "A. E." 's accustomed Sunday evening gathering. His wife had lain for weeks at death's door, and he had been too sick at heart to speak to anyone : now the doctors had pronounced her out of danger. Riding the wave of his released emotion, he talked like a man inspired : one dazzling extravaganza after another held the company breathless. At two in the morning " A. E." went to bed, but most of the party adjourned to a neighbouring house, where the conversation continued till dawn.

Society at all times acted as a powerful stimulant on MacKenna's brain, a stimulant which in his later years he dreaded and as far as possible avoided, alleging that it made him talk too much and too recklessly. " I never was able to behave like a reasonable being save en tête à tête," he wrote towards the end of his life to Debenham. He detested being lionised. When he lived at Harrow, literary hostesses who tried to collect him as an exhibit for their menageries were met by an uncompromising refusal. " Thank God," he would say with a shrug (for he was one of the few islanders who really used that gesture), " I have done with all this Lady business."

Between 1908 and 1913 the strain of leader-writing left MacKenna little energy to spare for the projected translation of Plotinus. He had become too self-critical for daily journalism ; often he would waste many hours in polishing an unsatisfactory article destined to be forgotten as soon as read. " I am driven to death," he wrote in 1912, "with cram work on Persian politics, flying machines, and the rest whereby I live." He had brought with him from Paris rough MS. versions of considerable portions of the *Enneads*,[1] and had at first spoken optimistically of " getting all ship-shape within a couple of years." There was no one to undeceive him, or to warn him against the enterprise into which he was being lured. At this time, so far as I know, he had among his acquaintance no single Greek scholar. There were in Trinity College plenty of men who knew Greek ; but they were reputed, with one or two distinguished exceptions, to be the sort of men of whom a Dublin wit remarked that " they read Homer for the grammar and the *Irish Times* for pleasure," a type uncongenial to MacKenna ; and it is in any case unlikely that any of them knew much or cared much about Plotinus.

Be that as it may, MacKenna was left to discover gradually for himself the overwhelming difficulties of his self-imposed task : to discover that the syntax and word-usage of Plotinus was a practically unexplored field ; that not a dozen people in Europe understood the details of his system ; that the text printed in the two German editions of 1878 and 1883 (the best available until the Budé edition began to appear in 1924) was in very many passages neither Greek nor sense ; and that the scholars of the world were holding their hand from either re-editing or translating Plotinus because they dared not risk their professional reputations in pioneering this vast tract of dangerous and notoriously difficult territory. " If there are to-day perhaps only twenty or thirty men alive who can read this author after a fashion, that is mainly due to the present state of Plotinian studies, which are at

[1] Most of these he eventually burned unused, as their inadequacy became clear to him.

the stage reached centuries ago in the study of Plato. We have no adequate text, no commentary, no grammar, no lexicon ; no other great author of antiquity has been neglected to this degree." So wrote the leading German authority [1] on Plotinus as recently as 1930. Before the war there existed no readable translation of Plotinus in any language, and none with any pretentions to accuracy save the literal German rendering of H. F. Mueller—an honest piece of journeywork, but one which in difficult passages merely reproduces the obscurity of the original.

MacKenna's notion of translation was quite other than Mueller's. He recognised that with an author like Plotinus literal translation, useful as a scholar's tool, was useless to the modern reader whom he had in mind. To make such a version was for him only the first step in the translator's task. He must not rest until he had " carried over " every nuance of his author's meaning, emotional as well as logical, into the idiom of another language ; and that idiom must be rich, flexible, dignified, above all contemporary—his most furious expressions of contempt were reserved for what he called (in a note written on the flyleaf of Tucker's *Choephoroe*) " the Verrall-Jebb pseudo-grand days-of-yore-ish sham." [2] He had put himself to school with the great translators, from Chapman to Wilamowitz, and he could not be satisfied with a less achievement than theirs.

It was in January 1912 that E. R. Debenham,[3] who was a total stranger to MacKenna but had admired the experimental version of the essay On Beauty, wrote to ask him when the complete Plotinus might be expected. He explained in reply that he could not give consecutive time to the undertaking. " At best," he added, " I work very slowly ; and nothing would induce me to put out

[1] Richard Harder, *Plotins Schriften*, i. p. vii.

[2] Cf. his judgement on Butcher and Lang's *Odyssey*, letter 51. On his own theory of translation see further letter 9.

[3] Now Sir Ernest Debenham.

any shred of Plotinus with whose form I was not entirely satisfied at the moment of publication (I already regret some failures of style in that little sample). All I can do is to go on working slowly as opportunity offers, hoping some day to get the leisure the task really requires." Discovering to his astonishment that this fastidious scholar was a daily journalist without even a university degree, Debenham became interested. He promised to find MacKenna the means of publication, and presently offered him a subsidy sufficient to make him independent for a while of leader-writing. The subsidy MacKenna firmly refused : " I could not, or would not, take a penny from Plotinus as long as anyone, unless a speculative publisher, stood to lose from the enterprise." When he was eventually persuaded to accept an advance payment he did so in the belief that it came not from his patron but from the publisher ; not until the first volume of the translation was in print did he understand that Debenham had financed its publication at his own risk.

Debenham's intervention transferred the enterprise from the domain of the impossible to that of imaginable achievement. But fate, who does not care to see men achieve the impossible, began at this point to play out her trumps, of which she held a long hand.

III

The first blow fell when MacKenna was ordered to hospital for an urgent and dangerous operation—the removal of a mastoid. It was successfully performed, but his recovery was slow, and he had not (so far as I can gather) long returned to work when the symptoms of acute neurasthenia began to show themselves—agonising headaches, sleeplessness or tormenting dreams, aboulia, inability to concentrate, and some loss of muscular control which caused him more than once to collapse on the pavement as he walked. These symptoms, which were to be his intimate enemies for the next ten years, he very naturally regarded as after-effects of his recent operation : to the end of his life he used to allege half seriously that the surgeons had cut away the best piece of his brain. Actually, while his lowered physical vitality no doubt favoured the emergence of the trouble, its real causes must have lain further back in his history. Mastoid operations do not make neurasthenics ; moreover, the man who wrote the journal of 1907-9 was already, as it seems to me, spiritually *maladif*. There is little mention in it of physical ailments, though he is "not sure of his health" ;[1] but the psychological weaknesses which tormented him in later life are already recognised there, sometimes with bitter self-contempt. They are the characteristic weaknesses of his type : the same weaknesses which an earlier introspective, H. F. Amiel, observed both in himself and in his predecessor Maine de Biran—"indecision, discouragement, over-dependence on sympathy, inability to finish things, the habit of watching oneself feel and live, and the growing incapacity for practical action."[2] Physical ill-health no doubt aggravated these tendencies in MacKenna, as it has done in others ; and it was to him, as to Maine de Biran, "most disquieting" to find his psychological states varying as a function of his physical condition.[3] But fortunately for himself he had one quality which most of the great introspectives conspicuously lacked, namely the sense of humour. It did not save him from periods of neurasthenia ; it did not always enable him to resist accesses of childish rage or humiliating self-pity ; but it made impossible for him any continuous or habitual yielding to such moods.

In the autumn of 1913 MacKenna's doctor persuaded him to abandon his work and go to London for treatment by Dr. T. W. Mitchell. Marie and he gave up their

[1] April 11, 1907. [2] *Journal of H. F. Amiel*, June 17, 1857.

[3] Letter 8 ; cf. Maine de Biran, *Journal*, ii. p. 340, etc.

Dublin house, and after a short visit to Paris they found a little flat in Kensington Square, " five minutes from Kensington Gardens where the dear dead Queen was born. . . . It is not central if you make learning or life your centre—'t is a whole twopence from the flame of the theatres—but it is central when, as me, you make peace your centre and must see sheep and dead leaves." [1] Here MacKenna passed an anxious winter of enforced idleness. He feared that he would never again be fit for work : " Guard your health even more than your virtue," he wrote to Bodkin ; " the one you can get back à volonté, the other never." His wife, feeling that he had " too much time to think," tried to take him into interesting society : among other people, they met at this time Epstein, Marinetti (who in Mrs. MacKenna's opinion " looked a brute "), and J. C. Squire. The first meeting with Squire was arranged by J. M. Hone at his house in Chelsea, an old Queen Anne house (now destroyed) where Tonks and Orpen had lived. Squire set down his memory of it twenty years later :

" Few men ever made so great an impression on me at first sight [as MacKenna]. He had tousled dark hair, a slight moustache, and brooding eyes : in a dim-lit room he looked into the fire and talked. He talked in imagery, and talked without posing : without any of that self-consciousness of charm which often accompanies Irish (or indeed any) charm. Sitting with him, one forgot the contemporary world, and explored all the abysses of Space and Time—or, rather, he did—for nobody wanted to interrupt him when, with the firelight illuminating his beautiful meditative brow, he talked, as it were to himself, in the loveliest imagery, about the bewilderment of the human soul in this mysterious universe, with which we find it so difficult to cope." [2]

Evidently this was one of MacKenna's good days. In the surviving letters of this period he is, I think, rarely at

[1] Letter to Thomas Bodkin. [2] *London Mercury*, May 1934.

his best : he writes like a sick man, and his gaiety has often a forced note. His health was in fact making little improvement, and early in 1914, on Dr. Mitchell's advice, he entered a sanatorium for nervous cases in Kent. The treatment here did him good, and presently he expressed a hope that he would eventually emerge " as one of those innocent-faced blue-eyed old fellows with lovely white locks who always look as if their mother bathed them and put them to bed at six after hearing their prayers." [1] On leaving the sanatorium he began to make plans for the future. His friends in Dublin pressed him to return : " Ireland seems a thin kind of place," wrote " A. E.," " with folk like you and Stephens out of it." Stephens, on the other hand, suggested that the MacKennas should join him in Paris ; and they might have done so but for the outbreak of war.

MacKenna and his wife did not react alike to the war. Mrs. MacKenna was for a time carried away, not so much by the flood of British patriotic fervour as by a strong sympathy for the France where she had spent her happiest years. She disapproved at first of Irish neutrality, and in 1915 she was writing anxiously to her friends in Ireland about " the awful advance of the Germans." Her husband, on the other hand, viewed the war primarily as a good European, and secondly as an Irishman. From the former standpoint it meant to him overwhelming and senseless disaster, whichever side won ; from the latter, he saw in it a fresh threat to the integrity of Ireland. He deplored the recruiting activities into which men like Arthur Lynch had suddenly flung themselves. " We never did fry our own fish," he wrote to an Irish friend during the first winter of the war, " but did be always jumping into the fire to yank out the herrings for the other man—and small leavings to ourselves when that one had them gozzled."

In the exasperated condition of his nerves he was reluc-

[1] Letter to Thomas Bodkin, spring 1914.

tant to return to a Dublin infected with war fever. "I am glad I'm not in Ireland just now," he wrote, "because I could hardly hope to keep one friend, and I want to keep 'em all." He was still far from well physically, and there was talk of another operation. The drain on his savings was heavy; his wife's income, already diminished through unfortunate investments, was still further reduced as a result of the war. They moved restlessly from one cheap boarding-house to another. "I get tired beyond speech of grinning and chattering, and really lose the health in a vain effort to appear young and gay and friendly and affable and obliging and pleasant and courteous and in general like a banjo which I'm not. You know the banjo: it says tink-a-tink all the time and is welcome in every boarding-house which again I'm not."[1] In the autumn they went to Hove. The prime motive was economy, but MacKenna was delighted by the change. "I am enchanted by the sea," he wrote to Debenham: "somehow I never felt it before except as a cold flat stretch of grey dampness: I used to read Swinburne's sea-hymns with a dull astonishment: now I feel the sea, its spell of magic; above all, the sense that at the seaside you live completely, seeing all the elements, land and sea and over all a great sky that you never knew inland even in the widest and barest park. It has been a sort of revelation to me, and at lowest a great peace, a quiet wonder." Again and again he attempted to resume work on Plotinus, and although the result was always to kindle "a little cerebral hell-fire" he clung fast to the project. "I do feel all the same," he told Debenham, "that I will bring out this great thing for my little life's work." In the spring of 1915 they moved to rooms in Hampstead, and spent much time sun-bathing on the Heath. By July Mrs. MacKenna reported Stephen's health substantially improved. As he gained strength he became home-sick for Ireland, and in the early autumn they returned to Dublin.

[1] To Bodkin, 1914.

MacKenna did not resume his position as leader-writer on the *Freeman*. That journal had followed Redmond in urging Irishmen to enlist: MacKenna disagreed, and once again sacrificed his livelihood to his conscience: "how could I work for it," he wrote to a friend, "when all its sympathies are English?" Eventually, he expressed his willingness to contribute articles "from the outside" (and therefore ill paid), sticking to non-controversial subjects. But his main energies were henceforth given to Plotinus. His health remained precarious. He had to sleep in the afternoon and keep early hours: "if I don't, I crumple up, look corpselike, fall about the place, and wish for a speedy death. I almost pray for it, but that I 'think nobly of prayer' and would not use it for such personal whims."[1] Money was very short: "we are desperately hard up," he confessed to Debenham, "live outwardly very well and inwardly very poorly, and can't get even a week's country change." The suburban house which he had taken on his return had soon to be given up for reasons of expense, and in 1917 he and Marie found a home in "a lovely little flat, quite howlingly swell" in one of the dignified Georgian houses of Merrion Square. He liked to live thus "in the heart of the little city," where he could step across the road to the National Library even on days when he felt too weak to venture far.[2]

To MacKenna, as to almost all those not actually concerned in organising it, the rising of 1916 came with the shock of complete surprise. He had indeed envisaged eight years earlier the possibility of such action, and defended its justice: "even a sage," he wrote, "might to-day take to arms for Ireland, if there were any hope that way."[3] Although he was never, so far as I can ascertain, a member of the Irish Republican Brotherhood or any similar organisation, he was steeped in the Fenian

[1] Letter to Debenham, c. 1916.

[2] Letters to Debenham and Mrs. Robert MacKenna, 1917.

[3] See *Journal* for February 14, 1908.

tradition : he had sat at the feet of O'Leary and Davitt, and he counted among his personal friends such men as Arthur Griffith, Thomas MacDonagh and Eamonn Ceannt, leaders of the new Sinn Fein party (as well as pacifists like Sheehy Skeffington and moderate nationalists like Edmund Curtis). But he was not in the inner councils of the movement. On that singular Easter Monday he stood among the bewildered crowd in O'Connell Street and heard Padraic Pearse read the Proclamation of the Irish Republic to the accompaniment of " a few thin, perfunctory cheers."[1] He stood there for many hours, wrestling with his thoughts. Austin Clarke, the Irish poet and novelist, has sent me this memory of him:

" It was about five o'clock in the afternoon of Easter Monday when I met Stephen MacKenna by chance in the middle of O'Connell Street, directly opposite the G.P.O. A restless, difficult crowd was gathered at the corner of Earl Street, and a few volunteers, armed with rifles and in full green uniform, were endeavouring to keep order. As I made my way through the scattered groups beyond the crowd, I saw Stephen MacKenna alone in a little space, lost in his thoughts and indifferent to those about him. He was leaning weakly against an electric tram standard, but he greeted me in his quick, sad way. He told me that he had hurried down that morning as soon as he heard the news, and that he had been there all day. He looked terribly ill ; his face was deadly pale, and it was obvious that only the intensity of his own feelings and of the event itself sustained him. The Post Office was already cold and grey in the shadows, and beyond passing heads I could see, almost obscured by the great pillars, the watchful figures of armed men at the sand-bagged windows. But clearly against the bright, blue sky above the roof rose the flag of the Irish Republic declared that morning. MacKenna said little to me, nor could much have been said. Thought and emotion could find no

[1] *Memories of the Dead*, p. 20.

other end for themselves than the words ' at last '. Certainly neither of us mentioned any of those friends who, as we knew, must be at their posts opposite us or somewhere else in the city. The historic hour existed with all its secret, countless memories of the past, in and of itself, so that even the feeling of suspense and of coming disaster seemed to belong to a lesser experience of reality. It is difficult now perhaps to recapture that emotion and thought from which even the crowd, dimly hostile or perhaps taken by total surprise, was scarcely a distraction. It has become quite easy to forget how completely the country had drifted away from its own individuality and national life—mainly I fancy from mere indolence and avoidance of self-responsibility. It is easy to forget how greatly the few awakeners were hated and abused. As I stood silently beside Stephen MacKenna, I was increasingly aware not only of that supreme event but of the terrible and painful emotion in his few broken words from time to time. I was still a student, and I had a healthy respect both for his scholarship and for the wilful anger which I had once innocently drawn upon myself. His tormented exaltation, though I secretly understood it, filled me with a superstitious alarm for him. Realising that his wife and others might be already searching for him, and calling suddenly to mind the imminent danger in the city, I tried to persuade him to leave. But by then he had almost forgotten my presence. After some futile and timid efforts, for I feared to irritate him, I went away full of compunction, leaving him to his thoughts."

It was later in the week—on the Tuesday or maybe the Wednesday—that MacKenna, propped on a stick (for he was half crippled that day with rheumatism), returned to O'Connell Street, approached the portico of the G.P.O. where a handful of men were still facing the certainty of defeat and the all-but-certainty of death or long imprisonment, and for the second time in his life proposed himself as a volunteer in the service of an oppressed nationality. Perceiving no doubt the uselessness of the sacrifice—for he was unarmed and untrained, even had he been physically fit to handle a weapon—the commandant rejected his offer. MacKenna hobbled away to brood on his own futility.[1] A few days afterwards, while he and Mrs. MacKenna were staying with his cousin, William Kelly, the house was searched for arms by the military. It proved to contain a number of rifles, the property of the Irish Volunteers, and all the occupants were arrested ; but the MacKennas were released as soon as it was established that they were merely passing guests.

A year or so later there appeared in Dublin a pamphlet on the men of Easter Week, entitled *Memories of the Dead,* by an otherwise unknown " Martin Daly." MacKenna's authorship of this booklet, suspected at the time, seems to me certain both on grounds of style and from the fact that after his death there was found among his papers a list of the " cuts " made by the British censor in " Martin Daly's " manuscript.[2] *Memories of the Dead* is an unpretentious little work : its object was to preserve for future historians some lineaments of the men whose blood was to be the seed of the new Ireland—not only of such as Pearse and MacDonagh, whom all the world had learned to know, but of humbler soldiers like Tom Clarke, the little old tobacconist of Parnell Street, and Peadar O'Meacin, a tradesman who " died for his ideal of Ireland as simply and instinctively as other men follow a bent towards a study or a pastime." The pamphlet is now rare,[3] and the reader may like to see a sample of its manner. The passage which follows is characteristic in its mixture of gentle mockery and imaginative exaltation.

[1] This story rests on the evidence of a single informant, but I know no reason for dismissing it as fiction. MacKenna was not the man to boast at large of his patriotism.

[2] Some of these are exceedingly quaint : thus a reference to insurgents who were shot " in the chill of a barrack yard " appears to have hurt official pride—the words " the chill of " were deleted !

[3] I am indebted to " Seumas O'Sullivan " for procuring me sight of a copy.

" I cannot quite think of the pipes with the calm acceptance one offers the violin or even the flute. When a long, grave man—well dressed, of religious mien, a native philosopher and mystic, showing in his luminous face and solemn presence the race of which he is sealed—stands massively on the platform of a garishly-lighted hall before a vast audience that has just been yelling with exaltation and defiance over political speeches ; when with thoughtful deliberation he takes the pipes from a gill, arranges the curious tubes and bags, elaborately tunes, solemnly begins to play—why, may the outraged spirit of the ancient Ireland absolve me—such a sight would normally make me smile.

" None the less :

" One of my cherished memories is of Eamonn Ceannt piping just so at the Ancient Concert Rooms a short time before the Rebellion. There had been eloquent haranguing, fiery response from the Hall, the thrill of an Ireland resurgent to virile plans and passionate hopes. During an interval princely Eamonn rose before the people, gathered his bags and tubes under his wing, tuned, played : and even then, not foreseeing even dimly how soon the desperate effort, the tragic end, was coming, even then I felt very sharply, like a knife slashing between the bones, that he stood in some quite rare way as the symbol of the times. So gravely, so religiously piping, piping as it were without enthusiasm, as a duty, as a solemn declaration of faith, almost ritually, he appeared before my mind as the grave ghost of the old Ireland rising to haunt the new and to awe it into homage and obedience. I do not know whether Eamonn piped well that night or whether he ever could pipe well ; I know only that long ago he lamented humorously the tragedy it was in one's life to take up the crustiest and most personally unbiddable of instruments ; but I know that that solemnest of all Irish pipers stands and will long stand before my mind like some colossal work of sculpture, some Mestrovich figure full of the entire meaning of a racial existence."

The emotion which the events of Easter week roused in MacKenna found expression also in another form. In July 1916 there appeared in the Gaelic journal *An Claidheamh* one of his very rare experiments in verse, a translation in the original metre of " The Merchant's Son " by Aoghan O'Rahilly (c. 1670-1740). It is introduced by the following note :

" ' The Merchant's Son ' may be taken to mean any such Saviour of Nationality from over-sea as the Gaelic Ireland of the 17th and early 18th century was ceaselessly awaiting. . . . A good deal, though not all, of the intricate Irish rhyme has been reproduced ; but any charm the version may have will be felt only on reading aloud and pronouncing the vowels with an Irish robustness, not with the mincing and slurring of Sunday-parlour elegance. The rhythm in the English here depends wholly on stress, no count having been taken of the number of syllables making up the foot. The translator has used, substantially, the Dinneen-Torna text (Irish Texts Society, 1911)."

I

A Vision sharp, limned on the dark, as I sink at heart for our smitten Queen :—
It brings her past me, with singing and laughter, in winning mastery of her skimming steed ;
Deep eyes aglow, sweet life aflow, all stately ripe in maiden sheen,
She tells the coming of The Merchant's Son with Spanish rage and steel.

II

Sweet her talk, her speech was soft ; my heart's love aye the dreaming maid ;
Ruler of Brian that schooled the Fiann—my grief to-day for a Queen's sad fate—
Under foreign yoke and murder's stroke, my flesh and bone in the Regal Race !
" But there's help to come ; The Merchant's Son will proudly run to my feet again ! "

III

The thousands are pining, worn down by their sighing and
bound to their dying for the face of their Queen ;
Princes are grieving, Clann Mílea is keening, strong wills are
leaping to raise her to freedom ;
But her doom holds her fast and the gloom will ne'er pass—
oh, the brooding will last—" Till the day we shall see,
When The Merchant's Son o'er the waters shall come and the
sorrowful face will be gleaming ! "

IV

Woeful the tale ; thrown down her fame ; lonely the eve of
her day,
Of music bereft, few helpers left, where her clans were once
cheerful and brave ;
Her holies all wrecked ; her soul in the net ; no fool but may
leer in her face,
Unmated, undone—" Till, one day, shall come The Merchant's Son to my gates ! "

V

The tall sons she cherished have fallen, all perished ; gone are
the stately and free,
Conn and Art, that governed stark and won their part in
raging fields,
Crífan strong that held Gaíll in bonds, Luíeach macChéin the
leal ;
Hope there is none—" Till The Merchant's Son o'er the
waters sails for me ! "

VI

By the shore of ships our Mourner sits, poring southward upon
the sea ;
Her baulked eye flits to the Eastern ridge and searches it
wistfully ;
Naught stirs : " O God ! But the Western rim . . . ? Is there
naught but the sand and the spray ? "
Thus her heart is wrung " Till The Merchant's Son shall
muster his heroes from Spain ! "

VII

Her kin all broken that still wore her Token, who filled up the sweet of her day,
No banquet is set, no flagon is wet, no lad in the land will meet maid ;
For love's sky is clouded, frolic is fouled in ill-come crape and keening ;
" But I trust in the coming of The Merchant's Son with thudding drums to relieve me ! "

VIII

Thus high burned her hope. But stern I spoke : " Return ? Mo vrón, he is clay !
The dirge in Spain has surged for your brave ; unheard is your wail, my liege, this day ! "
Woe with the word ! prone on the earth, bemoaning her dearth, my Heart's Dream lay !
The Merchant's Son will never come ; will no other one serve my Queen, for aye ?

Meanwhile, despite political distractions and the state of MacKenna's health, the Plotinus crept forward. There were endless difficulties with Lee Warner, the publisher, who after some correspondence with MacKenna decided that he was " as mad as a hatter," and told Debenham so. More than once the whole scheme threatened to break down. MacKenna on his side was frantic with impatience: " I feel the delay," he wrote, " eating at my heart like some fat rat inside me." Finally in 1917 the first of the five tall volumes saw the light. The luxurious and costly format was not MacKenna's own choice : " my own feeling," he told Debenham, " has always been that poetry should be published at 6d. a volume, and I'd like Plotinus at half a crown." The book was respectfully treated by the reviewers, and received warm praise from Inge and the one or two other Englishmen who were competent to assess it as a work of scholarship ; but the reading public in 1917 had little interest in expensive translations of Greek philosophers, and the sales were, to MacKenna's naive surprise, exceedingly small.

He swallowed his disappointment and worked on at the preparation of the next volume. But the conditions of life were becoming more and more difficult. The war now weighed on him like a nightmare [1]; and if the attempt were made to enforce conscription in Ireland against the Irish conscience he foresaw " a bitterness that will rage for a century." In 1917 he had a serious return of neurasthenic symptoms, and before the end of that year Mrs. MacKenna too fell ill and was " hurried out for an urgent dangerous kill or cure operation which neither killed nor cured." As soon as MacKenna was well enough he had to immerse himself in journalism to meet the doctors' bills and the now steeply rising cost of living. " We have been in dire straits," he wrote about this time : " for a while we were obliged to go very short indeed, even on food—not quite enough of the very simplest—only when we both got very ill did we rise out of that economy, eating, in a grim recklessness, enough to save the health." It was at this point, I think, that Debenham intervened and persuaded MacKenna to accept an arrangement by which for each volume of the Plotinus he received a payment of £250 in advance of publication.

In the autumn of 1918, Mrs. MacKenna had a fresh illness, which was doubtfully diagnosed as an obscure variation of Addison's disease. For several months she lay between life and death, much of the time in great pain. " We have had four nurses in the houselet," says a letter of this period, " and last sacraments all over the place." A further operation, in January 1919, was thought for a time to have been successful ; in March she was pronounced out of danger, though she was " still quite incapable, a mere whimpering yellow ghost." But six months later the dreaded symptoms reappeared ; once more she was " almost continuously in danger all the

[1] Cf. letters 4, 6 and 8.

winter through," and MacKenna was again confronted with the alternative of " the double relay of nurses, or the fantastically dear nursing home with its horrors of bullying ladies who terrify my poor old ghost of a wife." In June 1920 he wrote " The poor old lady thinks she is at last convalescent : the doctor tells me she is incurable and is merely ' enjoying ' a respite."

Meanwhile he was driving himself to continue the Plotinus work, though his organism revolted against it ; he had " constant hot pain and axe-split head by day, and the most appalling dreams by night," " at times such queer things going on up aloft that I have feared my brain was going."[1] His forced efforts rarely brought him satisfaction. " I'm plodding on with Plotinus," he says in another letter, " at what is often the 10th rewriting : the quick flash is gone out of my brain for ever : all the little I get is by toil, mosaic-work, smoothing, planing." He was in despair at his failure to make progress and carry out his undertaking to Debenham : " it burns shamefully in my brain that I have had so much and done so nothing."[2] He would gladly have abandoned the enterprise, but felt bound in honour to continue :

" I have bitterly deplored my ever entering into a contract, and I abhor myself for having taken your money, not only that personal subsidy but also the expenses of publication. Even in journalism I was never bound before : I always refused to contract for a certain number of words or any service at all ; I went to all my Russias and Swedens and Hungaries and the rest on the strict understanding that I sent what I liked and when I liked, and that if the editors did not get full satisfaction I must be allowed to resign at their nod with the full honours of war. . . . I had arranged with my wife that once she got over the danger-point we were to take no more of this money ; but there's the past and there's the contract.

[1] Letters to Debenham, July 1919 and June 1920.

[2] Letter to Debenham, March 14, 1919.

And there are the people who bought the first volume on the pledge of the rest to come duly." [1]

In the end the second volume was finished somehow. It appeared in 1921. MacKenna had thought of inserting in it an announcement that reasons of health prevented further publication, and paying back the subsidy by degrees ; but Debenham succeeded in dissuading him.

With the shootings of 1920 and the British campaign of terror in 1921 national anxieties were added to domestic ones ; life became " a daily and nightly burden of horror and doubt, personal and public." MacKenna believed the policy of armed resistance to be justified [2] ; but he dreaded the increasing spiritual degradation of a war of reprisals. " My dear horrible Ireland, our beautiful people so soiled. . . . Even the noblest Englishman could never understand the distinctions, reservations, allowances I'd feel obliged to make. . . . In the long run, all comes down to the elementary bedrock fact that civilised and moral instinct is just snuffed out when, rightly or wrongly, a people (or in extreme cases a single individual) feels the call of self-preservation against an unwarranted curtailment or denial of liberty." [3] He repeatedly urged Debenham to use his influence in favour of a settlement. " Even though England can crush Ireland to pulp," he wrote in 1921, " Ireland would still rise a nasty ghost and a persistent worry, for generations to come. Pulp does not settle anything where there is an immortal spirit to be reckoned with."

Throughout 1921 MacKenna, like a great number of other people in Ireland, lived in nightly expectation of being raided and arrested.[4] In March he had a narrow escape, which is thus described in a letter to Debenham :

" The other day I, as many others every day, was seized and pawed and shaken three times, exactly like a child, and yelled at and threatened with arrest for a crime

[1] Letter to Debenham, July 1919. Cf. also letter 11.

[2] Cf. letter 13.

[3] Letter to Debenham, March 24, 1920.

[4] Cf. letter 14.

of which I was utterly unconscious : I had looked at a group of men (11 o'clock of the forenoon in College Green, the live centre of Dublin), who it appears were disguised detectives ; had I lost my balance and been either too grovelling or too impudent, I would certainly have been dragged to jail, discovered to be carrying an Irish book —two in fact, the Bedell Bible and a book of verse—and I would be in jail still untried."

Later in the year it was thought that an oath of allegiance would be imposed. MacKenna could not take such an oath, and he made all arrangements against the event of his being imprisoned or interned as a non-juror. Debenham counselled him to leave the country, but he replied that this would be cowardice : "The purely negative service of my poor presence and my 'non serviam'—the admirable thing the devil said in some Psalm or other holy book—that purely negative service I could no more in conscience, the deepest and most sacred, refuse than I could expect you to bow to the Irish republican flag. I only hope," he added, "that you feel as I do that underneath—or above ?—all these intense national differences there may always be a deep personal regard in the realm of peace. 'I fought him, and fight him, bitterly on the lower levels, but we are in deep love above it all,' said Nietzsche of Wagner."

That autumn Mrs. MacKenna was temporarily a little better again, and in the hope of preventing or postponing another relapse it was decided that she should spend the winter in Switzerland with two cousins of her husband. The flat in Merrion Square was disbanded, and MacKenna moved first into rooms in Dublin, then to country lodgings at Enniskerry. He was at Enniskerry when the Dáil met to debate the Anglo-Irish Treaty, and the men who had been working side by side for Irish freedom found themselves of a sudden divided into two bitterly opposed camps —"Free-Staters" and Republicans. To the surprise of many of his friends, MacKenna declared himself unhesitatingly for repudiation of the Treaty. His reasons are set forth in two long letters to Debenham (Nos. 16 and 17). I add here some extracts from a yet longer letter which he wrote at the same date to an Irish supporter of the Treaty :

" I would even now accept this agreement if only it brought us an un-British freedom—just left the question of membership in abeyance, went on the unexpressed assumption that we were members and adherent—though I admit that in that case I wish we were even a little less sovran : if one means to do a man in the eye one would rather not get too much out of him before the happy day of the doing arrives. . . . I'm horrified when I think that we are asked to save even the language by the path of a declaration of 'adherence to and membership of . . .' The language is interesting and lovely in itself and in its potentialities as well as its stored values, but so is Arabic : I value the language not least because it says Civis Britannicus non sum : in an Ireland which should say 'O'Neil is a Briton, MacCarha, O'Brien, O'Murachu Britons,' I don't see any sense in the language except as there is in Greek, Sanscrit, Bantu. . . . The end of the historic Ireland should be the end of Irish, just as the Maori end was the end of the Maori lingo. . . . If the people of Ireland like being British I can only spew them out as I out-spew any Briton—or they spew me out as an offence and a danger to the body or soul of Ireland. Of course if we are many thus spewed out, it becomes a question which is spew and which is body : perhaps we Repudiators are not a spew but a birth—who knows ? "

For a few unhappy weeks MacKenna felt that he must abandon Plotinus, at least temporarily, and throw himself into a whirlwind campaign against the Treaty. But it presently became clear that his fellow-republicans intended to adopt methods of which he could not approve : he had hoped for " constitutional work for freedom, either by advocacy only or by 'passive resistance.'"[1] The civil war of 1922 filled him with shame and grief. There was no place for such a man in the Ireland of the gunmen. While, however, he was revolted by the brutalities that were committed in the name of republicanism, he was, and remained to the end of his life, "impenitently republican."[2] "Take notice," he wrote to Curtis in the autumn of 1922, "that I abhor now and for ever amen the free state[3] as the abomination of desolation seated in the High Places ; and if, now or ever, anyone says 'S. M. K. has verted,' then kindly spit in his right eye, kick him to the ground, kick him on the ground, dance on him, and cry in a loud voice 'Here lies a liar.'" But he never extended to individual supporters of the Free State his serio-comic indignation against the régime : his friendship with men like Curtis and myself continued unbroken, and "A. E." remained for him "a noble gentleman despite his utter inability to see our republican point of view."[4]

After his abortive excursion into politics MacKenna resumed work on the next *Ennead*. For a time it went well : "the present revision is joyful," he reports to Debenham ; "it is the divine Plotinus again." Mrs. MacKenna had returned from Switzerland convinced that she was cured at last, and they found quarters in Dundrum, a village close to Dublin. But by the summer she was once more bedridden, and her husband's old incapacity had reappeared : "there are weeks during which I can't hold the thread of an argument in my head at all."[5] For what was to be the last winter of her life she was sent to Bournemouth, while MacKenna, by her wish, remained in Dublin. "Distance from such things helps a lot," she wrote from Bournemouth to Debenham :

[1] Letter 20. [2] Letter 21.

[3] MacKenna refused even the dignity of initial capitals to this detested institution.

[4] Letter to Curtis, 1924 or 1925. [5] Letter 20.

"he cannot possibly worry so much over there, with cheerful letters (one learns to invent cheerfulness) from one every day." But on Christmas Day, 1922, she took a new turn for the worse, and MacKenna hurried across from Dublin: "I will never again be 12 hours away from her; her long sufferings and bitter disappointments have earned her all the help and comfort one human being can give another." [1] Presently he fetched his MSS. from Ireland and attempted to carry on his work, "trying to finish the book in snatches at the nursing home and in my own room." Marie's struggle for life lasted another six months, "always on the brink of danger, often given up, always battling back to a condition in which she just lives, too weak to be even lifted from bed to a low chair for a change of view." She died on July 4, 1923, and Stephen went back to his earliest Dublin home, his aunts' little house in Rathmines, to bury himself in Plotinus and to tend the ailing survivor of the two Dresden china ladies. "If the doctor thinks well of it," he wrote to his mother, "I'll hire a bath-chair and push her about for half an hour or so on a fine day as I hoped to push my own old lady."

His immediate reaction to his wife's death was, as might be expected, a sense of release. But the strain of the last years had exhausted his courage and vitality, and in the months that followed he came, I think, nearer to complete mental collapse than ever before. Whenever he ventured into society he broke down. "As time goes on," he wrote to me that autumn, "I get madder, not calmer, and I make disgraceful manifestations of grief or of nerve-wrack, and go away worse than ever in myself." "No religion or philosophy has any validity over my trouble, nothing gives any value to life," he told Debenham.[2] The new instalment of Plotinus was nearly ready, but it brought him no comfort. Like its predecessor, it had been done, as he said, "in isolated strips while my wife

[1] Letter 22. [2] Letter 30.

was five years a-dying and all a bleak muddle round me"; and in his depression it seemed to him impossibly bad. He now saw the whole enterprise as a hideous blunder: "It is not through my own fault that I am, in the fact, what I think I most loathe of all things, a humbug in scholarship. I took up, honestly, what was beyond my powers; I was taken up by others, and am caught in a net."[1] He refused to accept more money from Debenham, and reverted to the idea of handing over the Plotinus to someone else and paying off, by a return to journalism, what he persisted in calling his "debt of honour" to his patron.[2] A little later, after the death of his surviving aunt in February 1924, he offered, if Debenham would release him, to use the scanty inheritance which had come to him to pay a professional scholar for doing the work, leaving himself an income of between two and three pounds a week, on which he proposed to retire to some Irish-speaking village in Connaught.

IV

It was, I believe, Debenham's action at this point which saved MacKenna's health and sanity; he summoned him peremptorily to England and insisted on giving him a prolonged holiday in Dorset. Four months of complete quiet among green fields did much to restore his mental poise: "It has plucked me out of a slough of despond," he tells Debenham, "and set me in the places of hope." And in fact the worst period of his life was now over. He had before him ten more years of poverty and recurrent illness, and for six of them his tired brain had still to battle with Plotinus; but nothing that was to come was comparable with the agonies of the preceding decade.

He returned no more to Ireland. Apart from his dis-

[1] Letter to E. R. Dodds, 1923. [2] Letter 27.

taste for the new régime, Dublin was, as he told Curtis, "too full of memories," and he had too many acquaintances there—his experiences in the last twelve months had left him with a morbid dread of society, especially the society of intellectuals. "I don't care a button," he wrote in 1929 to his brother Robert, "about intellectual people, in fact they frighten and bore me, except for James Stephens, who tho' eminent is the simplest and friendliest soul alive; I would never care if I never met any living thing that had ever heard there had ever been an idea or a picture or a sonata in the world." To his surprise, he found the slow silent country folk of Dorset and Hampshire far more to his taste than the chatterers in Dublin drawing-rooms. "I admire the people of Hampshire immensely," he wrote to Curtis, "the plain people I mean, their dignity, mannerliness, comeliness; and yet at times I look on them with amazed reprobation, and on myself, saying 'your people are not my people, nor are your gods my gods, and the Lord alone knows what the devil I'm doing among yez.'"[1] He continued to see a few of his older friends, but at increasingly long intervals. On the other hand he wrote more, and I think better, personal letters at this period than when he lived in Dublin. To some extent the pen now discharged what had been the office of the tongue: he had developed a highly individual epistolary style which kept the inflections of the living voice. In the gay and nonsensical scribbles which on good days he would despatch to Curtis or some other friend the reader may come nearer than elsewhere to an apprehension of what MacKenna was like as a talker.

He had a further reason, as he explains in a letter to Octavian MacKenna, for keeping out of Ireland. He had made up his mind formally and publicly to renounce Catholicism, and he wished, characteristically, to avoid embarrassing by his presence certain pious Catholic

[1] Cf. also letter 49.

friends in Dublin to whom he was henceforth a " renegade " and in effect an untouchable. Ireland is a country where, with the rarest exceptions, religious beliefs are still (*a*) inherited and (*b*) taken seriously—almost as seriously as the political beliefs from which they are with difficulty separable. Hence MacKenna's " apostasy " really did cause surprise and scandal in Dublin. It was as though he had suddenly turned imperialist. I have even heard it charitably suggested that his brain had been addled by his sufferings and that for the last ten years of his life he was not fully responsible for his actions—an interpretation to which the concluding volumes of the Plotinus and the later letters in the present book are surely a sufficient answer if any is needed.

It is clear that the " apostasy " was not in fact that sudden renunciation of the beliefs of a lifetime for which it was mistaken. The tone of the 1897 Commonplace Book is already non-Christian, though the sentence which explicitly condemns Christianity may possibly be a later addition. And there is the Journal of 1907-9. After reading it, one asks not " Why did this man reject Catholicism ? " but " Why did he remain for so long a nominal Catholic ? " In 1908, though he still attends mass and is still moved by " the beauty of the ceremonies and their old meaning," [1] he looks forward to a time when the religions, " with their neat promises of future redressing," will have crumbled away and there will be only Religion—" men going in the evenings with eyes downcast and glowing." [2] The Renaissance, he holds, " brought sanity into religion " by reaffirming the Greek respect for the intellect, which he misses in Thomas à Kempis and in Eckhardt, though he finds in Rosmini " something that begins to look like it." [3] He is shocked by the Church's condemnation of socialism : " the Church now excommunicates, as I understand, those that

[1] *Journal*, April 18, 1908. [2] *ibid.* February 11, 1908.
[3] *ibid.* November 12, 1907.

preach the doctrine which Christ and the first Churchmen practised, the doctrine which the Young Man having Great Possessions was excommunicated for not accepting." [1] Catholic orthodoxy astonishes him: "can they really believe that the Once Human, now ravished in the Beatific Vision, do look down upon the upper room of No. 1, Goldhurst Terrace, Finchley Road, where the Wax Lady waits at the door? Amazing the things one can believe when one is called *homo*." [2] His "they" is surely decisive.

Seven years later, in the essay on "Experimental Ethics" to which I have already referred, he writes of such men as himself: "Despite all their instincts and longings they dare not, in the truth of their soul they cannot, take stand upon an eternal Aye or Nay. An infallible Catholicism presses upon them, perhaps; but reason will not bend. The Protestantisms show a certain bravery of independence with reverence, but seem fluid, fissible, an uncertain footing, a yielding staff. Oriental teachings, marvellously explaining all things, seem to leave their own warrant unclear. Mysticism lures, but shows too its threat of insanity or invirility. The vaguest deistic faith in immortality seems too definite for these sick souls' certainty. Yet life, with its men and women, presents its problems, and the inward war wages relentlessly, and something in the man cries for a law and for an emotional spur, for a table and for a whip, that he may know whither he would go and may be driven down the path he has chosen."

Nevertheless all through his years in Ireland MacKenna continued to call himself a Catholic, though he did not pretend to be a "good" one: in conversation with men of Protestant origins like "A. E." or Curtis or myself he would maintain with fervour that "to be a bad Catholic is the best religion in the world." *Intus ut libet: foris ut moris est*, he had quoted in his 1897 notebook; and for

[1] *Journal*, April 3, 1908. [2] *ibid.* December 11, 1907.

more than a quarter of a century he appears to have acted in matters of religion (though assuredly in no other) upon that questionable maxim. His motives were, I think, three. One was the "purely extraneous reason" given in letter 36, namely that "Rome is the best trench against Buckingham Palace or Downing Street." Catholicism was significant for him less as the Universal Church than as the church of his own small people; that is why it seemed to him, for example, right and important that Casement should have died a Catholic.[1] A second motive, equally extraneous, was the fear of distressing his wife, who in her last years especially clung to Catholicism as her only protection against the besetting fear of death. Thirdly, individualist though he was, MacKenna had throughout his life a longing "for a table and for a whip," together with a strong sense of the spiritual power generated by collective acts of worship. "I have never yet," he wrote to my mother after he had abandoned Catholicism, "been to any service, Romanist, Anglican, Unitarian or even Salvation Army street-howlery, without feeling a spiritual presence there, working from somewhence upon the crowd, and from the crowd, if not from that somewhence, upon me." The most perfect instrument of this operative power was in his view the mass; in contrast with the Roman rite, the Anglican seemed to him "smugly sure and at rest," whereas the deeper sort of religion "throws itself about in a kind of agony and must use magic."[2] And he still thought it "on the whole a very legitimate thing" to accept a religious system "as a vehicle of spirituality without intellectual adherence to dogma."[3]

When MacKenna left Ireland in 1924 the extraneous considerations had ceased to be effective. His wife was dead; and politically the Church had in his opinion betrayed its trust by siding with might against right and

[1] *Memories of the Dead.* [2] Letter 36.

[3] Letter 35. Contrast his later view, expressed in letter 71.

preferring expediency to principle. " Since the Bishops," he wrote to Bodkin, " entoned their *credo in unum Johannem Bullum omnipotentem*, I've become a Christian and read my Bible like George Moore and Mr. Wesley." But the removal of external restraints was hardly the main cause of his *volte face*. In the hour of its testing, discipline without faith affords but a slippery foothold. The abysses which had opened beneath his feet in the last few years had forced upon MacKenna the need for a deeper solution of his personal religious problem than was to be found in a merely disciplinary Catholicism.[1] During the last period of his life his strongest interest lay in the attempt to discover a creed which both his reason and his heart could approve.

His temperament demanded some form of " two-storied " belief. " I feel much more sure of God," he confided to his *Journal*, " and of some real Being other than that which I see, than of the Finchley Road." And twenty years later he wrote to my mother, " I could no more doubt the existence of this divine mind at work (or at play) in the universe than I can doubt the existence of a mind in humanity." It was, I conjecture, just this intuitive perception of the visible world as an expression of something other than itself which had originally drawn MacKenna to the study of Plotinus ; and in his years of tribulation he sought comfort from him, not wholly in vain—" As I'm tried bitterly in the furnace of trouble," he told Debenham, " I become more deeply a spiritual disciple of Plotinus than ever before." He thought that " a good Plotinian would be undistinguished in life and death from a good Christian, except perhaps in being better." [2] But as with Catholicism, so with Neoplatonism : while he drew from the philosopher true spiritual nourishment, he found intellectual acceptance of his premisses increasingly difficult. Plotinus' teaching left too many aspects of life unexplained. " He builds the soul a

[1] Cf. letter 30. [2] Letter 4.

fairy palace," said MacKenna once to Bergin : "enchanted, you follow him through the lovely labyrinthine structure ; you mount, breathless, by successive stairways of the spirit, each more pure, more tenuous, more aspiring than the last—but sooner or later there comes a time when you ask yourself where the W.C. is." It is significant that at the end of his days MacKenna turned from Plotinus to a harsher and less imaginative but more homely comforter—Epictetus, the lame ex-slave.

By the autumn of 1924 he felt sufficient confidence in his powers to resume work and accept Debenham's subsidy for the next volume. The expenses of his wife's illness had been, for a man of his means, fantastic—just over two and a half times his income, he estimated. And at her death her little capital passed under her father's will to the children of her sister. But his aunt's legacy brought in about £150 a year, and on this, with the subsidy and the scanty remnant of his own savings, he set out both to live himself and to make a contribution towards the support of his mother, who was now lodged with his brother Theobald in London. "Beyond living while the work is doing," he had written to Debenham, "I can't care a button about the money side. . . . I never did care about money as long as I could live and buy books and hear and make music." [1]

I have not yet mentioned that the hearing and making of music was from his schooldays onward one of MacKenna's major pleasures, and became in the bad years his last fortress against misery. He was, I am told, a very indifferent executant, but he made up in zeal what he lacked in aptitude. As I write, I recall my first meeting with him. In 1917 or thereabouts a friend brought me to visit him at his flat in Merrion Square. Entering what had been the drawing-room of some Georgian hostess, I saw a long lean man with grizzled hair and liquid brown eyes remote and melancholy as a peatbog : he was walk-

[1] Cf. also letter 41.

ing, with a peculiar grace of movement, very softly up and down the twilit room, swerving now and again in his course to avoid a jutting piece of furniture or a heap of books on the floor ; his face, upturned and serious, wore the illuminated look of an El Greco saint ; and as he walked he played upon a concertina. He did not interrupt his stride or his music for our entrance, but as the tune ended his grave mouth suddenly wrinkled into a grin of welcome. I gaped, uncertain in my undergraduate scepticism if what I had seen were pose or passion. Doubtless, like much of MacKenna's behaviour, it was both—passion inviting you to laugh at it as pose, in the secret fear that you might laugh at it as passion.

The concertina was at this period his chief resort in bad times.[1] Jack Yeats has told me how, calling once at Merrion Square when Mrs. MacKenna lay seriously ill, he was met on the staircase by faint strains of music. He mounted, but study and living-room stood empty. Guided by the muffled music he tried another door. The bedroom to which it led was also apparently empty ; but on the bed was a strangely shaped heap of rugs and blankets, and from the interior of this heap proceeded sounds as of a concertina being played very softly. He poked it and a head was protruded : " Come in under here, Jack," whispered MacKenna, " the way we won't disturb my old lady, and I'll play you a grand new tune."

He would allow no reflections on the prestige of his favourite instrument. When in some letter I spoke of playing the concertina in one's bath, he was indignant : " The concertina is not played naked, but in frock coat, top hat and lilac Oxford trousers : you mistake its rank. . . . Have I never told you that QUEEN VICTORIA and forty Ladies of Honour used to sit in a little circle round the throne with forty dukes behind each chair and the whole 41 playing 'There's someone in the house with Dinah,' the first piece in the Concertina Tutors of the

[1] Cf. letter 12.

time? 'Twill give you an idea of the rank of the Concertina."

Later he began to collect, and experiment upon, all manner of strange instruments. "I play," he wrote to me in 1926, "not only the concertina but the guitar, two kinds of mandoline, four kinds of clarinet, and the gramophone." Of the clarinet he wrote to another friend, "I think it is far more beautiful in tone than any human voice: the mischief is 'tis a spitty instrument, and variable: I suppose good players can control it, but with me it emits the most incongruous sounds, just when it has been behaving most divinely: 'tis a child, not to say a baby, incalculable, irresponsible." When he lost his teeth he had to abandon his assaults upon it. His last love was for the guitar, at which he and James Stephens toiled long and despairingly.

His desire for music attracted him to Bournemouth. He settled in lodgings on the outskirts, at a point where, as he told Debenham, "beauty and sordor co-jazz." [1] He had good health here during the winter that followed, and Plotinus moved steadily forward. But in the late spring of 1925 the familiar symptoms were renewed for a time: "I feel obliged to nurse my head as a little girl a dolly: I feel myself carrying it just so, as something not my own; perhaps like those that carry, I believe, eggs on spoons in races." He emerged from this bout only to be attacked successively by kidney trouble [2] and muscular rheumatism. To Curtis, advising him at this time on historical reading, he replies, "I never now will feel able to buy a book that takes more than 7 days [to read], lest I'd be called before I'd get the value of me money."

He was not called, but progress was slowed down, and doctor's bills were hard to meet. It was not until 1926 that another *Ennead* appeared and he started work on

[1] Cf. letter 38. He had to move later into cheaper rooms.

[2] The source of the "horrible tho' comic symptoms" referred to in letters 43 and 44. It eventually killed him.

" the ouf volume, i.e. the last." In that year he was reluctantly contemplating arrangements to set up a *ménage* with his mother in Brighton, when the old lady died. The event left him unmoved :[1] she was a woman of cold and conventional temper, and although he behaved towards her with a touching gentleness and deference, he had never loved her. Her death relieved him of some financial responsibility, and he felt able to buy himself " a pretty cottage, guaranteed damp and leaky," which he named Vinecot, at Wallis Down, outside Bournemouth.

It was at Vinecot that MacKenna first met Margaret Nunn, who was to take the place in his heart of the children whom his wife had not borne him. She has sent me the following description of the house, and of his life there as her youthful eyes saw it :

" Vinecot overlooked the moors, at the edge of Bournemouth. There never was such a cottage, from floor to ceiling each room was lined with books except where in spaces hung musical instruments, mostly stringed ones, guitars, mandolines, balalaika ; there were also clarinets and squeegees. And there were Lord Buddhas of all shapes, sizes and postures, and these were perched quaintly in corners where they caught the eye as you entered or left a room. All the doors had been removed so that the rooms led one into another. It was an old Hampshire cottage, thatched, with walls made of mud and wattles. Some of the rooms had been dark but in all he had had windows made, the glory of which he loved to show you. On the western side of the cottage he had built a sun verandah of glass, where bloomed golden chrysanthemums in profusion.

" Here we arrived, myself and a Unitarian minister, a great scholar and always called by S. MK. ' the holy man.' We talked from noon till night, we made strong tea and drank it out of mugs of which there were great variety, German pewter-lidded beer mugs with handles,

[1] Letter 48.

silver mugs, and mugs of diverse colours and shapes. We stood and discussed them and chose us one mug each, the one we fancied most; for S. MK. was whimsical—no little beauty, no little passing interest was missed by him, there was no routine in his soul. There were mugs for tea and you must choose your own and not be dull and commonplace and drink smugly and unilluminatedly out of a blue-lined cup.

" He played a Beethoven symphony on the gramophone; he had a lot of symphonies and played one each morning at his breakfast time, drinking tea and munching plummy cake.

" The gramophone was a Columbia though he had really wished for an H.M.V. he told us, but he simply could not bear their trade mark, the silly smug little dog gazing into the huge old fashioned horn—to have that on his gramophone and in his room eternally to look at, it was too common and unbeautiful. He simply hated that little dog; so he wrote to the H.M.V. Company and told them that he disliked their trademark and asked them could they supply him with a gramophone without the dog. They replied that they couldn't, but undaunted he wrote to them again that they were very unbusinesslike and unobliging and surely it would be better to sell a gramophone without a dog than lose the sale of one altogether to a man who would laud the H.M.V. Co. and their wonderful gramophones. But they wouldn't and he hated them for being so pig-headed and having such a horrid little dog. To understand S. MK. one had to realise his extreme love of beauty and hatred of vulgar incongruity."

The " holy man " mentioned by Margaret Nunn was Henry Hall, a minister of unusual intelligence and cultivation, for whom MacKenna conceived a warm regard. For a time he attended Hall's chapel regularly and astonished his friends by writing them long letters about Unitarianism—or rather, about a creed of his own which he called by that name.[1] " My Unitarianism," he told Curtis, " isn't a thing to be publisht má's gá'é,[2] as you seem to imply ; the very contrary : it's to be dragged down and bellowed forth ; it's to be painted in red letters on every green pillar box ; to be worn on your brow, inscribed in the palm of your hand, stamped on free state stamps, publisht like a Republic, like a Rhododendron, like an unBerginal joke, like a Thingumabob on a Whatumacallit, like everything public, gá' and gan gá',[3] from Sunday noon to Saturday midnight, to be Broadcast, Radioted, Listened in to, though all Ireland die of Heart-shock and the Pope throw himself with snarls of baffled rage into the Tiber." But when Hall was transferred to Trowbridge MacKenna's chapel-going quickly ceased, though he resumed it for a time half-heartedly in London. He found it impossible to digest " the too minute and dictatorial prayers, and the slushy-wushy sloppy-poppy hymns " ;[4] and he was revolted by sentimental gushings about " Jesus Christ, who is to me offensive." [5] His fellow-worshippers in London appeared to him " a disgusting set of imbeciles gathered under the divinest banner." [6] His final judgement on Unitarianism is expressed in a letter which he wrote in 1931 to his brother Robert :

" Unitarianism is of course a lost cause—largely, I think, because like the concertina (a most noble instrument of the most astonishing capabilities) it has fallen into the hands of idiots and never been given a fair chance. It will utterly die out, I feel sure, in less than a hundred years. That is, in its organised form : as a matter of fact, being the core of all religion of the western type (and being able even to absorb, easily and fittingly, eastern ideas) it will be in essence the religion of the future

[1] Cf. letter 50.
[2] Irish, " in case of necessity."
[3] Irish, " necessity or no."
[4] Letter 61.
[5] Letter to Robert MacKenna, about 1929.
[6] Letter 73.

—but under another name and form, or under no name and form."

The "eastern ideas" exercised a strong fascination upon him. The *Journal* shows him already interested in the Yoga system.[1] In 1913 he read the *Bhagavadgita*, but concluded that it was "all in elementary Christianity, only in another metaphor."[2] Later on, when Stephens had persuaded him to study the Indian scriptures seriously, he revised his opinion. While, however, he learned to value Yoga as a mental discipline, he rejected its supernaturalism as firmly as he did Christianity.[3] He preferred the contemplation of Buddha to the contemplation of Christ: in its Indian form the human ideal was not blurred for him by what he was accustomed to call "that bloody lamb business." But despite the images of Buddha that accompanied him in all the migrations of his last years, he was no Buddhist: he saw no reason, as he told a correspondent, "to believe in Karma, reincarnation, and all that."[4]

About eighteen months after MacKenna had acquired Vinecot he found himself obliged to sell it again: "I have drawn on Plotinus in advance," he writes to his brother Octavian, "as much as I honestly can, and must therefore sell to live." He had to move into two unfurnished rooms in a bricklayer's house in the village of Ringwood; he expected this to be his permanent home "as long as I permane, which I don't wish long." The change was accepted with a philosopher's cheerfulness. "I have pleasant enough rooms here, and find more ease than in my cottage, where I couldn't get any service, and was fast becoming a household drudge toiling over lamps and oilstoves and tea-mugs. Yet the little place had grown pleasant and serviceable (bar the service)."[5]

Some ten miles from Ringwood lived W. K. Magee

[1] April 11, 1907.
[2] Letter 1.
[3] Cf. letters 79 and 80.
[4] Cf. also letter 70.
[5] Letter to Debenham, spring 1928.

(" John Eglinton "), who like MacKenna had declined to be a citizen of the Free State, though for an opposite reason. He considers that he " did not quite succeed with MacKenna," and indeed no two men of intelligence could have differed more in temperament and outlook. Yet there was a certain liking between them, and at this period they saw each other fairly frequently. Mr. Magee has been good enough to send me the following reminiscences of their meetings.

" MacKenna, with his important work as a translator, his gay letter-writing gift, his musical instruments, his liking for the society of humble folk, reminded one a good deal of Edward FitzGerald : but FitzGerald managed his life better than MacKenna, who, after his wife's death, was sadly in need of someone to look after him. He had established himself (' for ever '), after various unsuccessful experiments, with some people in a pair of cottages beside the bridge at Ringwood, which the river often threatened with inundation : you could see his books and belongings from the road, bulging against the windows of both houses. The lumber of books and miscellaneous articles in his gloomy living-room was agreeably relieved, soon after my first visit to him, by a happy and daring innovation. I had noticed in my neighbourhood the disappearance of a little building of corrugated iron, lately used as a Catholic place of worship, and when MacKenna invited me to see his ' church,' I was amazed to find that he had purchased the building (' for £40 ') and set it up in his back-garden. He had closed off one end to make a little bedroom, and the rest of the building was a longish apartment lined with his books and with comfortable seats—as fine a working-room as a writer could wish, though in cold weather we had to come back to the house. MacKenna with his priestly appearance suited it well. What his real design was in this edifice, what he hoped from it, he had never perhaps quite worked out in his own mind. He was framed to be the centre of a listening circle, and in Dublin I had often heard his talk caught up into inspired harangues. There were people in the neighbourhood who would have heard him gladly : a well-known novelist lived over the way, and the Rector of the place (as MacKenna told me, not without some apparent gratification) turned out to be a student of Plotinus, and much interested to hear that MacKenna was his neighbour. But association with his neighbours would have involved entanglement in social obligations, which he abhorred.

" I once brought out George Moore to see him. The two were naturally antagonistic to one another, MacKenna being one of those who denied all value to Moore's authorship ;[1] Moore, on the other hand, smiling persistently at all the musical instruments lying about, and even conceiving a doubt about MacKenna's Greek, suspected him of being not much more than a picturesque charlatan. I daresay he was saying to himself all the time what a lovely couple of pages it would all make. They talked pleasantly together, however, especially when Moore found that he could not insult the Catholic church in MacKenna's person, and our host regaled us in a garden-restaurant on the other side of the road. But the point is that the little stir of this visit pleased MacKenna : in this reception of a visitor from the outer world, one of the unavowed intentions of the ' church ' was for the moment realised. As it was, it only served to bring home to him his loneliness."

This account attributes to MacKenna a sense of isolation which I think he felt only rarely. He made friends with all the children of the village, and with the gypsies who had an encampment close by. He continued also to see a good deal of Hall and Margaret Nunn. Much of his time, the latter tells me, was spent in tramping by himself at night : " often he would set out at midnight and not return till four a.m. : there was a road by which ran a

[1] This is perhaps an overstatement : see letter 83.

river, and beyond were flat marshes, and beyond again a low hill covered with pines ; here he said God was always brooding, and here he liked to walk." It was not until after Hall's departure to Trowbridge that he found himself " getting cranky " at Ringwood, and " began to hate everyone." [1] He moved first to rooms in north-west London, to be near Stephens ; then in the autumn of 1929 he bought himself a little house at Harrow—" Ellendene " or " Eldene "—for under Debenham's skilful management his finances had improved somewhat, and he was tired of " swallowing other people's foods and moods."

" Eldene " is thus described by Margaret Nunn :

" It was just a little modern house, not an old cottage full of character like the one at Wallisdown or later in Cornwall. But there was no need to get any further than the front door to find that this was no ordinary house : the letter box had been made large enough to receive parcels of books without calling anyone to the door, and you could easily put your hand through and unfasten the door as well ! Inside, the walls of every room, including the bedroom, were lined with bookshelves that reached from floor to ceiling. . . . The collection of Buddhas always increased, and here they were everywhere, on the window sills, in odd corners, and in the kitchen solemnly meditating among the domestic utensils.

" To Eldene every Saturday was invited anybody who could play a guitar. We played and talked, got ourselves tea and later supper, in the summer sitting long into the night in the sun-room,[2] the stars shining a little distortedly through the glass roof. Quite regularly came a Portuguese boy, a Russian, the Russian's father-in-law who was an Austrian, a young English architect and his fiancée ; sometimes there was an Italian, a very good guitar player, who came when he was in England. At

[1] Letter 63.

[2] A glass structure built on by MacKenna at the back of the house.

these parties S. MK. was delightful : we spread ourselves all over the house and garden talking and playing, and he would prowl round happily, commending or criticising ; he wouldn't play himself, though he could get the shyest performer to. But he would tell us of the hours that he practised with no result except that he found the loveliest melodies and occasionally produced a note of the divinest quality that mortal man ever heard. He had a wonderful collection of music, which included a wealth of folksongs. We always strung his guitars for him : he simply couldn't manage to tie the knot and twist the other end into the hole at the top and secure it. He said he often longed to send for one of us when a string broke."

The last volume of the Plotinus—a long and particularly hard one—was ground out slowly at Wallisdown, Ringwood and Harrow. In the autumn of 1928 I received a despairing appeal for help[1] : " I'm in agonies over the Sixth, and not the difficulter parts. 'Tis all too difficult for me and I wish I were dead—tho' even that has its risks : I figure myself sometimes flying down the corridors of Hades pursued by Plotty and him roaring." More was wanted than the slight occasional assistance by way of criticism and suggestion which I had been able to render in connection with one or two of the earlier volumes. I introduced MacKenna to a young Plotinian scholar named B. S. Page, and Debenham so far relented as to allow the two to collaborate in the translation of the last *Ennead*. I had feared that MacKenna might not be an easy person to work with ; but I was wrong—the partnership between the young university-trained man and the self-made scholar proved a very happy one, and resulted in a better version than either could have produced unaided. In May 1930 the last proof-sheets were signed. " The work will be creditable," wrote MacKenna to his patron, " but there's no disguising the fact that a few more decades could well be spent on bringing it up

[1] Cf. letter 60.

to a really fine polish." He thought of adding a brief personal postscript to this final volume, but decided against it : " the whole thing has been austerely impersonal, and that impersonality is very personal "—what had Stephen MacKenna's victory over fate to do with Plotinus ? He had judged the achievement " worth a life " : he had given his life, and had achieved.

Whether in fact MacKenna's Plotinus is worth the enormous price that was paid for it—not only in effort and suffering, but in the sacrifice of the other potentialities that lay in his rich natural endowment—is a question which I will not attempt to answer. But two things are certain : it is a noble monument to an Irishman's courage, an Englishman's generosity, and the idealism of both ; and it is one of the very few great translations of our day. " I lay down for myself," wrote MacKenna at an early stage of the work, " the general principle that I must have the courage of my own decisions, of my own idiocies or ignorances. . . . Of the things I have done against the general view of scholars, many will be finally accepted, while others will no doubt be spat out of the ' final mouth ' as grotesque blunders." [1] Blunders there are in plenty—some of them inevitable in any pioneer work on such a text, others of a kind which a lesser man, given the ordinary academic training, would quite possibly have avoided. Yet taken as a whole it is, with all its faults, not only an astonishing performance for a journalist who had never crossed the threshold of a university, but an important contribution to the understanding of the most obscure of major Greek writers, and one of which any professional man of learning might well be proud. Its claim to permanence, however, rests not on its scholarship (in the narrow sense of that term), but on other qualities, which the learned too often lack. " In the matter of accuracy," said an authoritative reviewer in the *Journal of Hellenic Studies*, " Mr. MacKenna's translation, which in English

[1] To Debenham, about 1916.

at least is virtually pioneer work, is not likely to be final, but for beauty it will certainly never be surpassed." As Dr. T. E. Page put it once in a letter to Debenham, " You could possibly find half a dozen scholars who could translate Plotinus accurately ; but to reproduce him, to make him live again, to catch something of that unearthly beauty which attaches to his words—this needs something more than accuracy or scholarship, and Mr. MacKenna possesses it." " I do not think," said Sir John Squire, " that any living man has written nobler prose than Mr. MacKenna."

His friends in Ireland had already tried to give expression to their sense that the Plotinus had, in W. B. Yeats' words, " conferred honour and dignity " on a small country in which the union of scholarship with literary art is perhaps even rarer than elsewhere. At the national festival of the Tailteann Games, in August 1924, Yeats announced that the Royal Irish Academy had "crowned" MacKenna's work and awarded a gold medal to its author. It was recognised that he would in all likelihood feel obliged to decline the award on grounds of principle, and for this reason he was not notified of it in advance. He did decline it, explaining in a letter to the press that while he was " pleased by the compliment from so distinguished a body " he could accept no honour " from a Society whose title seems to imply any connection between Ireland and the English throne." [1] Despite this rebuff, he was asked some years later to accept membership of the Academy ; but this too he felt bound to refuse.[2]

With the completion of the Plotinus, MacKenna was liberated from the last strands of that network of conflicting obligations—obligations to his wife, to his country, to his patron, to his own imperious dæmon—in which he had felt himself entangled since the " moral upheaval " on his thirty-fifth birthday. The thing that he had set himself to do was done, and in the doing, though he had

[1] Cf. letter 34. [2] See letter 83.

worn himself out, he had " shaped his own image " : he stood at length free and entire. Despite growing poverty and increasingly frequent illness, the four years that remained to him were the calmest, if not the happiest, which he had known since 1907. " My work isn't much, but it stands done : now on milk and eggs and with music and Irish I can idle and wait, in peace of conscience." [1] Once only his peace was disturbed, when it was proposed that the Plotinus should be republished in the Loeb Library and he felt that he must undertake a revision ; but the project, like some earlier negotiations to the same end,[2] eventually broke down.[3]

His Irish he had kept up as best he could since he left Dublin. At Ringwood he bought linguaphone records in Irish and French : " I was determined not to lose my French, tho' it is improbable I shall ever have to use it again in speech : same with the Irish ; I always swore I'd die a fluent speaker of bad Irish." [4] A Gaelic calendar hung by his fireside to be " a defiance and instruction of the damned Sasanach." [5] While he was at Harrow he tried to discover in London " a learned well-bred speaker of Connacht Irish " with whom he might converse in that language on all manner of subjects. He failed to find a native speaker ; but O'Rinn introduced him to George Thomson, a youthful Fellow of King's College, Cambridge, who shared his dual passion for Greek literature and for the Gaelic speech. Thomson became a great favourite, and figures frequently in the letters of these years, now as " Dante " or " Geoffrey Chaucer," now as *fear na feasóige*, " the bearded one " (in reference to the beard which learned men should by tradition possess). MacKenna

[1] Letter 92. [2] Cf. letter 9.

[3] See letters 73-75, and 82. Debenham and Dr. Page wished to reprint MacKenna's version as it stood, *vis-à-vis* with the fifty-year-old and now obsolescent Greek text on which it was based. MacKenna felt—in my judgement rightly—that account should be taken of the work which had been done in the interval on both text and interpretation.

[4] Letter to O'Rinn, 1928 or 1929. [5] To O'Rinn, 1931.

and he cherished in common the dream of fertilising the revived Gaelic culture from the same sources which at the Renaissance had given new life to the literature of France and England. Something of this kind had long been in MacKenna's thoughts. Many years earlier he had embarked on an Irish version of the *Antigone*—the characteristic choice of a lifelong rebel against authority—but was discouraged when Padraic O'Conaire told him that "it didn't mean anything, least of all anything Irish." He had also tried his hand at putting Epictetus into Gaelic,[1] and had even planned a grammar to be used for the teaching of Greek to Irish children through the medium of the national language. Stimulated by Thomson's example, he now returned seriously to these ideas. At the time of his last illness he was at work on an Irish version of Horace's *Satires* and *Epistles*: he believed that Gaelic idiom could be made to yield a perfect equivalent for the gracious colloquial style of these poems, and that the mellow humanism of the Latin author was exactly what the new generation in Ireland needed to counteract Catholic supernaturalism and the evil heritage of bitterness and intolerance left behind by the years of violence. He also hoped one day to produce a volume of essays in Irish.

When Thomson, with a quixotry worthy of MacKenna himself, left Cambridge to bury his talents in Galway as a lecturer at a small and remote university college, MacKenna was momentarily tempted to take the advice of his Irish friends and follow him. But he was too old and too ill; he resented, moreover, the increasing interferences with individual liberty which were imposed in the name of economic nationalism or of Catholic piety—"you to buy this and not that, to say this and not that other, to think one thing only and not that yon."[2] "I couldn't bear to live," he wrote to Mrs. Erskine Childers, "where

[1] Letters 47 and 59. Cf. Preface, p. xvi.

[2] Letter to "A. E.," October 1932.

I must ask a minister of Church or State whether I may or may not read Anatole France."

Poverty, however, compelled him to sell the little house at Harrow. His life there was of the simplest, with elementary meals—" I live mostly on eggs and milk and brown bread, and feel young and gay on it " [1]—and no service, save for a woman who came once a week " to give a big clean up." But there were innocent extravagances which he could not resist—books,[2] Buddhas, sun-parlours, and above all the luxury of generosity, in small matters and great. He insisted on paying his charwoman at 33⅓ per cent. more than the standard rate, since it shocked him that any human being should work for less than a shilling an hour. He bought (to the alarm of his friends) a motor bicycle, decided (to their relief) that he could not ride it, bought in its place a motor tricycle or " pram," and presented the discarded machine to a neighbour's son. He tried to contribute £100 towards the education of a village girl at Ringwood whom he thought more than usually intelligent.[3] And when, on the death of his brother Theobald, his minute estate was divided among the surviving members of the family, Stephen voluntarily offered to forgo his share of the inheritance in favour of two struggling brothers in Australia.

He now discovered that he was eating into his capital, and decided that he must remove himself from London and its temptations to expenditure. I tried to persuade him to buy himself an annuity with what was left of his

[1] Letter to Debenham, October 16, 1929.

[2] MacKenna was throughout his life a passionate book-buyer. But he was no bibliophile. He bought books as tools, and treated them as such : it was his habit, as he once warned a prospective lender, " to strew cigarette ashes and pencil faugh's and hurroo's over the pages." Nor were his Buddhas a mere mania. Their purpose was not to gratify a collector's vanity—few of them, I believe, were of much value as *objets d'art*—but to people the empty house with serene presences.

[3] Letter 64.

money, but he felt that he must conserve it for his heirs in Australia. He found a workman's cottage in a Cornish mining village, where he was able to live on an income of two pounds a week while he awaited death. It had a kitchen, a cupboard-like parlour, and two tiny bedrooms, one of which became his book-store ; and he built himself one last sun-room. He lived completely alone save for a pair of tame robins which hopped in and out of the sun-room : his soiled clothes accumulated in a rain-water barrel and his soiled crockery in the sink until these receptacles were full, when a neighbour's wife was summoned to come and wash them. He was cut off from Margaret Nunn and Stephens and the gay guitar parties, but he found companionship in the Cornish moors—which he would visit on sunny afternoons in his " pram " —and he made friends, as everywhere, with the village children. He interested himself also in contemporary psychology and economics, and in contemporary literature. Deeply as he had loved Greek poetry and Greek thought, he refused to admit the finality of classical standards. " Inspiration for the life of to-day," he wrote during his last illness to O'Rinn, " is in this day's best—and that best judged and ranked not by any ancient standards of thought or expression but by the simple test question : is this a hard-hitting Beauty or Awe of to-day, or is it merely (*a*) antiquarian research or (*b*) the crimping and cramping of the present and the future by laws, ideas, values once possibly useful but never more than provisory? Someone else's old clothes are not the wedding garment."

He had given up trying to interpret the world and his own life. " Looking back," he wrote to Robert MacKenna,[1] " I find no reason, touching my own satisfaction achieved or service done, for my ever having been blown hither from the peace of nothingness : 'tis to nothingness I'd like to return, and that dam quick." But there was no resentment in his attitude, and no denial of value to

[1] January 27, 1931.

the world's life. "I abhor this universe," he had written in the bitterness of an earlier mood; "I feel I could make a better one out of mud and waste paper."[1] This blasphemy he now vigorously recanted: "I'm a secularist agnostic: I don't know anything about the Soul or the Divine or Immortality or anything of that order, and I do believe in this life: I hate those who hate the world."[2] In the falling away of all dogma, what remained to him of religion was the sense of awe in the presence of nature. In his last letter to "A. E."[3] he wrote: "The older I grow the more I find of wonder everywhere, and no explanation: my last gasp will be one of astonishment. To-day an absurd bird sang—on Dec. 31—as if God had already wakened out of his winter snooze; and I was paralysed with a sense, utterly by me inexpressible, of the wonder of the world, the least and the biggest thing alike: so that I ended by saying 'Nothing is big or little: all is infinite grandeur, infinite mystery, infinite insanity.'"

In the early summer of 1933 he had an operation which cost him, with nursing home charges, a year's income, and did no lasting good.[4] He returned to his cottage, but he was weak and in frequent pain, and had often to spend much of the day in bed, getting up at intervals to make tea—for he still would not afford himself an attendant. In September, hearing how he was situated, I went down to Cornwall to see whether I could do anything for his comfort. I found him lying in a deck chair in his sun-parlour: he was gaunt and worn, dressed in a tattered shirt, patched trousers, and an ancient pair of bedroom slippers, but he had kept all his old courtliness and charm of manner. Our talk ranged over many topics—Plotinus, Ireland, his boyhood in Liverpool, Cornwall and the plight of its unemployed miners, the Russian experiment, the future of religion. He had been deeply moved by the

[1] To Mrs. A. F. Dodds, December 21, 1923. [2] Letter 95.

[3] December 31, 1932. [4] Letter 92.

spectacle of unemployment in London and in Camborne, and although he did not consider himself competent to express opinions on questions of economics, his sympathies were definitely socialist or communist.[1] Had he youth and strength, he told me, he would go back to Ireland and try to start a campaign " against God and for social justice." He knew that he was dying, and we spoke of the approaching end without embarrassment. He said that he had no wish to live longer, and when I asked him if he did not fear to die alone, he replied that he preferred it : he had always been spiritually alone, and his one dread was that the " black crows " might scent his deathbed and pester him with unwelcome services. He hoped, and expected, that there would be nothing after death. I asked him whether, if he did find himself surviving, he would attempt to establish the fact by communicating with me through a medium ; but he begged to be excused, on the ground of a distaste for mediums and a congenital incapacity for scientific experiment.

To mark the importance of the occasion, a neighbour's wife had been asked to cook us a chicken. When we had consumed the meal—or rather, when I had, for MacKenna scarcely ate—he rested on his bed and I was sent out for a walk. On my return we made tea, and strolled among the falling apples of his little weed-grown orchard. Then it was time for me to go back to Camborne, and we set out together through the village, he looking like a monk of some strange heretical order (for he still wore the threadbare dressing-gown which he had put on for his rest), I staggering under the load of books which he had given me, along with a beautiful old china plate, as a parting present. The village had evidently accepted him: the children who ran out to greet us and open gates seemed to do it less in mockery or the expectation of apples than in pure friendliness. When we reached the top of a little rise he showed me the loveliness of the

[1] Cf. letters 81, 82.

landscape under the autumn sunshine, and repeated his assurance that I had no occasion to be distressed or anxious on his account; then he went back to his cottage, and I went on to Camborne.

Two months later he entered a London hospital for a further operation. He survived it, and for a time was expected to recover. But his endurance was at an end: the doctors reported that their patient had no will to live, and on March 8, 1934, he quietly slipped through their hands. True to his resolution, throughout this last illness he had kept his whereabouts a secret from his friends, and he would have died without seeing anyone, had not Margaret Nunn discovered his address from his landlord at Reskadinnick and sought and obtained permission to visit him a few days before his death.[1]

[1] See letter 99.

JOURNAL

PREFATORY NOTE.

The following excerpts are taken from a manuscript book which was found among Stephen MacKenna's papers after his death and was kindly placed at my disposal by Mr. C. V. Thomas. It appears that he kept this journal partly as a spiritual exercise, as an aid to self-understanding and also to mastery of expression; partly in the hope that the written word would preserve for his own later memory "a secret warmth of the mood of which it is the dry extract." The entries were made sometimes daily, sometimes at much longer intervals: often he finds no mood worth recording, or no skill to record. The journal was composed without thought of publication; but in 1915, having re-read it and made some stylistic corrections, he pencilled on the first page a note (which he subsequently struck out) "I think there is much printable in this book"; and from some numerical calculations on the last page it may be inferred that he thought of printing about one-third of the whole.

He never proceeded with the idea, but my own judgement coincides with that which he formed in 1915: what follows is about a third of the total bulk, although my selection can hardly be identical in detail with the one he would have made, and many paragraphs would undoubtedly have been remodelled before he surrendered them to the printer. I have had to omit or abbreviate many entries which were still in the rough, and therefore failed of concentration or clarity. I have also omitted some which lacked personal quality, being purely exercises in style; some which gave alternative expression to thoughts already set down; and a very few which appeared too private for publication. With what remains I have not tampered, save in occasional matters of punctuation and in amending a few obvious oversights.

E. R. DODDS.

JOURNAL

PARIS 1907–DUBLIN 1909

Ἔστι δ' ὅπη νῦν
ἔστι· τελεῖται δ' ἐς τὸ πεπρωμένον.
οὔθ' ὑποκαίων οὔθ' ὑπολείβων
οὔτε δακρύων ἀπύρων ἱερῶν
ὀργὰς ἀτενεῖς παραθέλξει.—Aeschylus.

Too much thinking doth consume the spirits, and oft it falls out that while one thinks too much of his doing he leaves to do the effect of his thinking.[1]
SIDNEY's *Arcadia.*

PARIS :

January 27, 1907.

One of the very most surprising things in life is the contented aimlessness with which it is so often, almost always, lived. Few live for joy in life, fewer still for something to be done with their life : most live, and apparently in content, not as free animals live who must be doing something, but as tram-horses or trees or as monotonously flowing waters... and without the beauty or dignity of trees or of flowing waters. No doubt there is use in what most are doing, keeping shop or building bridges or spending money idly, but there is not aim, or the aim is mainly personal and wholly bounded within time. A father perhaps keeps shop for his children's sake, that they may be better or happier : but if he had any deep sense of value in life he would be so long occupied, and so intently, in making this value clear to himself that his shop would fail ; he would make his living wait upon the clarifying of his notion of life's values and meaning. It is well for the playing of the piece to the end that the actors

[1] These mottoes are prefixed to MacKenna's manuscript.

do not stay to think what it all means and leads to : they themselves meanwhile remain mummers, idly mumbling, cutting ordered capers, and the more violently, sonorously, the less men. Monastics are nearer manhood, if to be man is to act for an end : whether theirs is a wise manhood, probably nobody knows : but it seems wise to make action wait for the wise pointing of action.

There is a sort of reason in the American sect—Hindoo too ?—that refuses generation and grows by adoption : those withdrawing from the common pursuit of idle procreation have at least the moral manliness of restraint ; those adopted live, by the fact, in an atmosphere of grave thought ; they are snatched from the common drifting. It seems one of the clearest proofs of an ultimate meaning in the comedy that so few stay to ask its meaning as they play their parts : what driving power is there in man except one of which man is only the vehicle or the driven ? If man had a clearer motive for all he does, we might rest on that and never talk of a beyond. He might be God or the proof that no God is : he might be Life : but Life he is not, nor is Life in him : it is without him, blowing him against his will, without his care or knowledge.

If a man is happy and content selling cheeses or prattling in an evening dress, it is that a greater uses him : the meaning that is not in him is without, and his gyration or his placid movement on the set path tells of a great wind blowing.

January 30, 1907.

I find that everything I write either is full of gross faults against the logic of expression or else is muddy and clogged—in either case is unreadable, even to myself. Of old I wrote, I suppose, even less correctly, but there was a certain liveliness, a certain glow : running the eye down the page, one caught the gleam of pretty words like the faint burst of colour here and there that showed in the old metal plate I bought, dirt-encrusted, in Moscow.

I am inclined to put the change down to three main causes, cable-journalism, the use of the typewriter, and a failure-bred distaste for all writing. The sense of the tariff checks the picture-making faculty, hinders the easy play of fancy : the typewriting seems to lead towards the lapidary and away from the fluid : journalism, especially of a low and impersonal kind, long pursued, necessarily rusts the imaginative faculty, for it creates the dread of any statement that is not warranted by some outer evidence and of any phrase that is not stamped in the vulgarest mould.

February 2, 1907.

It seems incredible that he could ever write, out of his own fancy and sense of fitness and beauty, anything that could touch the heart or please the fancy or even satisfy the intelligence of others. He should remember that he is sane and that therefore, if only he be at first simple and sincere, he will not maim good sense ; that he has talked and pleased, and therefore may please when he writes ; that he need not seek to touch the heart by any very sorrowful imagination, and that so, not making the extreme effort, he may easily save himself from the supreme fall and yet find beneath his easy-going feet the little herb rue now and then, enough for his simple purpose. If it be a question of craftsmanship lacking, craftsmanship is above all the thing won by work. If he foresees that he will never do great things and that so his work will be wasted, let him remember that his work can never be wasted, even though it never show outside himself, and further that it is not necessary for him to do great things : he will always have done his best, been most himself, cultivated his garden, and the devil take the rest !

February 5, 1907.

Reading to-day the *Areopagitica*, it seemed to me that this is the noblest prose I know—with the flow and power of Bossuet and with no touch of the borrowed : it is music, power and personality all at once : not only is there no cliché in it, there is nothing that could ever become cliché ; and yet it is not harsh, forbidding, strained : it flows, though very massively, with the true simplicity of a pure and entire expression of the thought and emotion ; but the thought is too fine to fall into phrases that would ever quite fit a broad general need, and the phrases are too grand for any common use. Milton has now and then a sophist-trick : in him, in the pomp of all that sturdy work of proof, the trick has a delicious air of frolic, of gaminerie : as if he knew the thing would carry but knew, himself, that it should not.

Buying books to-day—a Corneille, a Molière, a Montaigne—shivering a whole afternoon along snowy quais, wind-swept, a memory of the Fontanka [1] : a body pulled out of the Seine in front of the Institut, a "jeune fille" the people said gaily : two dogs came up to the skirts of the crowd, sat together on their haunches for a contemplative moment, sniffing towards the sacking, then bounded off merrily, floundering over each other in supple play.

February 6, 1907.

It seems to me after all that there was much good sense in the old school law of using by choice the Anglo-Saxon words as the main stuff of writing. It is not so much that they "touch the heart," "strike home to men's business and bosoms," and so forth : it is that the Latin words and phrases are precisely the most common, the most hackneyed, go most readily "home" and, sinking expected into a prepared place, make no dint : only jagged words and phrases that bluster in like storming-parties make themselves felt as they pierce. And there can be no art, no cry to brain, unless there is violence. The hard thing is to do violence in the neatly right degree : you

[1] A street in St. Petersburg.

must tap your man's skull but not crack it : you must wake him but not daze him : he is to be made to hear, he is not to be deafened. The Latin forms, too, are the ready masks of unclearness in thought and of grotesquely mixed metaphor, the two main sins, I take it, against good writing ; the twin brethren of blur and blundering, at whose entry all hope of making picture or of casting spell flies out of door. Latin forms, too, come readily, first, unsought, into the writer's mind : to let them flow out on to the page unchecked, unquestioned, is to abdicate artistry, to be slave not master, not a person but a patient, not a writer but a fountain pen—very certain to blot and to run dry.

February 7, 1907.

There seems after all something childish in yesterday's law : we must not restore the Heptarchy in an edict : it would be a sad day when one felt oneself bound in every case to say "wobbling" instead of "oscillating," "red" —is "red" Saxon ?—instead of "vermilion." And of course the true way to meet the danger, lurking in the Latin, of slovenly thought and bungled metaphor, is to use no word, from whatever tongue, that has not been dusted and studied and approved for its place.

February 8, 1907.

I perceive that he is very superstitious : it is not the demon-dread, the δεισιδαιμονία ; thirteen and Friday do not frighten him : it is rather the contrary, an instinctive, unceasing, foolish feeling of good spirits watching over him very kindly in the smallest matters. When he stops to reason, he waves the whole hierarchy of them away with a smile : but every day and all day long he is paying them a silent homage : if he has the notion of laying a log across another on the fire and it insists on falling flat, he lets it stay, not out of indolence but out of deference to another will : if in typewriting, when he has to point back to 15, the index shows 16 against his will, he bangs the letter with a conviction, unquestioned for the moment, that the thing is ordered so. All day long a score of little obediences and obeisances are so offered : he waits ceaselessly on the little gods of the fire and of the desk and of the bookshelves, of the omnibus and of the shop. Is this a mere idiocy, or a stupid outward acting on a true deep intuition ? There seems, in any case, to be need of a word less pejorative than "superstitious" and less pompous, or hieratic, than "spiritist"?

February 17, 1907.

It is, very likely, a grave mistake to read any one writer too often or too deeply : perhaps Schopenhauer is wrong: if one thinks over, "studies," another man's thoughts while his phrases are still fresh printed on the brain, one almost surely fails to find oneself in the matter then, or perhaps ever afterwards : *he* has taken up all the place, and one cannot hear oneself for the noise he has made : for years afterwards if one has taken, in one reading or in several thinly spaced readings, the hard impress of his idea, the strong wash of his phrase, the brain chambers reek of him, the thought runs too easily in the channels he has cut, a network of his setting pegs down and maps out the lava, that can then no more follow its own natural paths. I begin to think that, in all reading undertaken for other than historical, critical or purely fancy-feeding and joy-giving purposes, one should merely skim and put by. Some little one will always hold, enough to breed thought, not enough to stifle it ; what one takes in mingles, instead of crushing down in a hard lump : the reader will be an original, not an echo. The more temptingly a writer lures the more swiftly one should flee him —except, always, for the poets, for the pure artists of poetry or prose. Every writer, who has other ends than to paint pictures and tell stories, is plotting against the freedom of every reader : the thing is to take from him not what he wants to force on you, but what you yourself need : if you don't cheat him he cheats you.

February 19, 1907.

How we are fooled by words. Bourgeois, bourgeoisism, how hateful in our Latin-Quarter days, however un-Latin we be in heart and act. I always saw, however, that bourgeoisism is a hardened mysticism : nearly all the virtues of the bourgeois are true virtues of the poet too ; the artist is deeper as well as saner for being the faithful husband of one wife and keeping healthy hours and temperate diet. The mischief is that the bourgeois too is fooled by words : he lives his virtue (and judges others) by formula, not in the freedom of the children of the Light, and formulas are starched robes ; forced upon a lovely figure, they will often make it look out of law and ugly. The thing is to be bourgeois in act with a free soul : and especially not to measure another man's life by an iron bar, but by a silken band that will ripple over the ruggednesses and, if the man be true, will show him true by the numbers, though all the build be strange.

February 21, 1907.

One great use of keeping such a record as this is that one learns what blank things most of one's days are : reading, talking, eating, writing without interest or emotion, the days go by, blank : and it is life that passes : days make life, and if the days are blank—it is terrible. The only good thing in life is to have a vivid mental activity and some human love to warm it : all the rest is cold as fuel without fire. I believe it is a moral duty to think and to love ; because it is a duty to live, and these are life.

February 22, 1907.

I have vowed to give one half hour at least every day, at any cost, to reading Irish and mod. Greek alternately. I cannot bear to think of not being able to read Gaelic fluently before I die, and I will not let modern Greek perish off my lips—if only by way of homage to the ancient holy land and in the faint hope that someday, somehow, I may see it again with clearer eyes and richer understanding.

February 23, 1907.

Reading Coleridge's "Biographia Literaria": it is a rich incoherence, a style that sometimes suggests Sir Thomas Browne and sometimes Ben Jonson ("Discoveries") and sometimes Plato and sometimes some subtle modern, perhaps Pater, and often an ambitious schoolboy or an illiterate inspired contributor to some village paper. If I chanced on this book by the luck of the counter, I would almost certainly have fingered it a while, shaken my head, and put it down with a sigh for crude talent: how many as rich writers may there not be who, because they have not had the fortune to be poets and so to have made a hearing for themselves for all they put out, have perished having given none of their good to living soul. To last may be only for genius, but genius itself will not last unless it show in a mellow style, clear or exceptionally powerful and above all *one* in its texture—unless, of course, as in C.'s case, from some such other circumstance as having fought a good and resonant fight or having fine poetry to be lamp to a dirty rich prose.

February 24, 1907.

De Quincey, now, seems to me to be almost, of all moderns whom I know, the man who most writes; as some pictures give the feeling that every brush-stroke was thought and judged and tried and only after such a test allowed to stand, so every de Q. sentence tells of thought and choice, and every word in its place seems willed. And what delicious phrases that paint or sing or smell sweet, or have a quiver of moonlight on them, or go with the solemn splendid glory of a great brave pageant: and always, I think as far as I have noticed, prose is prose and all falls featly, simply, as falling from a rich and a gracefully-stocked mind by the will to be full and true and very exact and persuasive, never in the spirit of self-display, never in a tawdry oriental embroidering.

February 28, 1907.

Writing for the *Freeman* : of the choice of matter, I say nothing, and nothing of the wisdom or folly of my views, but I notice, with the beginnings of contentment, that as the words fell on to the paper they fell with a certain neatness : I said more nearly what I meant to ; there was more grammar, more logic (within, possibly, a large unreason) ; metaphors were truer, cleaner, clearer ; there was, with no brilliance, little or no dirtiness ; the thing seemed to me to bear the mark of a careful gentleman. Hence I pronounce this, that as old experience doth attain to something like prophetic strain, so all comely facility traces back to long pondering ; intuitions are the reward of ancient gropings. I pronounce this also, that ill-paid work which does not shock one's taste is pleasanter far to do than the vulgar which much enriches—especially, perhaps, when the vulgar gold still rolls in.

March 8, 1907.

Politeness, deeply searched, is but savagery. Instinctively we neither ask it nor use it in our dealings with our nearest ; the easier manner that rules within the household may be a lurking danger to peace and lasting goodwill, but it is the seal and token of a friendly union to which savage domineering and savage placation are alike strangers. To the enemy outside our own cave we come with smiles and bowing, either as a sign that we are not going to club him this time or as a prayer to him not to club us. The merely ceremonial observances, therefore, as apart from a kindly care of not wounding or harming, are a declaration of enmity with a plea for truce—sometimes indeed a treacherous plea, for we are never so polite as just before we club. Politeness turns the enemy's eyes away, and the blow falls the truer. The husband who is polite to his wife is out of love with her for the moment, and a mother is never polite to her child. Business is always polite : it is " dear Sir " and " your favour of the 6th " and " yours faithfully," and bang goes your sixpence. You cannot think of anyone being polite to God or God to anyone else : it is because there can be no war and perhaps no hate between Good-Power and Littleness. Before the divine, savagery is burned away.

March 9, 1907.

Is it mysticism or is it madness or is it both ? He finds himself quite often sunk in long rambling dreams opened up by such strange objects as bottles. The sight of a row of wine-bottles, empty, ranged on the lid of a coal-box, stirs the question—why does everything we drink go in bottles, in glass and of one of two sizes and forms ? Tiens, it must be because drink is fluid. But why are drinks fluid ; why must fluids go in bottles and not in boxes ? What is the essential difference between a box and a bottle, between a fluid and a liquid, between a bottle and a fluid, between a man and a bottle or a fluid ? And so on, until he might grow old listening to his thoughts. He thinks, deep down under all the bottle-thoughts, that he is drawing near to the Secret : he wakes to be afraid of the fool's-coat.

March 10, 1907.

Often it is not foolish to prize the shadow over the substance. The pigeons strutting on the floor of the balcony, or sidling along its iron-work with cautious peering out of inquiet eyes, are welcome visitants : but there is almost a catch at the heart when, as they fly by unseen, there sweeps over the walls of the room the shadow of their wings. To-day, too, in the Luxembourg, as I looked at the sun-lit trunk of a tree and there fell for a wing-beat on the bark the black shadow of a bird minding his own business between the tree and the sun, I had a sense of an angel passing. That is it, the shadow is often the angel of something nobler than any substance : the shadow of the wings tells not merely of a passing body but of sun and of infinite space and of strange laws and of free wild life and of all life and power and law. I suppose the shadow is often the awakening of all the mystic sense of a child : I remember well being haunted by my own shadow and angry with it, and entranced by the shadows of trees lengthening and devouring the yellow-green of the sunny grass.

March 14, 1907.

There are trees that are all a-strain upward like a prayer ; there are trees that rise only to flow eternally downwards, drooping like death ; there are trees that are all a-twist, an agony of contortion, writhing, serpenting now towards earth and now towards sky, inwards and outwards, upwards and downwards, tortured uncertain lives, very dreadful and very beautiful : but in all the trees there is beauty, and the birds of God rest and nest and sing in all.

March 18, 1907.

I find I haven't the art of rest. When I'm too tired to work at something which must be done but is distasteful, I give it up and work just as hard and long at something else : I take a defeat of the will instead of the frank brief rest that would make the distasteful work possible. Probably the great workers of the world have been the great masters of the art of resting.

March 23, 1907.

When a man has nothing to write it is that he has not sufficiently lived : most of our days we are dead. I can imagine very well what joy there is meant in the Christian Beatific Vision or the neo-Platonic ecstasy : it is the fulness of living, a ceaseless straining of the burning point of the unsheathed spirit, the cumbering body shaken off, the diverse earth now passed out of sight, distracting, luring, dazing now no more : it is the flame of the mind never quenched or downed or twisted awry ; it is the intent living towards the only life. And it seems hard and strange that so noble a hope, once come into the world from the heart of men, should have no truth beyond the world. *Credo quia humanum est.* But it is a hope full of terrors : what if one were never to be worthy, what if——.

March 28, 1907.

It seems a token and habit of older age to feel very deeply the charm there is in every display of life : I love it yearly more and more—in the antics and questions of children, in the roaming of a baby's surprised eyes, in the sparrows (now as I write) cracking seeds on the balcony —so busily, happily, jealously, pugnaciously—in the white shimmer of apple-blossom I saw yesterday at Clamart, and in the garden there in the dusk, when we walked under the chestnuts and wondered at the noble curves of their spring shoots, flowing, naked long withes of an exquisite bend topped with a fresh green tuft which was borne upwards in a proud gesture of happy achievement and glad homage, towards the sun. When I was a child, a boy, a young man adolescent, I felt at no time that I had any right or place in the world : now it seems to me that only for such is the kingdom of earth, for those that are filled with the life of youth, and for all things that show no beginning of morose decay.

March 29, 1907.

There is something high fantastical in the thought that if every day of my life I had a good hot piece of gossip, about some millionaire fool or some powerful business man at play, to cable to New York, I should be well off and considered from New Year to Christmas ; but if I put comely English about Plotinus and give him for the first time—and perhaps for all time—entire and clear and pleasantly readable to America and Australia and England, I shall certainly go about in old clothes and shrink from facing a post-office clerk. When I did very little, and that better left wholly undone, I was a fatted bourgeois : work begins only when " the dear little cheques " that paid me for an ugly idleness cease to flutter in.

April 4, 1907.

There is a sort of restless kindliness, imbecile and lowering to the human person : do not in an April shower run out to hold an umbrella over a bee.

April 6, 1907.

Three things alone seem to me unquestionably great in Greece : Plato and Sculpture and Pindar ; and a fourth seems to me probably very great too, a life of beauty and harmony very generally lived—though when I read Aristophanes I wonder how much of this is our fond dream. Sophocles seems to me great in *Antigone*, and Euripides in the *Bacchae*, and Aeschylus, though with some reserve, in the *Prometheus* : but in all the rest I feel an uneasy sense of incompleteness and blundering and stammering, and I doubt sometimes whether I admire very sincerely, whether I do not cheat myself, force myself, whether a large part of my pleasure is not perhaps in the mean triumph of the child pleased with the dull thing he has himself spelled out because he has spelled it out. But Pindar—he seems to me wholly, authentically, with no reserve great, great in almost every moment, line and word and movement and meaning : you think of magnificence when you read him : you think of every art and of every personal nobility : he moves you as some infinitely rich and powerful music.

April 11, 1907.

The Yogi outlook on life, the Yogi disdain or unconcern, seems sometimes a huge lie as a height or a lowness inhuman. Yet M. for all but a few moments each day goes very quietly about his Pindar or his Corneille or his Shakespeare or his Gaelo-Romaic half hours,[1] though he stands at a very doubtful turn of the short road—just about to lose a well-paid employment,[2] stepping from financial peace to moneyless labour and anxiety and to many inevitable disappointments, not sure of his health, not sure of making for wife and mother the easy graceful way of life he should and must. . . .

Nothing in him really cares, nothing in him is even occupied by the crisis. Is it childishness or is it wisdom ? Is it perhaps both, because the two are one ? Somehow, from some source unknown, the man has a conscience : these outer things, however dire they look, have never really troubled his peace : yet let him think that in any way he has done wrong, in a word, in a frown, in a gesture, and he suffers deeply. This is a natural Yogi-ism : if only it were at call for the little daily trials of temper as it is for the great threatening disasters, the man would be a rare fellow. The fact, however, that he isn't able to keep the daily peace, " having his own will with perfect sweetness," shows that there may be here at least as much of weakness, thinness of blood and dulness of brain, as of virtue.

May 4, 1907.

To-day Arthur Lynch takes my bishopric and I am free, and from to-day I begin to think how best to make straight my ways both towards livelihood by the pen and towards some useful and interesting work in Irish politics. Despite all my roamings, my heart has always been in Ireland, and though I cannot renague Greek and Plotinus

[1] See above, p. 99. " Romaic " is modern Greek.

[2] As continental representative of the *New York World* : see memoir, p. 31.

I do greatly deplore that in and by their reign I have broken, not in heart and not in thought, but as far as persistent act goes, my early vow of loyalty to Fodhla.[1] Henceforth it is to be first Ireland and second politics, supported by journalism (or literature, if the gods were good), and then—third but very dear—Greek and Plotinus. And I like to set down for my own later memory this true word : that though my thoughts of making a career in politics are due, unquestionably, to my breach with the *N. Y. World*, yet I act in entire honesty, believing that I may serve some good end and make my life in every spiritual and " teleological " way better, as being vowed to a noble cause which has always had all my love and hope.

May 20, 1907.

A fruitless, costly decade in London. M. R., Northrop, S. Gwynn. Now begins the task—to make money by writing, to learn Irish and master the problems and politics and personalities of Ireland, to keep Greek bright and Plotinus simmering, to watch modern French literature and not to let modern Greek slip out of mind. I am to read much English literature, especially the rich older writers, but with the greatest care to save myself from the snare of " specialising ": my one end, ever clearly in view, must be, after enjoying in all simplicity their beauty, to pluck their mystery from them, to learn in my degree their art and to harvest me their words, their rich strength: they are to be to me not a " subject " but for delight and for use. Worked only about 2 hours, on a story.

LONDON :

July 17, 1907.

I have left this book unwritten for more than a week —a week of Irish political study—and every day as I have

[1] A traditional poetic name for Ireland.

fingered it, trying to get courage to write, I have found a deeper unwillingness, a sort of stiffness in the joints as it were winter—fattened limbs labouring to drive a mud-clogged bicycle. The spirit has been unwilling and the flesh weak. Even a little needful letter-writing has been painful and the outcome poor. It is clear that study, the taking-in with ever so much zest and with careful thought, is perilously impersonal : a man to keep his brain in working trim must not merely think, he must also act : thought without some putting-out (whether of the matter mainly dwelt upon or of some other) settles soon into a kind of torpor. The mind knows at once the body's drowse, and may shake it away ; but there is nothing within the mind by which it may know its mindlessness ; its only means of seeing itself is, like the eye's, a mirror : and the mirror of the mind is its act put outside of itself, at once its outcome and its looking-glass. The sun is seen only by its own light, and the mind is appraised only by its own outgoing action. Unfortunately there is so little good talk that the outward act must be most often done on paper : talking, one is most often benumbed by others' stupidity or by one's own, and in either case there is no faithful imaging : the unoffending paper takes all and adds nothing, in almost no way reacting upon the thinker, and so gives a nearly true picture of the mental state. And hence the wisdom of the *Nulla dies sine linea.*

August 6, 1907.

I think the finest things and the subtlest, not less than the thin fare of the ungrown mind, may be carried, and best, in simple wording and in clear sentence-building. The very noblest of the classic French literature uses scarcely a word and never, I think, a sentence-flow that could call even the least read reader to even a moment's halt : all that such a one can miss is the soul, the deeper meaning and the warm feeling that give life to the plain words. And there is no reader so awakened or so eager that this may not readily slip out of his sight under cover of mist and among the folds of rocky ground.

A certain strangeness, that perhaps must play always over good writing, is not obscurity : rather it makes for a clearer understanding ; it calls for slow-going that there may be thought and enjoyment, but it does not bewilder so that even for a second there be a doubt of the way ; it is for freshness that wings the meaning, not for a murkiness that dulls and dims.

August 7, 1907.

Murkiness may sometimes have a place in good writing, as heavy shadow, a religious gloom, sometimes in a cathedral : but it must be used, not merely allowed to slip in, and it must be rare : it is a " figure of speech," like " personification " or " rhetorical question." And the way must be opened to it very carefully, so that it shall be a half-light, a softening of hard outlines, a side-chapel off a clear nave, not a pit of forbidding darkness.

August 13, 1907.

If a violinist tries to make his instrument " speak," making literature under his chin, he becomes loathsome, sentimental ; if a writer tries mainly to make his sentence ripple and sing, laugh and groan, he is very near to becoming merely sensuous ; and the sensuousness of the violin will always be the nobler. Every art knows its own secrets.

August 15, 1907.

Everybody reading the Bible I suppose is pulled up by an uneasy feeling that morality never elsewhere came holding out so many gifts. It is a ceaseless bribery : Keep the Sabbath and your days will be long in the land ; Be chaste and you will become a woman of three cows ; Serve God and He will serve you. It seems to me that England and America owe to their Bible reading their curiously commercial virtue: Celtic nations, in their vices as in their virtues, are less calculating, more instinctive,[1] because they have not had this century-long training in the cash-down system of morality. I am tempted also to find the beautiful melody of the Authorised Version a hurt to its spiritual power: there is something of a lulling sing-song, very fatal, in long use, to the upspring of an eager morality speaking out of and growing in itself, apart from all book and tradition: the singular rise and fall of sound, very grave and cloisterish, weaves a spell that puts thought to sleep: active feeling for right is quenched in a comfortable sentimentality: the flow of the sentences, whether one reads for oneself or for others, calls for a chant, and chant breeds cant, or at any rate dulls the edge of the soul: all except the hard matter-of-fact in this morality becomes as it were a mere Sunday anthem. I think the Catholic Church is wise: much Bible-reading would not be good for the mass.

August 17, 1907.

Once I was placid over the stupidities of others and did not feel any in myself, now I rage over both: I become bitter as I grow old, more bitter still when I foresee for myself a peevish, snarling old age. It is very well to make rules for keeping outward peace, and the rules may do their work; but what a dismal thing to have to live under rule lest one become a raging curse.

August 19, 1907.

Platitudes are, after all, only the neat packing of good sense so that it can be carried about: they are useless, like a portmanteau, until you put your own key to them; then by them you live and work.

August 20, 1907.

A man's notion that he has this or that quality, seems to be almost always the stirring of that something really

[1] Marginal note in MacKenna's handwriting: "Are they, though?"

there : perhaps it may be true also that the desire of something to be within him is the sign, not yet clearly read, that the something is there, though deep-down, crusted over and not yet wholly able to shine out in the unmistakable brightness of the idea itself. Desire would be as it were the dim life of the thing of which idea was the clearer fuller life : from the desire of the thing to the idea of the real presence of the thing is not a great step : from the idea of the real presence of the thing to the use and enjoyment of the thing is hardly a step at all. Herein is much magic.

August 24, 1907.

Consider how ideas come : they must be at least partly from within, something within the man catching at outside things, or caught by them, and taking from them some image to be worked within the man into a feeling, a thought, a piece of will. This idea (feeling, thought, will) then comes largely from the strange Me, is a part of the unknowable Me : when I welcome it, brood over it again, I am merely tending to be Myself ; whatever idea I seek to foster towards strength is already in being within me, and it grows strong and stronger by the very fact that, of all the Me, this part rather than another part is fostered by the Me. I am ready to believe that something like this is meant by the doctrine that in single-heartedness and little-childhood is the way to Salvation : it is not meant that children by their innocence are near to heaven, but that all good is gained by those whose thought and life are kept pointed close to one main thing, not scattered abroad upon a thousand. Spill your thought, let your idea go straying in a maze of zig-zags, and there is no one central point from which the Me governs all—there is almost no Me, because there is no Me holding all the powers and faculties in one firm grip. The Me that came upon the earth has been whirled about and is dizzy and faint, and asks only for ease or for the not-being towards which it is drifting. Until it come, perhaps, to non-being after death it will never have the ease it sighs for: its ease is in its being, and in its activity after its kind, because only so does it know its being.

September 27, 1907.

I am not interested in facts once I have sucked the good out of them for myself; therefore I make a poor hand at all that kind of journalism which coasts upon reporting. I have too little imagination, insight, mastery of masses, too short and dim a sight, and too little courage and self-trust, to create any powerful work of literature. There remain only, in the writing life, the work of reasoning upon the daily happening and the work of lightly touching in very simple style upon the grave things which true literature handles in a strong grip. I have the essay and the "leading article." An múineadh[1]—do 'em.

October 6, 1907.

Our spiritual troubles we may, or some of us may, put off from us—"Come unto Me, all ye that labour and are heavy burdened, and I will give ye rest": but no one died for our brain's peace, and there is no one upon whom we can put off, any one of us, the rubbing burden of our mind's discomforts. This thought alone is enough to make religions seem thin and untrue as dreams are.

October 8, 1907.

Never, I think, was man born to be, more than myself, a Waiter: I am like the Princes of Greece round Penelope, a ten years' Wooer: I am always in my mind waiting for some bell to ring that never rings, for some wonderful thing to happen that never happens. I try to show myself that luck follows work as harvest comes by ploughing: deep down I have never believed it; I cannot believe it; I cannot make myself believe it.

[1] Irish, "the moral."

November 12, 1907.

Blake says, " Men are admitted into heaven, not because they have curbed and governed their passions or have no passions, but because they have cultivated their understandings." This is very widely a mark of the modern mysticism : it is not found in Thomas A Kempis, and not in Eckhardt : it is, or something that begins to look like it is, in Rosmini. It is, however, under all Plotinus ; and knowledge, science of natural things, is a main step in his Ladder to the Beyond. It would seem that here again the Greek mind, even borrowing from the Egyptian or other Eastern thought, still kept its σωφροσύνη : the mind of the Middle Ages, coloured from the monastery, filled with the idea of giving up the world, not of using it, is really a sort of Orientalism : monks are Yogimen : the Renaissance brought sanity into religion as much as it brought back the idea of joy into the arts and into the morals of the daily life.

November 13, 1907.

There is something accidentally deep in the saying put into the mouth of the Irishman who, hard-pressed about Transubstantiation—" How can Bread be God ? "—answered, " What else would it be ? " It sometimes seems that all there is in the world that is not God is man : I feel a queer little quivering of God in a buttercup and an oak-nut ; it is not common to me to feel any in myself, and when I read of a mass of men—say at a public meeting—I always shudder in a horrid thought of perforated lumps of flesh : I can't bear the thought of human beings except when I think of beauty or intelligence or rare and cloistral goodness in them—and one cannot think of these lovely things shining in a crowd.

December 3, 1907.

All the labour and thought I have spent upon words, these many months past, upon choice and setting of words and on the clear flow of sentences, stands to style only as scourging and fasting to holiness : these are steps in the purgative way : style is far beyond all this ; it is personal thought and emotion breaking out into beauty and new power, as naturally as the sun's heat breaks into rhythmic cascades of lovely sovran light. When a soul is fallen and soiled within the body, it must cleanse and redress, but it must not glory in the cleansing or even in the being clean : it has still very far to go.

December 4, 1907.

Synge once told me that all the sadness he had in the thought of death was that while he lay there cloistered the seasons would come and go and he know nothing of it all : his tone and look as he said it made it to me the sorrowfullest thing I ever heard of death. Sometimes to myself there comes a curious thought that in the grave I may hear no poetry, read no more philosophy, care neither for the Elizabethans and Wordsworth and Browning nor for Plotinus and the mysteries ; and when I think sometimes that perhaps I may (in some sense or some other) "go to heaven," the thought that then I may have gone so far beyond as to have no more care for these things comes to me as a fear. I suppose, though, that this is sad childishness—or is it the human dread of a dreamless Nirvana—the fulness of knowledge so close to non-feeling, almost non-being ?

December 5, 1907.

Whenever I look again into Plotinus I feel always all the old trembling fevered longing : it seems to me that I must be born for him, and that somehow someday I must have nobly translated him : my heart, untravelled, still to Plotinus turns and drags at each remove a lengthening chain. It seems to me that him alone of authors I understand by inborn sight, I alone of possible translators —though I am forced to see that Principal Caird is not far behind me. Would I had been born a leisurely Protestant parson, a scholar in an oak-raftered parsonage library.

December 6, 1907.

There is no beauty, and little use, in the virtue that's always muttering of laws and running off to turn over text books : such a virtue there might be in a fiend afraid. The only goodness worthy of a human soul, or a human Best, is the quiet fruit of a ceaseless contemplation : beautiful thought left ever in the sun ripens surely ; it is only the apple fallen from the bough, unkissed by the light, untossed by the high-blowing winds, that unripened rots.

December 10, 1907.

I wonder has any one studied the history of Remorse, I mean of mental penitence. It does not seem that the asceticism of old was penitential : men went out into the desert, or scourged themselves, or begged their way naked, for self-mastery's sake, and not for expiation ; not to atone, not to pay, but to cure themselves : it was a medicine of the soul, and there does not seem to have been more shame over the past sickness of the soul than we have over the sickness of the body. In any other sense than to re-make oneself (putting away the evil and doing good), to repent for past misdoing is like spending new-found health in living over again the misery of old illnesses. The duty of Remorse and of penitential humbleness must have been invented by some hard-hearted Righteous Man [1] so that the Prodigal Son might not have the best of it all round—riotous living and fatherly feasting both untainted by a due melancholy. I wonder did Christ preach, as John seems to have done, the penance of the mind : he orders the bringing forth of " fruits worthy of penance," I know—and that seems a great deal more healthy than " penance " pure and simple. Plato

[1] Marginal note in MacKenna's handwriting : " I suppose Remorse is Jew, *tout simplement*."

and Plotinus did not ask for long faces or sick brooding, nor, I think, did the Stoics : you must put away the soil of the soul and live nobly ; but from that first conversion-moment you were Katharos, and unless you lapsed again you might go very cheerfully along the upward path. Their virtue was at once active and intellectual : it was not of the heart so much as of the deed and of the brain. There is something of this too in the Catholic idea of confession and absolution, and then great gaiety till you sin again.

December 11, 1907.

Found myself, surprised myself, with a prayer on my lips, a prayer to Plotinus that I might translate him : I am certain it would be as well to pray to him for any virtue as to pray to St. Augustine or St. Patrick, but I think Plotinus would not be pleased with this my prayer : it would seem to him a worldly thing, still. It is very strange to me as I write this to feel that perhaps very truly he looks down upon me writing : at least that is what the Catholic Church means with her " Communion of the Saints and Intercession of the Saints " : can they really believe that the Once Human, now ravished in the Beatific Vision, do look down upon the upper room of No. 1, Goldhurst Terrace, Finchley Road, where the Wax Lady waits at the door ? Amazing the things one can believe when one is called *homo*.

December 16, 1907.

I am lost in wonder at the mystery of Patriotism. Why should I care what Ireland is now when I do not live in it, or what Ireland may become when I am dead ? Yet I do, with a passion of love and pity and rage. This is the only thing that makes me see any sense in the Comtist idea of humanity in the long future as a compelling object of religion.

December 18, 1907.

I notice that these notes become steadily more careless in style : they were meant for gymnastic as well as for true recording : the gymnastic has slipped away, and I hurry the bare noting of ideas. Reform it, altogether ?

January 15, 1908.

36 to-day, and nothing done. I feel that my life is one long series of beginnings : I am always planning for next year, always working towards something, never *at* something. The one clear reason—whether 'tis an excuse or not, I don't know—is that nothing that is within my power interests me or seems worth doing. I am interested in Plotinus : to translate him into beautiful English and then to interpret him and press him into the use of this century seems to me, has always seemed to me, really worth a life—but I have not been able to give the work all my time and thought : I must write bosh and run about the world on stupid people's tracks. So also, to write good English, and with it to say some good simple thing, seems to me well worth doing : I must bang out rubbish for a scant market : I cannot yet write English, because it does not come naturally to me and I haven't time to learn at peace. Gaelic literature would seem to me worth a life—to master it, expound it, put it to use for Ireland : and Ireland itself—to be doctor and expositor of Ireland's need and claims and methods, to help by writing and speech and action at putting the new soul into Ireland, that too would suffice me, but I must first live or try to make a living. I utterly lack the power many or most men have of working indifferently well at some one trade for livelihood while keeping two or three passionate efforts always marching quietly but surely on towards the great ends that are the real meaning and use of life. And, deep down, I cannot find in myself, in power or vision, any reason for believing that I can really add anything to the world, do any service : and anything less than such

an effective service as will reach far beyond myself seems to me utterly unworthy. I have no interest in trifles, in trifling things or trifling people, and, being below or outside of the serious, I become trifling myself. The others I quietly scorn; myself I scorn bitterly, angrily. I have just sent off to the *Freeman* an article, whose subject is quite good, whose underlying meaning should make it useful for Ireland, whose style is such that to put it out from the workshop deserves a beating.

January 14, 1908.[1]

How deeply the primal curse is smitten into us—like Milton's "forked arrow sore smitten into the Kingdom's sides." To-day has been a desert of morbid moping, nothing done: except for a couple of letters, begging for work, nothing even in my mind to be done. And because I have done nothing I am most unhappy, ashamed. In the darkness of the back streets of Kilburn, as there suddenly crashed in on me the thought that I had eaten and not worked, I blushed vividly, hotly: it was like being "convinced of sin," it most likely was exactly the same mood, not more and not less spiritual or moral than that Christian process. And I ask myself, why? Why is it not enough to live as the animals do—as the plants do, in their lesser life? Is it because the plants and animals are, given the world, self-sufficing, and have, so to speak, always earned their own dinner? It seems a base morality that is always looking into the kitchen and counting the saucepans: "have you filled a larder by your toil? Then you are a good man, bless you!" "have you eaten without earning, then you are low!" Yet somehow the larder has to be filled: why may I eat what another has got together? Why may I have others to serve me, when I do not serve them? Yet to follow on that trail is to kill all learning and all light of the mind in the world—at least until the day when the whole social

[1] There is a slip in the dating, as the order of the entries shows.

system shall be new-shaped so that every man can live by the work for which he is most fit and shall not be a slave even to that. Until these things are settled for us, by those that have the knowledge and judgement to settle them, we, who through our fault or our peculiar merit are not skilled in economy and psychology and statecraft, must merely do our little best in the world as we find it, and live for our best spiritual and mental health and well-being in an ill-based society, as we would live for these things in a society more justly disposed.

February 9, 1908.

No doubt a man must for his happiness and his dignity find something to do in the world and for the world ; but there may be men whose nobly-borne poverty is their work, whose playing with ideas is all their task as it is all the task of a child ; it may not be pleasant to know oneself born to be for ever of the Little Ones, but there precisely the virtue may be, in living honourably faithful to the duty of being always at school, learning painfully, humbly, in the Great Taskmaster's eye until he, as Browning says, shall somehow, somewhere, find use for the learning.

February 11, 1908.

If the consecrated religions are doomed to pass away, and dogma and liturgy to become matters of learning or of poetry, there will still be mystics and mysticism : already, indeed, we see that the crumbling of the old faiths has enriched the soil for many strange forms of lawless, emotional religion. Men will believe something about the nature of the Cause and about the high meaning of man. But apart from this, which is perhaps vanity and hybris, there is another reason why Mysticism will always be in the world, and will grow as the shared, the communal faiths wane. Through religions and through literature and the arts and through the ceaseless widening of the common knowledge of human life, there has sprung in men a greater pity, the beginning of a deeper love : and once the religions with their neat promises of future redressing have ceased to set consciences too easily at rest, there must come a new brooding over the meaning of the world, a new searching after all justice and beauty and perfection. Henceforth men must always find in themselves a gnawing greed for a good that the world does not give ; if they cease to pray to God, they will all the more, and all the more imploringly, consult their own Highest, which is but God more nearly seen ; all the old words of the mystics they will re-read in their own, the new sense, and they will find new words of their own for the new revelations of life's meaning and duties. There will still and always be men going in the evenings with eyes downcast and glowing. And there will still and always be men and women in cloisters or hermitages or deserts, men afraid of life but not cowardly, men who cannot think they have anything to do with the world but to flee from it humbly—not that they are idle or scornful, but that they feel no power to help the world and are afraid lest they soil it or soil themselves in it.

February 14, 1908.

There are two kinds of peacefulness—the peacefulness of the sheep and the peace of Plotinus. The first is, in Man who is Nature self-acting, a vice ; the peace of the contemplative is at once the most beautiful and the most fruitful act of man. Even Tolstoi's peace of non-resistance, allowing for the moment all injustice, is in any but a savage and incurably cruel society an active force : I may kill a raging man whom I have raised in passion against me ; I may kill a crawling insect that in some way thwarts or vexes me : but I cannot long have peace in killing men who stand with folded hands to show me with reasonings like my own that I am doing wrong. There is a peace, however—which I do not take to be

Tolstoi's—which is simply injustice masked : it arms the wrongdoer by its silence, and the dagger which it has put into the hand of Injustice will make more than the one victim. The just peace speaks its mind very boldly ; it has thrown away the sword only the better to beat down injustice by its reasonings. Its method is slow—sometimes so slow that even the sage must leave it for awhile and take to arms, as a sage might to-day for Ireland, if there were any hope that way—but its victories are lasting and are themselves fruitful, bringing forth ever new victories, offspring of the once-sown seed of reason and beautiful conduct.

February 16, 1908.

Sincerity, one is apt to think, the utterance of the plain truth of one's thought and vision and feeling, is all that is needed for the raw material of literature : add a little grace of style, and you have the thing you seek, the book that is worth the writing and reading. It is true—that is just the mischief of it. For this very utterance of the thing you see and feel is the whole matter of genius : nothing seems easier when you think of doing it, nothing seems easier when some one has done it : but try to do it, and you find it is like the creation of the world : it is selection from a chaos, it is seizing the eternally fluid, it is bringing from deep places to the plain daylight things whose whole secret meaning was in the dim half-lights, it is to clothe for beauty something whose excellence and life it is to be nakedly itself, untouched. And what a sharp sight must that be which shall see clearly down in the dark where the self lives and flickers.

February 18, 1908.

There is in Ireland, in politics, in criticism, in the treatment of differences in religion, a bitterness, very striking at first sight both in talk and in writing, which alone is enough to show that we are a backward people, paying by our lack of wisdom for the waste of force to which our history and our temper acting together have led us. Because in various ways we have been kept fighting, we have not, as a race, been learning : keenness has been made more keen, and passion, as Yeats says, is hot in Ireland—though not, as he would have it, because the Irish are Celts—and imagination, of the less useful kind, has not faded ; but we have not mellowed in studies, and there is no graceful equal interchange of thought among us ; we live in embattled camps and beat angry drums : it is exceedingly rare to find a Nationalist of any one school able to conceive that the non-Nationalist or the Nationalist of another policy can be sincere, upright, a well-wisher at heart to the country. They tell me, and I see many signs of it, that to value Synge's work is to be dreaded and disliked by the entire Gaelic League. Sinn Fein no doubt begins to think of using for practical purposes whatever aid Unionists may be willing to give : but it thinks it is using these strangers as unconscious tools, and its personal attacks on Parliamentarians seem to become all the fiercer, all the more stingingly bitter, all the more nastily personal, as if to make good the lessening or stifling of its hate towards certain Unionists by pouring out a deadlier stream of vitriol against the heretic Nationalist. We have yet to learn in Ireland that the greatest strength in almost all fights is to be strong nobly. We lessen ourselves, the better, we think, to meet our low enemy ; and behold, as we lower ourselves he rises with a sublimer head. This, I think, on both sides : hence we are for ever punching the air : no one wins because no one fights : only Ireland always loses.

February 19, 1908.

I find that Ireland is still mediaeval, beautifully and dismally mediaeval : the people is fantastic of speech, frank and simple and yet curiously respectful of dignities, superstitious and brawling and readily cowed : humorous, neighbourly, not shrinking all the same from cruelties towards man or beast, too quick moving and thorough-going to be stayed by tenderness or far-seeing prudence in moments of passion : cleaner of soul than of body, yet pagan and near to the earth, but to an earth worked over by gods or spirits, an earth heaving with divinity. I am enraged to-day reading the Lenten Pastoral of the Bishop of Clonfert who, telling of the decisions of some Conference of Bishops, calmly warns the people that it is "*henceforth a mortal sin*"—and reserved at that—to give out alcoholic drinks at a funeral or at a wake : a clergy that can make upon a day a new mortal sin has surely the keys of hell and is very courageous in thrusting souls down into the fires of the hot place. And the curious thing—a little comforting—is that there will still be drinks at wakes even in the diocese of Clonfert ; good Catholics who on one side of their minds know that the Church can save or damn will, in the other side of their brains, mix drinks with glee and good fellowship : it is strange. I would like to see that bishop.

March 26, 1908.

Churches, liturgies and private devotional habits spring probably and have their use from the soul's curious trick of playing truant. If we have a soul at all, it is fairly certain that we have it not always : it flits away sometimes, or shrinks down within us, exactly as the mind does ; and as there are absent-minded moments, so there are men and moments absent-souled. The mind may be very active, working at full power, but we know that we are dead at the time : there is no movement where the soul once beat with its wings—bare ruined choirs where erst the sweet birds sang : something is certainly changed in us ; we are lessened, lonely. I do not find that the soul in its going or coming plays with the mind at all : sometimes when the brain is quickest, eagerest, there is most lift and radiance of the soul, the deep, warm sense of things above the mind ; sometimes when the brain is sunk to a dull puddle, the man is comforted with the sun and knows that somewhere, in some way, in some shape or kind " his Redeemer liveth," and in his flesh he knows the eternal things. The spirit bloweth where it listeth and we can only wait and hope. But it is well to have one's litany or liturgy for a safeguard in the dull times : the soul—if it be, or as it must be if it is the best and highest in oneself—will come back the sooner if the place be swept and garnished and the arm-chair set for it pleasantly by the fire : the exercises which seem quite foolish when the soul is there become the only saving when the place is empty and cold : they invite or compel the return—and, as we can never foreknow the truancy of the soul, the disciplines are to be done always.

April 6, 1908.

When one has tried long, and failed, to make for oneself a personal style by which to set down one's thoughts and feelings with graceful power, or perhaps has tried long, and failed, to form out of the mists of living some strong thought or picture worthy of a noble setting, it comes to seem better to try no more : a man's life must be for worthier things than wrestling hopelessly with an unkind nature and adding to the grief of weakness the torture of envy and wasting bitterness. But it is to be remembered that a man lives by running : when we stand, we are dead, as most of us are dead : I think that unless in one thing or another we are straining towards perfection we have forfeited our manhood. . . . Our perfection is in being imperfect in something whose perfection is to us the highest thing in life. Sometimes, for this, all life seems to me utterly a dream : the soul has come down and robed itself in flesh and folly to rest from its own high living, as a man might plunge himself in drunkenness to get rest from the strain of the world : our work here is but a dreaming in the soul that remembers and plays over again its old high activities : it isn't the kind of the work that is prized in the eternal records, but the working : when something stirs, anything, it is to be known that the soul is the less heavily drenched, lives under the sleep, and will wake someday, by death, to a freshened life.

April 18, 1908.

Yesterday was Good Friday, and I was at the Westminster Cathedral for the morning office : quivering often with emotion for the beauty of the ceremonies and their old meaning and all the old human *ripae ulterioris amor* they tell of ; but quivering too over the mere distant sight of a noble old Irishman—woolly white hair, domed front, delicately pointed lower face, most beautifully chiselled features, simple black clothes, unbroken poring on his book—who stood to me for all that was ancient and noble and sound in Ireland, all that is Celt. And I couldn't separate the two emotions, or count one more holy than the other.

DUBLIN :

June 23, 1908.

The need of newness is the thing that most clearly marks off mind from either body or " soul " ; beefsteaks for the body, the devout brooding over a few old truths for the " soul "—but the mind needs new problems, new answers ; its life is in a ceaseless changing. The body is the mystery we know nothing of ; it works its own will and goes its own way, like a cat or a god ; as far as we know or have power over it, its joy springs from the secrets of its own dark life, it dies by its own calendar, and when we most think we are ruling it, it is obeying the order itself first gave. If we doctor it, we are but giving it the food it asked for, we don't know why ; if they cut into it for us, it must be trimmed only so far and no farther—an inch more and something very strange comes upon us. It gives itself its own laws, and we obey them and it : the mystery is the body : it is the stranger : we can only gape at it when it stands in our doorway, and do our best to keep it in good humour, the awesome, powerful, venerable stranger. There is something Egyptian about the body ; the mind is the Greek, childishly playing, running always after the new thing, growing daily, but usually not to a finer beauty. There is something in us that seems deeper and truer than the mind, and we call it the soul : I sometimes find myself thinking that the soul is nearer to the body than the mind is : perhaps it is the eternity of the body : for, like the body, it is self-centred, dark, little changing, little answering : it too goes its own way, muttering to itself, and the mind playing by its skirts can guess only dimly at its thoughts. The mind seems little more than a flickering, babbling stream that may sometimes catch and throw up for a moment the Image of an Image : the body, I have thought, may be God or, as the Hebrews seem to have deeply conceived, the Image of God ; sometimes the body seems beautiful enough to be mysteriously That ; always it is strange enough to be That, or the fallen image of That, for it is shapely and stately and most wonderfully coloured and it has too its strange share of ugliness, of evil : beauty and ugliness, The Good and The Evil, is there not in that strange blend something akin to the God ? but the body dies ? And if it does ? is it not good Pauline lore that it shall rise again, even as the God that died rose again ? *Et homo factus est.* Christianity has curious depths. But it is better not to sound them.

June 27, 1908.

The more I read—in every language I trifle with, English, French, Latin, Greek, even the rather lush Gaelic—the more I see that I really have yet no skill at all in writing. It is not merely that I have no art ; I haven't even the first base craft : it isn't that I'm not a sculptor ; I'm not even a mason, a neat chipper of the stone. I read nowhere, outside of the very sorriest reporter-work, any prose less like prose than mine is: my work hasn't even the clearness and easy flow which are the first need of decent writing, as calm manners and clean clothes are the first marks of a "gentleman." All I have, after all these years with their practice if not their effort, is a great enjoyment of the skill of others, with a quickening sense of the materials that lie to the prose-writer's hand. Perhaps, too, I have a large, ready stock of words. But the store is not the main thing: it is the use that counts: what is it to a man that he have a hundred thousand bricks, if he hasn't the skill to set them neatly, evenly, strongly one upon another to the building of a useful wall, that he have Shakespeare's richness of words, if he cannot put together a single comely, cleanly sentence? For years I played foolishly with "the Phrase," seeking the bubble, self-esteem, even in the canon's teeth, defying all the sanctities if only I might anyhow please myself with a yell and a flare and a fit of ribald glee: now only I begin to know that it is not "the Phrase" that counts to any good; it is "la Phrase"—the Sentence, the orderly, suave and gracious setting of the true word in the clear meaning. This is the anatomy of style, as anatomy is the beginning of medicine and of surgery, of painting and of sculpture. The glory is to come later, if it ever comes; as a man must first be sober before he can be a saint, and learn to behave himself before he climbs into the pulpit.

July 8, 1908.

When a man has no clear view, he will find no clear word. Style can't put forth what the mind has failed to take in. If I am to see at your will, you must see first, as if I am to be rich with your coin you must get a coin. Don't think you may trust to the force of a rough stroke to print in fresh strength on my brain things I have seen, known, loved of old: if you have not seen hard and clear, seen all, you will not light on the thing that worked on me, that still puts its spell on me. I will not leap to your rich gift : at most I will earn it with small joy ; I will have toiled to dig up the crock, and by toil I will be tired, too tired to care. If I see at all, I will see two things—in a dim light I will see what I was told to see ; but, most, I will see my rage at the cheat that is put on me. Work kills joy : and the man that writes must set me at ease, or I cannot love him or prize him or see or feel with him. It is in the bond that, for the nonce, he is to work, I taste his fruits.

August 10, 1908.

I find myself haunted by the desire to write well—if only with simple clearness, in sentences that can be read aloud. I don't understand why I feel so deeply the need of writing sentences that will pass the test of the " gueuloir ": it is not because all the writers on style dwell upon it, for they irritate me by their dwelling on a law for which they give no reason : it seems simply that I feel the desire equally with them while, like them, I know not why. It's true that in writing for the *Freeman* I always have in mind the thought that people are apt to read aloud at the breakfast-table a passage that has pleased them ; and when I am saying something I would like to see acted out I try very hard to ensure that, if a man should wish to pass it on to others, the form may enable him, even tempt him, to give it as I wrote it. But I know that this mere chance motive in the special case can't be the motive of what I feel to be a need in every case : I know that if I were writing a book, with no thought of more than one reader, I would still toil to make sentences easy to the voice : in vain I ask myself why. Can it be that in our blood and in our bones there is a memory of the long-past days when all writing was uttered, mouthed ?[1] I notice that for myself, unless by bringing force and

[1] Marginal note in MacKenna's handwriting : " Perhaps memory of early reading-lessons."

thought to the matter, I don't listen to a man's cadence: I have frequently approved, when reading without the voice, passages which on the test have refused the mouthing, have stuck in the throat or tripped up the breath, or, again, have annoyed my ear by ugly or useless repetitions of sounds or of words, or been feeble by the tags and tails they drag after them. Often enough, my own printed matter, even, though it has satisfied my eye-reading, has angered me when I have put it to the voice. And sometimes when I have worked the "scazons" over and given them a robust and easy gait I have found that I have lost, even to my own momentarily twisted or perverted sense, merits of colour or of meaning more worth than any merit I have acquired in sound. It sometimes seems that this law should be counted binding only for drama, poetry, oratory and perhaps newspaper articles; and that all subtle matter, all intimate, dreamy stuff that is not in its nature read aloud, should be free of all such gyves. *Haec cogita.*

August 13, 1908.

A day of nothingness, of prehumous death: pains and laze and brainlessness. Probably I could have saved this day and given it some value, had I but frankly from the early morning proclaimed a day of rest: it is always nobler to rest diligently than to work listlessly. Life is in activity, and if one can't be active in work the only living is to be lively in play. If one can't write seriously, one can read seriously: if one can't read long, perhaps one can think long: if one has no thoughts, one can read lightly: if one can't read light things or talk pleasantly, then better go to sleep, thus at last doing something seriously useful. If sin is sin by dampening life, then a morose dawdling is among the deadliest of sins; it is a very subtle shaft of the *Gillie nach chorp.*[1] Few acts could sink a man further from God's service, or from the mastery of himself more fatally or more miserably, than spineless discontented actlessness.

[1] Irish: "the Devil."

August 22, 1908.

Cycling late through Stillorgan we passed a full tavern, the door wide open, sending out a flow of yellow light on a dark road ; young girls and young boys, clearly fresh and good, lounging inside and on the steps ; one jovial rascal leaning with the naive ease of drunken enjoyment half over the counter, his face, full in the light, turned towards the road, grinning : 'twas a Teniers. I thought of the Russian *traktir*,[1] of far things : somehow there was something utterly continental and strange in the scene ; an animation, a grouping, an ease that seemed poles apart from the stupid English pothouse I have seen of late. I longed to go in and be a part of it all, for observation's sake : the mischief is that if ever I did go in, all the life would go out : men are born to their little boxes and like the different tribes of animals, snails and cows and bees, are strangers always.

October 1, 1908.

A month almost without writing and without thought. Let it roll away. In a long life there are some 600 months of truly conscious living, and there comes a time when it is wise to think that a great pile of months : if one looks on 600 as a small number, the waste of one would seem a too hideous loss to be borne with sanity. I find myself often saying or vaguely remembering that of Whitman, " As the trees and animals are ": even our wasted months must have their use, or nothing is of use ; the waste must even be perfect use, it seems, or nothing is of use. This, however, is one of those metaphysical consolations which serve little enough in physical, actual griefs : it always remains a fact that if one's service can conceivably be at once useful and visibly null, then one belongs to the lower calling : one touches the animal or the vegetable. Perhaps if one were aware of some lofty sanctity or other purely spiritual use and service, the blank month might be felt as a noble retreat, a beautiful brooding, a ripening,

[1] " tavern."

a full time of delicate effusion, a giving forth of fragrance to a world that is half a stench : but without that, what is there to live for but to do, sowing or reaping or giving to eat? Myself I feel ceaselessly, sadly, that I have really no use or meaning in life, and that mainly because I have neither conviction, nor even sufficient acting-belief, of anything at all being useful in which I am able to help. The one thing on which I have never wavered all my life —the whole body of my Irish faith—is altogether beyond or outside of my working-power : I do not know how Ireland is to be freed or built up : I do not know whether it ever can : all I know is that I cannot imagine myself happy in heaven or hell if Ireland, in its soul or in its material state, is to be always English. Of course I would be fairly safe in throwing myself with all my power into the Gaelicising movements, but then I have no power : I have wandered too long in other countries and loitered down too many bye-ways, and I have never been able to be or do many things at once : there is Greek and there is Plotinus and there is English literature and there is the art of English writing and there is the vast field of things to be known of which I am ignorant—*que faire, mon dieu, que faire ?*

January 3, 1909.

Reading of late : G. Meredith's verse : Soph. *Oed. Cols.* : Thos. Becon (Parker Socy.) : Eurs. *Bacchae* (third time) : Canon O'Leary's *Seadna*, double-translating Gaelic to English and English back : Plotinus, dipping into here and there : W. Morris (Tauchnitz) first time : Swinburne : Frank Norris, *Octopus*, Christmas : Egerton Castle, some sixpenny novel : Milton *P.L.*, for third time as a whole I think. Much Yeats, prose and verse, and wrote 1500 word review in *Freeman* this January.[1] Great amount of newspaper and review matter : India, Balkans, unemployment, etc.

[1] Cf. memoir, p. 38.

Trend of thought : how to write short-limbed, clear-cut, readable, simple English : what are the bases of national wealth and prosperity : the bases of morals.

January 6, 1909.

At the Gaelic League, Mícheál O'Briain, scamping his class and getting rid of the dull studious people, gathers two or three round the fire to talk. It is all on the decay of the race. In his own Irish-speaking island, he finds his own generation falling far short of their fathers and mothers : they are not so handsome, so massive, so strong of body, they are not so quick of mind, they are not so gay. The reason ? " Oh, they have too easy times of it. The old people faced the weathers and bore every sort of hardship : there was no tea in the morning before they went out to work : there was no white bread, but buttermilk and wheaten-bread (?). The young people must have their cup of tea before they'd look outside the door of a morning : they have everything to their mind, every sort of luxury (! ! !)." Mícheál says that when the " old people " do know any English 'tis much better English than the children of to-day will ever get. And much more to the same effect—a youth rising up against youth like a Hebrew prophet against the Hebrew.

Putting apart all question of personality, pleasant or unpleasant, I find myself revering every born speaker of Irish : I value them more than any historical relic : if it were good for them I would feed them in the Prytaneum : they are miracles of survival of a noble ancient thing : their intellectual pedigree dates from 2000 or 3000 years. And God alone knows whether in fifty years or a hundred the whole line of them may not be ended—ended in an English-speaking, English-thinking Ireland, to which these few or remnant would be a kind of savages.

April 1909.

I notice, with curiosity, that the longer I live, though many hopes fail and fall away and at last are almost forgotten, two stay firmly with me and grow. Neither is held by my reason ; both have to do with the heart and are for the impossible, as reason says coldly. I hope for the freedom of Ireland, soul and body freedom, Gaelicism and a flag : and I hope even yet to be able some day to write well—in English !—even though I should never use the power, never write anything for more than its one day's life. The first hope I cannot account for : " this bird has built its nest with me." It can be only a reach-back to the dead sons of Enna through centuries of Gaelic life. The other hope seems to have a moral foundation. It is hard at best to find any meaning in life at all ; impossible, unless by way of some action, something by which one especially lives, bringing out some singular quality, and something by which one adds to the sum of life, shaping by some personal means the larger form of the world.

No doubt to live " as the trees and animals do " is to be a Shaper : you have to get out of the way of a cow, and you think of a dandelion : but to rest contentedly in such service or power is to forget the intelligence, the personal heart ; it is to be content at one's lowest level. The thing which the French mock in the English mind seems to me very sane and healthy, the ceaseless weighing of goodness against cleverness : I still think a man must be one or the other to be worth a red cent : to be either mainly is to be both in a fair measure, and there is service and self-expression by either : to separate them is useful to speech and even to thought but, like all contraries and opposites in a world which is still one, they run together in the end : there is a great work of the brain in only keeping perfectly " good," and there is a great goodness, of life and of service, in putting out the fruits of the brain.

June 15, 1909.

It is strange and saddening to find, when one sits to write with leisure and entire freedom of choice, that one has nothing whatever to put down, or nothing but the despairing statement of an utter emptiness. What sort of a thin life is it, what sort of a muddy brain, what a chilly soul, that can give in twelve waking hours no single thought or feeling that a man may write for his merely technical exercise. For a great part of our life we are merely animal or quite dead : immortality in another sphere does not seem so certainly a boon as would be immortality during our present life. It may be that a good working guide to conduct might be framed on this ideal of living to the fullest here and now : it is likely that the soul seeking admission among the bodiless immortals in another world would be elected at once on the strength of having kept itself from death in days here below.

LETTERS

Prefatory Note.

The letters which follow have been selected from a much larger number which were placed at my disposal by the recipients. They cover the last twenty-one years of MacKenna's life. Of letters written earlier I have discovered, to my deep regret, only a few isolated examples, mostly of minor importance ; the most interesting passages from these have been quoted in the Memoir. It is also matter for regret that certain of MacKenna's most frequent correspondents in later years—notably James Stephens—have kept no letters.

The letters are printed as they were written, save that I have silently corrected occasional slips of the pen or eccentricities of spelling, and that I have altered the highly individual punctuation so far—but only so far—as appeared to be necessary in the interests of clearness. MacKenna's phonetic spelling of Gaelic words has been retained. Where for one reason or another it was necessary to omit part of a letter the omission is indicated by asterisks. Dates in square brackets are supplied by me ; many of them are only approximate. The majority of the original letters are undated, and dates like " 29th or 30th Feb. 1924 " and " Wednesday ?th of ? 1915 " are not infrequent.

E. R. DODDS.

LETTERS

I

To " A. E." (GEORGE RUSSELL)

39, KENSINGTON SQUARE,
LONDON, W. [1913].

MY DEAR A. E.—I'm a long time now trying to make up my mind to write to you, or rather to wake up my pen to obey my long-made-up mind. I have left all my friends without a word ever since we left Ireland ; and only now I begin at haphazard to send here a card, there a brief scrawlín, in the hope of forgiveness. In your case we were most accursedly sorry : had I had the ghost of a notion beforehand that you were coming over here, we would have early communicated ourselves to you in the hope that we might see you. We didn't know before it was too late, until you were all but here : then I had a very good reason not to write : 'twas that we had tried for tickets for the Albert Hall [1] and had been too late or too suspect or too something—and I dreaded lest you should think I had communicated for my advantage, my need. I would have given a goodish little sum to hear you, though—very probably in my ignorance of all the conditions—I didn't approve of that meeting : a sick nationalism and a dreadful fear of proselytism and general dislike of English fingers in Irish pies, the cause to me of my disapproval, passive only : I mean that I wouldn't have said anything except to my own soul on the matter, wouldn't have dissuaded one soul from going. All which is quite unimportant : I know nobody that is less certain

[1] The reference is to a meeting in support of the Irish Transport Strike, at which " A. E." delivered a remarkable speech.

of himself, his own mind, in all these things : I know only one thing, my own little thing, that I want Ireland Irish and Irish-speaking, and would prefer it also to be just, based on justice : therefore am platonically with the workers, and yet unable to make up even my own poor little mind on any such deadly practical matters as those you were up to.

I hear by the way that you have, very good-naturedly as would be your way, very gently, blasphemed my Nationality, saying that that Kind always flies out of Ireland : gently and kindly and playfully you did me a wrong : you have not acquired merit : your crown of glory will have one weak spot : you will have to keep your hand hovering about it lest your fellow-beatified would say now and then, " Why, brother, your crown has a crack in it," and you would have to say, " Oh nothing, just a little injustice I did to poor MacKenna, the decent poor fool God help him." I left Ireland for Ireland's good, in some sense : not that my state matters much to Ireland, but that 'tis a simple fact that matter or not I couldn't get my health there, to serve or play at serving, but must, absolutely MUST, have a large change, to try and get the brain back to something like working order, the nerves in tune or tone again, the spirits bucked-up : and I haven't the means to go gallivanting about *and* keep up an Irish establishment, even tho' climatically and otherwise that would (which it wouldn't) serve the need. It is of course very cheap and easy to say that one's heart is in Ireland ; but that only proves that sometimes truth *is* cheap and easy, mercifully. I will be back in Ireland yet before I'm much more grizzled than I'm now. * * * *

This is the end : you see there was nothing in me to say. I am not a man of the pen : I can say more in five minutes with my little tongue than with the longest fountain-pen in the world or the most ponderous typewriter : I hate writing and its tools : 'tis extraordinary how these paraphernalia freeze the flow of ideas and emotion : I suppose in a few centuries or so we will argue wirelessly over infinite spaces and publish our thoughts to all nations by some psychic channels, translation thrown in. Which foolishness reminds me I just read the Bhagavadgita through and copiously annotated it myself, on the top of the copious annotations of one Tookaram Tatya. Norman once gave me the Bh. to read, and I couldn't : the soul has its times and seasons and will not be forced : that which is its beatitude becomes its bunkum, and bunkum is seen to be beatitude the next day but one. I don't know did I ripen or rot when I fell into the ring of this curious book : all the same I remain true to the old heresy : 'tis all in elementary Christianity, only in another metaphor : my change is that now I read and to some degree understand another language for the old thing : a useful process in other things beside the Way of the Soul. I suppose you know Rudolph Eucken : if not, and if your wars and threats of war leave you time, you really should consume a pipeful over him.

I see I didn't succeed in ending this scrivín [1] after all : I sometimes think I will be prosecuted for keeping a disorderly house, my mind. Abandon Hope all ye that enter here : nothing clear or sweet is to be found, but only confusion upon confusion piled : you pays your money and you takes your choice and heaven help you. If you knew the dignified sensible letter I meant to write you, you'd be grateful to me : my intentions were good.

As I read " The City " [2] I remembered how you read it, with what fervour and organ music : it reads in the cold print nobly also, a magnificent thing, not less for the beautiful human things in it than for the spiritual splendour.

Long life to you :

STEPHEN MACKENNA.

My wife, were she in the now, would want her kindest good luck to go to you.

[1] Irish : " little screed."

[2] A poem by " A. E."

IA

From "A. E."

"IRISH HOMESTEAD,"
DUBLIN [1913].

MY DEAR STEPHEN MACKENNA,—My halo is indeed cracked—cracked along and across, but not because of the sin you impute. I may have uttered a wail that all my friends were in Paris or London or Berlin or New York ; but I'm sure I never blamed any of them whom Destiny took by the scruff of the neck and marched off with them, as one of James Stephens' policemen would take one of Larkin's men to Mountjoy : " There is no armour against Fate." James Stephens I may indeed gird at because he went with no knuckles at the back of his neck compelling him ; but not, believe me, any person who leaves of necessity because the purse is lean or the health has flown. You did not say how you are. Is not this unkind ? Is not this a crack in your halo that you suppose your friends don't care whether you are getting better or not ? You will have no advantage over me in Paradise * * * * I am glad you find the Gita more readable. Of course it is in its essentials one with the Gospel of John, but it was six hundred years earlier. I think you would like the heroic literature of India better than its religious literature. The Gita is an episode in the long narrative of the Mahabharata. If you read the last two books of the Mahabharata I think you will agree with me that there is no nobler epic poetry in the world. Edwin Arnold, a mediocre poet, translated them in his Indian Idylls, and even through his facile verse one sees the noble original, as the beauty of Cophetua's Queen shone through her tattered garments.

Ireland is a new country since you left. The land is shaking with the tramp of volunteers. Labour is drilling. The Hibernians are drilling, so are the Sinn Feiners. The Ulster men are also at it still. Ireland seems to have forgotten it had any brains, but places all its confidence in its muscles. I am all for other methods ; but all my friends are so enthusiastic that I can only look on and hope that the Lord means something good for this unfortunate country out of it. Dublin is split up into Labour and Capital, and one goes about these days with a burden on the heart all the time. You would feel it if you were here, and in a way I am glad you are not, for you would worry over it all until you made yourself ill. It is a new Ireland shaping itself rapidly before our eyes, like a country re-forming itself in an earthquake where old hills are rent in twain and fissures open in the long established plains—and there will be more fissures and cracks to no end before we get the new human formation. I once, about twenty years ago, had a series of visions about the future of Ireland. I saw a figure descending from heaven and standing on the earth, and at that moment a mother held a child in her lap. Then I saw the old Queen Victoria toppling from her throne, and other things—then a gigantic figure stalked across Ireland beating a drum and there were flights and alarms and smoke and burnings ; then after a silence the mountains flung up their rays as Brigid saw in her vision. I think the figure is beginning to beat the drum, and I am in hopes the mountains will fling up their rays to heaven when it is all over. I wonder will I see the avatar when he begins his labour of freeing Ireland. I would know him if I did see him, because the face of the vision impressed me so much that I was able to draw it. The drilling put me in mind of these twenty-year-old visions. But I am horribly sad at heart over Ireland just now.

Thanks for the good words about my verse. I would rather have the good word of a few folk like you than mighty columns in the papers. I am only a John the Baptist before the true spiritual poet comes to Ireland. The old prophecies of spirituality in legend and faery tale require some greater fulfilment than Ireland has yet given.

Our story began with epics and tales of the gods, and it ought to end in a blaze of intellectual and spiritual light to make our last days worthy of our half divine beginnings. Well, I was glad to get your note and I hope you are coming to yourself again, and that you will be back in Ireland not for the cracking of skulls but for the later spring of the spirit.

With kind regards to Mrs. MacKenna,

Yours ever,

A. E.

2

To THOMAS BODKIN

64, LANSDOWNE PLACE, HOVE,
SUSSEX, ENGLAND [*December* 1914].

MY DEAR TOM BODKIN,—My grief that I am little in touch with you : perhaps I'd write more often if you didn't change your address quite so much.[1] This is just a Christmas word, though I loathe Christmas and all Christmessiness. My lady friend, it is true, went out, and I at her heels, to buy you a Christmas card ; but neither Brighton nor Hove contained any one, even at three pence itself, that we could honestly declare worthy of you, so we let it go : we didn't think you would want a robin surrounded by tulips in a network of lace nest, or an old lady knitting, with a movable grandson and granddaughter poking out roguish curly heads on either side of her abbatial chair ? If you would like either, however, don't hesitate to wire me : I could get 'em at once. There is also a John Bull with a hat, and in the hat the flags of all the Allied Nations, and Herself serving a great plum pudding, the same flags stuck all over it : " very appropriate to the moment and selling very well "—sort of " useful Christmas present " I gather. We hesitated but

[1] MacKenna continually changed his address ; Bodkin never.

didn't buy : this you could have also at once : we'd even go three of them as they are only a penny.

I thought we were an intellectual and hightoned people, we of Hove, but really—for I was not quite serious above —I got a shock when I saw all this—and nothing else. We did ask in a sort of blush Had they any old masters—for, we thought, an old master always looks toney and saves the dire exercise of personal taste : but only one shop, and that not one of the big ones, had ever heard of Old Masters, and when we saw them they turned out to be indecent postal matter, hair-lifters from the Salons—the nou oh Salong ! Very nou indeed and not rapturously lovely. We did indeed buy one or was it two of the nous, but we are keeping them for ourselves—et pour cause.

I read a communiqué from your house, or from one of them, about the war : in the *Chronicle* it was : are them your sentiments too ? I don't like the suggestion that it's either cowardice or German gold which keeps some of us back from swearing terribly in Flanders. It may be idiocy, hereditary idiocy, but taint any taint of tothers. Well, peace to all men of good will : I haven't the energy to fight with anyone, and I wish to God they'd clear up all the mess and say nothing about it, as they did with the precocious productions of the prodigy in *Tristram Shandy*. I'm heartbroken over the war that has enabled his Most Reverence and Eminence of Armagh to declare with undeniable truth that Ireland will always leap into the breach in loyal devotion to the British Empire. I read this in the *Freeman* and it gave me a heart-ache, even unto real tears coursing down my innocent nose.

My son, I can no more : God make you good and happy, and may all good fortune rain down upon and soak into your house and household and all that is yours, and may all that you want be yours and nothing you don't want. All this very sincerely with true and grateful friendship.

STEPHEN MACKENNA.

3

To THOMAS BODKIN

[No address],
[*Autumn* 1915].

MY DEAR TOMBODKIN,—We are back. I'm dotty in the doe-nut again. Forgive my English : I've just been in England. Therefore—I want light reading. If you like come on Saturday. You know the kind of book. It must be light. It musn't be silly. Don't want any tragedies. Let it not be French. To hell with Art. No translations. Don't bring many. Let everything be just right. I'm sure you understand.

Nothing about Ireland. Anything about parsons or priests is good. I don't mind a *story* about art or literature. Don't let it be by the author of *Elizabeth's Garden.* Have you any Snaith ? Snaith is an author. I've read his *Wm. Jordan.* Have you any Butler ? But I bar something of his with " flesh " in the title.

Yours ever,
S. M. K.

4

To E. R. DEBENHAM (SIR ERNEST DEBENHAM)

24, CHARLEVILLE ROAD,
RATHMINES,
DUBLIN [*January* 1916 ?].

DEAR MR. DEBENHAM,—I was glad to hear that you got the Porphyry :[1] you do not say whether you liked it or not : I like it myself, tho' here and there it will be touched up.

I have had another bad relapse with a deadly pulse: for about a fortnight I was to be packed off coûte que coûte to Battle Creek, Michigan, to which all neurasthenic

[1] MacKenna's translation of Porphyry's *Life of Plotinus*, published along with the first *Ennead.*

Ireland goes, with Horace Plunkett at the head regularly —but they pushed the pulse up to something just tolerable, and so I am reprieved again. I do not feel ill, only languid and weak. I am however able to go on once more with my two hours or three every morning and so the work very slowly goes ahead, slowly but in my judgment very well—as I have said, to much better results I think than the " Beauty Xmas-card ".[1] I hoped to have been able to give up the first Ennead by this Xmas but have been disappointed : a good spell and I might finish the revision in a month : I hope for that anyhow.

As for the Lee-Warner question—I don't know at all : I couldn't possibly have more than one other Ennead, the second I suppose, ready within the year now beginning, for if I have health enough I really must get to work on something to bring me money down : we are making a great deal of sacrifice, even over this wretchedly long piece of work—I mean rather that my wife is—and that sort of thing can't go on ; it becomes unendurable, a shame and a torture to me, all the more since herself takes it gaily. I cannot myself imagine anything more deadly, or deadening, than the thought that one drags a bright wife down to a sordid sort of mutton-worry, watch-your-bus-fares existence. Of course we have a host of good friends here, many where-to-go's when I at least am well enough.

I hope you and yours are well and as happy as the dismal times allow : myself I sicken at all the blood, the mowing down of the youth of Europe, the stop, dead, of all we have thought of as civilisation, the multiform, wide as the world almost, agony and desolation. Plotinus mocks at all such emotions—if I weren't too lazy I'd transcribe a passage ad hoc, very fine as literature but dreadfully unreal to-day, at least to my lower sense—and this tho' Plotinus had been a soldier and seen, ce qu'on appelle vu, on no small scale too, the horrors which his

[1] His translation of Plotinus' *Treatise on Beauty* (*Ennead* I. vi.), published separately as a *ballon d'essai.*

" Sage "—really our " Saint " tho' one daren't use the word—declares a trivial ragged fringe on his beautiful inner peace. For my part I find this war, with all that it entails to the world and to my own poor little land, setting me blaspheming. I see men as trees walking—soulless motion merely, and no purpose over it all—perhaps beasts ravening would be better, nearer to my mind, and no thought ruling the rage even to some sound material end. I suppose in the light of history all this is absurd—and then Plotinus would be right—all comes out smiling at the end, and the fall of one civilisation is the beginning of another : if the Yellow Peril that once was a music-hall joke turned into a Yellow Actuality and all the world was yellow, there would be once more arts and religions and contempt for the ancient and passed thing with lyric celebration of the triumph of light at last. The world certainly renews itself, and always manages, with relatively brief periods of disaster and ugliness, to keep a sober average—but at the moments of ugliness, it is no pretty thing, no cheerful sight, and we get a sharp reminder (which our history is generally too dead in our minds to give us) that all our " truths " are merely dreams and that nothing is sure but birth and death, both sure but dark in their meaning. The God of the world is discovered to be an incalculable : we do not know what he is up to, or whether there is any care up there at all : *ὁ δ' οὐκ εὐσεβής*,[1] says Aeschylus of the man that thinks this, that Gods do not deign to care for the good and ill doings of men : I'm afraid I'm *οὐκ εὐσεβής*. Of course, by the way, so is Plotinus in this : his Supreme is too great and different to care : it is man that must care ; and on that Plotinus gets as stern a moral code as others get out of the God who is offended and appeased and always working at the wheel of the world. The Father's house has many mansions and still more approaches : all roads lead to its peace, and a good Plotinian would be

[1] " But he is impious " (*Agamemnon*, 372).

undistinguished in life and death from a good Xtian, except perhaps in being better. This is a long wildness I've indulged in—I don't know why.

All good wishes and many sincerest deepest thanks for your persistent interest in this odiously long-trailing affair.

STEPHEN MACKENNA.

Even yet I find I'm not done : I notice from a former letter of yours I just turned up that you are anxious about cadence. If it were not for two things, I could have printed a year ago : they are perfect clearness and expressive cadence : perfect clearness to those, bien entendu, who will take the trouble to understand the terms and what the whole is about ; cadence that shall help to clearness, and that shall further be a satisfaction in itself. I am labouring more for cadence than in the famous Christmas Card : the Card itself is rewritten mainly for cadence' sake. I think the new cadence far better than the old ; others may like it less ; on that point I can say nothing except that I will, permanently, continuously, disagree with them. I like pebbles in my brooks and little bends in my roads and raggedy edges to my clouds, and I don't like Noah's Ark trees or wooden legs and regular spots on my cows.

This my testament littéraire.

5

To EDMUND CURTIS

63, M[ERRION] S[QUARE],
Friday.

MY DEAR CURTIS,—I begin to fear you have Colahanised us—meaning that your excommunication is not valid, not accepted. My wife says I behaved very badly : she says if I don't apologise on the ground of nervous irritability I will break up an old and valuable and delightful friendship. She says also that if I do what I am going to do I will add insult to injury and throw the whole of Rockefeller UnLtd. on the slumbering flames.

Here's then—despite the wife—the whole truth : I was as she says nervously irritated : but for the reason that—

Enormously, incalculably admiring your gifts and honouring your conversation for its searching ideas and able and entertaining expression (so that I have frequently said that Boyd, Curtis and Séamuishín [1] were the three Giants of Dublin Talk), knowing and valuing the intimately for long years (my hair grown grey since that remote beginning),

Yet we had met at least four times within seven days, and I am constitutionally and for ever incapable of meeting anyone (except my wife alone in all the world of people that ever was or will be) of meeting anyone outside of business or quite exceptional other conditions, of meeting anyone (and especially of meeting anyone of set purpose towards long and intimate talk) more than once or twice in the longest week that ever existed. There's no one whose friendship I would more miss and lament than I will yours—but I'm afraid if a man has one leg and one eye and one wig and one hump and a large purple scab on one cheek and the hand of a long dead codfish, I fear that anyone who has him as a friend must accept these deficiencies and make the best of them. I'm also, plus these defects, constitutionally unable to hide them : my oneness of eye and leg and hump and my superfluities of facial colourishness hit anyone inevitably in the eye : I can't pretend to have two legs and no facial ulster as other men can, and so I can't possibly conceal my distaste for too much of the best heart and brain and charm in the world. Recognise yourself there and forgive me for being me,

S. M. K.

[1] James Stephens.

6

To AMY DRUCKER

63, MERRION SQUARE,
DUBLIN [? *Autumn* 1917].

DEAR MISS DRUCKER,—Delightful to hear from you : and the article very welcome though the poor man that did it exhibited himself as most of them do, no more capable of noticing a philosophical book than the soldier-monkey of an Italian organ grinder. I hope if you do me the honour of looking into my book you will not stick at the first tractate as most people do, sticking *in* it : Plotinus was no yellow-journalist ; he puts uppermost the dreariest and least tempting of his wares : believe me there are mighty fine and succulent things as you go on : I'd skip the first tract [and] read " Evil ", " Happiness ", and the " Preller-Ritter " Extracts which combine as I fondly imagine passages of great beauty and moving power—though these Preller-Ritter things have not received my dernière main. Your old lady at the library irritates me with her " best translation " she had read : there's no other : there's only the pretence of one other man, Taylor who " mar yeah " as we say (i.e. soi-disant) translated a good many treatises—not by any means all, but all vilely, neither English nor fidelity to the Greek nor understanding of the sequence of the thought. I will imitate the frankness of artists and say boldly " I am unique." There is one Plotinus and one MacKenna his fidus Achates and only nursing mother.

We hope you are not being pelted from the air in your centrality ? We gathered the last raid was a terror ? but at this distance we often gather London things that were never there. I'm in trouble : my radiant wife is losing her health : she is ill at present : and away from me : not in a hospital but being nursed, or rather gardenised into health, at my ancient Aunts' : the doctors do not take the thing alarmingly, but it's dreary to see her losing that splendid *go* of hers and that glorious flash of urgent intelligence and quick emotion in the shining face. I suspect war food as the cause of the primal internal trouble, and war-grief as nerve-wracking her so that she does not cure as naturally as—would seem natural. She really does grieve over the carnage, the hold-up of civilisation, the nasty silly passion of victory keeping the big men from lifting the finger that would save the world's young things from death and dismemberment. She's a public spirited old thing. Really a deep mind and a great heart.

This is all about ourselves—a " self and partner " scrawl. Disgraceful. But " such a man I am ". I have no ideas outside my own back-garden : some one counted (and printed the count) 97 I's in one speech of John Dillon's and argued that therefore he was not fit to lead a mighty people : I'm not fit, I see from this letter, to lead a puppy by a string. All good wishes and all thanks very much from my heart.

S. M. K.

7

TO E. R. DEBENHAM

[63, MERRION SQUARE,]
DUBLIN, 26 *January* 1918.

DEAR MR. DEBENHAM,—Yes, we " crossed " and all but crossed again. I was going to write when yours arrived —my purpose mainly to say that after three months or more of worklessness I am beginning again, and hope that the wretched health may still leave in my power the punctual keeping of my engagements.

Unfortunately the little work I can do is necessary : the times are very hard and threaten worse ; I am positively afraid. Had I good health I could do the two main things easily, but I will never have good health again.

I do not understand how I stand with the Medici people, whether I am to get something from the sales or not, but anyhow it would be mighty little or mighty slow : I was bitterly disappointed by the figures : I was not working (or planning the work) for money but for " Plotinianism "—those pitiful figures represent to me a tragic failure.

I never had any intention or thought of translating the Bouillet notes and illustrations : it would be a service to Plotinian studies I think—but not the best service for myself to set out upon.

The second Vol. should be very good : there's only one really dull or futile tract, and that very short : there are sublimities : but it is dismal to me to see that I am now handling, revising, work done in the rough, most of it, 10 or even 15 years ago—done in Dublin, Berlin, Moscow, Odessa, Paris. Had I been able to devote myself entirely to my only real interest (of the writing order), had I been able to live in Plotinus, Plotinus would have been done 10 years ago, and probably Proclus too by now.

Curious this having a passion for a fine thing and no way to live it out rightly !

My wife is convalescent but still weak and thin.

All good wishes,

STEPHEN MACKENNA.

8

TO E. R. DEBENHAM

63, MERRION SQUARE,
DUBLIN, *February* 1918.

DEAR MR. DEBENHAM,—* * * All was completed in the rough (and some several times revised) years ago. It is only now a question of intensity of the clarifying and " beautifying " power ; but unfortunately this is the uncontrollable thing ; it requires all my energy, a quickness of mind and feeling amounting to almost what we call inspiration in the poets. And I can't bear to think of putting any Plotinus forth that is not quite as noble, as lucid, as generally readable as the best mind in me can, under its best inspiration, produce.

But the weekly doses of electricity seem to give me a good deal of that energy, and if it were not for money worry and the hateful, crushing incubus of this War and world-wide horror, I feel that I could go ahead very well. It seems to me most disquieting that electricity should quicken the soul, and an outside horror deaden and blunt it—but so it is, alas ! I can't think why you Magnates do not end the appalling business : surely we owe as much to our own world (its arts and its lives) as to the world of our sons ? I have myself a brother [1] in this war—the only brother of 10 that I care a button about, but he is, I think, as dear to me as a son. (He is *much* younger than I.) He is the father of a young family in Australia—he will probably die in the " Great Onset "—for what ? He has written to me from the Front *asking me to tell him* why he left his profession, his wife, his intellectual and mystic life, his " kids ". The war magnetises the emotional, the best, but to their second and belated thought it does not justify itself.

I think all Europe ten years hence will be stupefied at its own folly of 1914-191— ?. I look upon it as a drunken fit : the most hateful thing to my mind in all the category of individual vices, and a thing utterly fatal when it is an entire world that has fallen into it. The widespread, daily growing and wider-spreading anarchy (first mental and then practical) of the times, this seems to me far more grave an evil, a war-induced evil, than any that the war is piously believed to be crushing out. Another year of it, and you will have such an upheaval as will appal history, and make the little differences between Hun and Hunter seem like the finger-to-the-nose of vulgar little boys.

I hope you and your clan and concerns prosper. My wife sends kindest regards.

S. MACKENNA.

[1] Octavian MacKenna.

9

63, MERRION SQUARE,
DUBLIN [*April* 1919].

MY DEAR MR. DEBENHAM,—Strange : when your envelope was given to me I had just flourished the signature to a letter to yourself, mostly twaddle about the state of the Universe, but telling you that Plots. is humming again, my wife (with whom Plots. never suspected his relationship) being at last on the sure path to recovery—I mean a good deal less ghost-like, though still very tottery and un-vital. All going well, I added, I would soon be able to have the 2nd and third Ens. type-copied, there to stand the last magic-working touches. Now :—Some months ago I got a most honouring letter from the Loeb people to much the effect of Dr. Page's letter to yourself. I wrote back truly : greatly flattered and the rest of it, but hadn't yet completed the work for you and could not, as yet, see my way to reform my ideas of translation ; was, however, willing to allow (subject to your permission) publication with any corrections they liked, *provided* they inserted very visibly an agreed formula stating that the original translator was not to be held responsible, to credit or discredit, for any phrases or interpretations differing from those of the Lee Warner edition. I got no reply to this. Probably it deserved none—I'm not grieving over that.

It is cordial to me—a tonic—that a man at once so distinguished and personally so charming as Dr. Page should speak so delightfully of my work—I must show his letter to my poor old ghost at Kingstown who will be cheered towards life by it, and I wish I had the energy or perhaps the idleness to copy it as a sort of pedigree for my posterity (collateral). But his conception of translation is poles apart from mine : what he calls artistry etc., I call simple veracity—that is, on the assumption that veracity does not mean a kind of transliteration but means conveying the full of the author's meaning, emphasis, mood, Stimmung, etc. Of course I know that some translators working on some books—Mackail's Specimens from the Anthology is an almost perfect example—can produce at once truth to the spirit (with beauty) and nearly verbal exactitude ; but this is quite beyond my art. I still itch to rebuild my first volume ; but precisely in the contrary sense to Dr. Page's. After all, I have had for years all but the whole thing literally translated and wanting only a few touches to make it publishable by that ideal. But my labour, my agony, is precisely the contrary—to " deliteralise "—in the interests of the higher veracity, as I judge.

I take it that once a student has gripped Plots. as a whole, the system, and become habituated to Plots.' queer uses of words and of sentence structure and paragraph structure, few authors are more easy to translate in that fashion called literal ; but I think no author that I have ever touched is one-eighth so difficult to carry over into another language. All existing translations or fragments in translation seem to me pitifully unjust, except for Dr. Caird's occasional extracts ; I don't think even the meaning is at any point conveyed (except to those that know the Greek) in any translation but Caird's and my own. (Mueller and Kiefer seem to me deficient as Bouillet, tho' in other ways. Yet they set out to be " literal ", and in the common acceptation are so).

I so utterly differ (believe me, with very great diffidence and the greatest respect) from Dr. Page that even on a secondary point—peculiarly however in his province—I differ toto coelo. As thus :—If I personally read Greek translation I'm always uneasy lest I'm reading the translator's ideas, not his author's, getting the translator's palette effects, not those of the original : if I have the Greek text en vis à vis I am at ease ; I can colour up or down as the Greek indicates to my temperament that the translator has over- or under-coloured, raised or lowered the tone. I think the Loeb people could give their translators a far wilder liberty than Mr. Debenham ought to be allowed to allow me.

I read a good deal of Greek in Latin-Greek, French-Greek, German-Greek and English-Greek texts as a constant suggestion of tricks of the translation-craft, so I consider myself quite an authority on this point : my total testimony would be that nothing could serve the classics more than superbly free translations—backed of course by the thoroughest knowledge—accompanied by the strict text. The original supplies the corrective or the guarantee ; the reader, *I* find, understands the depths of his Greek or Latin much better for the free rendering—again, I think of a chaste freedom, a freedom based rigidly on a pre-servitude.

I constantly find myself unable to read, unable to understand, translations which would appear to satisfy the accepted ideas of " literalness " : give me a free translation by a man of first-rate knowledge, and I'm quite often amused to find that out of the freedom I can reconstruct the Greek original almost verbatim. In other words, a good free translation can I think be proven to be much nearer to the original than most literal translations: it is paradoxical, yet it is truer than people would think who have not tried it. I would add—all this is from a long meditated and never written essay on translations from Greek—that I think it can be shown that the literal school

(1) necessarily by their principle exclude from the translator's use vast and important or even essential territories of the English language, idioms and words alike, and

(2) include hosts of words, idioms, and " attack " generally, which are no longer English.

So that " literal " English turns out to be (1) Liddell & Scott English or (2) a bastard English, a horrible mixture of Elizabethan, Jacobean, fairytale-ese, Biblicism and modern slang (not slang of word but, what is worse, of phrase or construction).

Totally then : (1) I cannot myself re-write my translation in the Loeb sense. (2) I am quite willing (and greatly honoured) that they use it, suiting it to their ideas ; but distinctly not as mine, but as their own modification or correction of mine (I have no vanity whatever on this point and don't in the least mind being "corrected" publicly : indeed I'm astonished and rather scandalised that I have not been so handled). (3) I can't see that the question rises unless they can wait another year or so until we are ready with the whole thing.

I hope I have not been too long—read me in chunks ; a sort of pill after each meal till all is in.

Have you read Wells' God the Invisible King ? I believe Wells hates Plots. (by name at least) but he's not far from him all the same. I found the book suggestive and in places up-building, "edifying."

Cordial good wishes.

S. M. K.

P.S. I will without fail return the letters to-morrow or next day after revivifying my ghost with them.

10

To E. R. DEBENHAM

63, MERRION SQUARE,
DUBLIN [? *Autumn*, 1919].

DEAR MR. DEBENHAM,—I cannot possibly accept this cheque—I have not been able to work. My wife got apparently all but well some 3 months after her operation —a month ago even so nearly well that she began to "type" my MSS.—suddenly got ill again, and is at present so ill that this very afternoon I thought she was dying in my arms. It will be a miracle if she lives thro' the winter. I can't work. If she dies I will shut myself up and finish my three volumes, wherever I can find a quiet nook—England or Ireland, where I need see no one and can hear some music.—You see what a state I'm in, rambling on like the village idiot.

Many thanks,

S. M. K.

II

To E. R. DEBENHAM

63, MERRION SQUARE,
DUBLIN [? *Winter*, 1919-20].

MY DEAR MR. DEBENHAM,—I had hoped by Christmas to send in the MS. for the second volume. I have it type-written complete—but not ready : I could not publish it in its present state : it is still rough : I can't get it smooth. * * * *

The strain of the last two years has been terrific : we have had seven of the first doctors in Dublin to examine and some three to treat my wife, and they combined and singly can neither say what's the disease nor do more than temporarily relieve the symptoms : it was given out by three doctors to all Dublin that she couldn't possibly live through October : she is still alive, and a week ago was even " walking "—really stumbling with a stick—about her room : two days ago we had a return of the mysterious swellings which in September ripened into horrible ulcers ; she is flat again, and I am again cold with anxiety. I know, or hear, that there are heroic men who settle hoti's business with their own or other people's lives in jeopardy, dead from the waist down, but hoti leaves me cold at these times—or, to be more accurate, simply tortures me, shames me, fills me with self-disgust.

I want to say also roughly (since I can't find the smooth for it) that you *absolutely must immediately* instruct your qui de droit that all monies to me are to be stopped : somewhere towards May a cheque would roll in else, and it *musn't*—I must know *now* that it won't : it is dangerous : I am too poor and too slovenly to be able to stand that sort of thing : I find—and do not find it essentially dishonourable, simply an ugly fact of nature or grey nature —that if a man gave me £1,000,000,000 on condition that I would twiddle my little finger three times a day for a week, I'd take the money and honestly forget to twiddle the finger.

Had the calamities not fallen on us I would, as far as I know, have finished the work—but the calamities have undoubtedly deadened my sense of responsibility, or rather my power of acting out my constantly present and even urgent sense of responsibility. (Even now I cannot make my meaning clear, so as to clear myself as I see myself fundamentally clear).

Anyhow I must have it quite firmly fixed as a fact in my mind that there is no more money for Plotinus, and that immediately. At every possible moment I tinker with the typescript, and find it slowly getting better—a second typing (to embody the improvements) ought to see things right before too long. If my wife dies I will bury myself in the work, the second volume and the third, which third ought (by the accident of its matter and the stage my MS. stands at) to be easier than the dry second.

Cordial good wishes,

S. M. K.

12

To THOMAS BODKIN

63, MERRION SQUARE,
Wednesday.

MY DEAR TOM,—You'll think me strange : what harm if I am or you do ? I want you to do if possible a thing for me, and if not, then for ever hold your peace.

In this time of trial I can't settle my mind on things of

the intellect : I must settle it or I'll unsettle it. I pine for music. I have a place wherein to make it, or its base imitation, and no one a whist the wiser.

But I've lent my concertina away where, and under conditions whereby, I can't immediately or for a month resume it. I have heard that your sister Norah has been at times possessed of a concertina, one of a most silvery sweet song. Could you discreetly discover (1) whether she still has it and (2) whether having it she would unhave it for a spell : i.e., not to hide my mind, whether she would lend it to me. I heard, it is true, that she had thoughts of selling it, not for her personal gain but for the Sinn Fein funds or the WAACKS or some such worthy purpose. If this is so, I implore you to breathe no word of my ghastly secret, this ill desire : if it isn't so, you will break the news gently to her, as gently as you'd break a suspected egg, and see which way the wind blows, and if ill then nip it at the thin edge of the wedge instanter.

Above all you're not to laugh at me—though I *am* laughable—for in truth I'm also very wretched : the news here is neither good nor bad, but the suspense is awful : I'm amazed myself that I can think of concertinas ; the mischief is I can think of nothing else, apply to nothing but tune.

Kindest regards,

S. MACKENNA.

13

To E. R. DEBENHAM

63, MERRION SQUARE,
DUBLIN, *March* 1921.

MY DEAR MR. DEBENHAM,—* * * * To-day is a bad day : 6 boys hanged : the great, strict, un-rebelly judicial lights all say, I'm told, in their privacy that only one of those could conceivably have been death-sentenced or at all sentenced by the ordinary Civil Courts ; and that in the case of the one, civil judges would recommend reprieve since the evidence admitted doubt. I imagine no one in all England, not even the extremest of the little pro-Irish party, can understand with what a personal touch these things come to us : this morning my wife and a servant and a charwoman are all in tears—and I sit shivering by the fire, scrawling this farrago but thinking deep down all the time of the tragedy of Ireland, mourning for the young lads. I suppose this is funny or horrible, immoral, to the outsider : " murderers " settles it : we know that in their hearts (assuming the very doubtful assertion that they were in that particular ambush and ignoring the undisputed fact that there were no casualties whatever there), we know that even if they did kill, there was no murder in their hearts, that, rightly or wrongly, they, all such men, think themselves soldiers, killing as a Belgian might kill a German, killing in a war of liberation.

We know that all such think so, and thinking so are good men sacrificing themselves, answering a call of the spirit, of a possibly misguided spirit, " bamboozled by the Divine in them " as a man said to me in humorous allusion to my Plotinianism.

Until the English understand this basic fact of the Irish psychology, they will understand less of Ireland than of India or China, and, however they may finally crush us down in slime and blood, they will never hold us down : I am grey and sad waiting for the freedom of Ireland, but the little boys and girls in the street are flaming with the same old spirit—their very play tells it—and generation after generation will rise as generation after generation has risen, striving for the same thing.

Very cordially,

S. M. K.

14

To E. R. DEBENHAM

63, MERRION SQUARE,
DUBLIN [1921].

MY DEAR MR. DEBENHAM,—* * * * The fact of the matter is (as I meant to explain and I thought I did explain) that I had allowed myself to use you as a safe-deposit. Raids by night and day are the order of the night and day : the most incredible people are raided—high Government Officials, quiet Unionist old ladies : it is often a matter of the most irresponsible or purely malicious denunciation, as in the case of the Master of the Rolls the other night. The forces of the Crown are sometimes highly polished gentlemen and sometimes the savagest kind of uncontrolled brutes : they tear up Irish everywhere, and I am full of Irish books and MSS. If I were denounced or suspected there would be little left of my papers. I fear for Plotinus, who would probably pass to their eyes as a low Gael plotting crime in a fantastic alphabet.

I am surprised and rather humiliated at not having yet been raided and sacked. I have never concealed my mania for either the Irish language or Irish freedom ; the fact that I'm entirely out of all touch with active politics would not enter into the matter : I'd have to prove that, afterwards. And by the way, tho' it is as true as any truth and all truth, I'd have difficulty, I couldn't prove it. I couldn't cite men who are inside to give me a testimonial of outsideness, incidentally incriminating themselves : all that could happen would be that of course the authorities couldn't prove the contrary. But the ruin would have been wrought.

It maddens me to think that all this horror could have been averted by un bon mouvement at the middle of the war or on the Armistice or even much later, on the Sinn Fein election victory—the touch of justice, or simple recognition of fact, giving a thoroughly good measure of self-government.

I am ashamed of expressing shame for my delays : I can only hope that domestic and national matters will leave me peace enough for reasonably consecutive and speedy efficiency.

My wife slowly gets strength—no sign whatever of relapse ; if she goes on as well till the turn of the year, we will cease to worry.

Kindest regards and all good wishes chez vous,

S. M. K.

15A

From "A. E."

84, MERRION SQUARE,
DUBLIN, [*Monday* 1921 *or* 1922].

MY DEAR STEPHEN MACKENNA,—I make haste to acknowledge the gift of the second volume of your translation of Plotinus which came this morning. I have not yet done more than steal the time from my writing of *Homestead* leaders to read a few pages ; and I find there the same pure and cold intellectual distinction as I knew in the first volume. You are one of the few people who can write with an austere dignity appropriate to the subject, and I read it with the refreshment of one who drinks cold water after being poisoned with rich and corrupting liquors. It is a pleasant thing to think of, that an Irishman in the midst of all the turmoil which distracts our country has the spiritual energy to persist at such an intellectual labour. I have not half your power of concentration, and a book I began two years ago is not half completed because I allowed myself to get involved in matters which in the heart of me I feel were not proper for me to deal with. But this dereliction of my own duty, this wandering of mine from the guidance of my own star, makes me respect you, who have persisted in your proper work, still more. I say to myself " It was done for the beloved Motherland, this errantry of mine," but I know in my heart that the service I gave was an easier and lower service than doing the best and highest it was in me to do. The translation of a thinker like Plotinus may not make one's name be shouted in the streets ; but your work may make some who read it of nobler mind and utterance, and they may bring a reflected light of your work to others who perhaps could not benefit by a direct study and whose ideas must be diluted if they are to digest them. I owe whatever dignity of mind I possess to a study of Plato and the sacred books of the world, and I feel your translation may kindle others as I was kindled when a boy coming on the *Banquet* and other dialogues. I will read it closely, this translation, as it must be read, and I thank you for your kind remembrance of the poet who strayed into politics.

Yours sincerely,
A. E.

15

To " A. E."

COLLINS' HOTEL,
ENNISKERRY,
CO. WICKLOW,
[1921 *or* 1922].

MY DEAR RUSSELL,—Your generous letter of to-day touches me deeply—believe me or not, all but to tears ; actually to emotional chills down the spine and the tingling of my top-knot. I take it as a passport into high places : God knows I never had, never understood how anyone could have, any desire for reputation, I mean in the sense of fame : but I have wanted to do my hackwork with just " dignity," " austerity," a certain degree of nobility : and these are the things you find : a great joy to me. Of course—I don't know whether I said it to you—that second vol. is (relatively, and for the greatest but not only part) poor stuff: the first, third, and fourth are the finest Plotinus, than whom there is little finer in the world. As I grind at the revision of the third I tremble sometimes, often; grandeurs; lovelinesses; humanities; raptures; great doors flung open suddenly—but we are hurried by with scarcely time to look; that is always to me the test of a spiritual value, that we scarcely dare to look at the thing, down the vistas, into the Infinities. . . .

But this is not what I meant to write about at all: I set out to say only that I'm very sorry you don't appear to understand the greatness of your own life and the profound and future-looking value of your own service. I have quarrel enough with you; all the Papist Celt in me shudders at your failure (as I see things) to grasp the spiritual splendours and values of our befogged old Catholic Church—the artist in me, too, the historian, several other people and potencies in me are shocked and chilled. I look upon all that as a most deplorable and inexplicable failure—this I say for honesty's sake which is a jewel; for conscience' sake:

but: as a preface to the future truth that I have always thought of you, always in all these long years, as one of the noble expressions of the divine mind (the Supreme Intelligence of Plotinus and of course of all the metaphysically informed mystics); and further that to me it seems, has always but especially of late seemed, that no little part of that greatness is precisely in your devoted and inspiring service in what foolish separatists call the petty side of things. I remember once reading a parody of Ruskin in which he was made to say, "But a sewer is an entirely holy thing." I always thought parody, there, had spoken wisdom: without any practical taste or skill myself, I always look with admiration, almost reverence, on the man that has it and uses it even for his own sake—the big business man, even the despised shopkeeper, the middle-man (though of course I don't think that *he* is eternal: only that in the present state of things even the middleman who keeps things humming seems to be respectable, valuable, a worker, a server) :

but when all this practical power is consecrated, then my reverence is unbounded. Yours has always been so, and if there were only the dairies and the unfailing brave word for this little people of ours, why I'd humble myself to grovelling. But, again, when all is conveyed in the noble terms of a spiritual passion (to say nothing of purely technical or artistic power), when we are taught to make butter and to defend our national soul and potentiality in the name of the Soul and the powers behind it—towards the working out of a sublime will behind all the shows—why, my dear man, I can only think—again in terms of Plotinus—of men that are " not merely without fault but are Gods." I don't quite deify you yet, you know : I think you have a spot or so : but a few millions of aeons in a good hot Babylonian hell will burn those out, and then—ah, then . . . ! I cannot think with you that your work has been of the easier order, unless in the sense that the noble way is easiest to the noble : I am certain that in your books, in your articles, in your organising and regulating and correcting, there has been the highest spiritual value ; and that Ireland, if there be such a thing, will rise up on the Last Day, if such a thing there be, to call you blessed. * * * *

No need to write : this is my homage : it never occurred to me that you could think little of your service.

Sincerely,
S. M. K.

16

TO E. R. DEBENHAM

COLLINS' HOTEL,
ENNISKERRY, CO. WICKLOW,
Christmas Eve [1921].

DEAR MR. DEBENHAM,—It is a matter of simple honour to tell you what may not to you seem honourable, that for the past week and for the immediate future Plotinus is suspended : that would not matter, " a Christmas holiday," but that unfortunately there are signs that I may not be able to resume the work for some little time and possibly may not at all. I told you I was not in the remotest degree in touch with national work : I have to be, from the moment of the signing of the London proposals. It is to me like the call to the English to break off their work and their loves and all their life to fight in France. To explain adequately would be long and useless. In a word, I never concealed from living soul my intense desire of the utter freedom of Ireland—I felt like a Pole to Russia, etc.—and I encouraged cordially every form of effort towards it ; this solely, for the past ten years, in speaking and in an occasional article—and for the past hot time not even that, since my wife was dying and I ill. At the same time I never concealed from the extreme party of my choice (tho' sometimes from the moderates) that I would be for accepting some adequate form of self-government that I then thought might be known as Dominion Home Rule. Now that they bring us home Dominion Home Rule, I could no more be a party, I find, to accepting it than you could to accepting internal self-government, the fullest, within and under the name of the German Empire. " Adherence to and membership of . . .", allegiance to K. George *and his heirs*—all that is merging *us* by *our* consent for ever. I, no politician, did not understand that D. H. R. meant anything so funereally final as that. It was a grave error, a most blameable ignorance. Most of the men and women of the Dáil who are accepting the Proposals are saying that they are not morally bound by them and are intending only to use them : I and a great many others, thank God, cannot descend to that. I have been invited to co-operate with the honest Repudiation Party ; I cannot refuse the call—cannot in conscience. If we secure Repudiation, we will all have marked ourselves for the most drastic treatment by the English Govt. or army here : if we fail, we will have to carry on the struggle to upset a British Dáil—by what means I do not know. But even if by means which do not cause our arrest by the Dáil, yet the work will be severe. Plotinus will be interrupted. I will write later when I see the future more clearly : for the moment I merely expose, as in honour bound, the situation which obliges me to break our contract, the one-sided contract in which you have had all the loss and I all the gain. Should I be long out of the Plotinus field I will be able to make arrangements to repay that last most unhappy advance ; this certainly ; my wife, in whose interest mainly I took it, will be able to do that : for what preceded it, I can only hope that slowly the returns of the 2 vols. will leave you finally not at any great loss.

Disaster has weighed heavy over this whole thing, this Plotinus business—but I could not know when I agreed with you that to an increasingly scrupulous literary sense, and desire of the finest scholarly accuracy within my extremest power, revision would really mean triple and quadruple re-writing and often more even than that. Nor could I predict my own nerve-failure, the post-operation neurasthenia rooted in the constitution, and the terrible years of my wife's lingering malady—now all past in her case. If you can understand the call of my conscience in such a matter I am intensely relieved : I remember writing to you that I could never take an oath of allegiance—much less can I side with my country's doing so. If you can't get into our skulls to see, why all I can do is to say from the depths of my heart that the princeliest soul I ever knew, one of the very noblest characters I could imagine, was known as an Englishman E. R. D.

My kindest regards and warmest thanks,

S. M. K.

I know Mrs. Debenham in all her manifest kindliness could not endure me : you must tell her, if you speak of the matter to her, that if I was jauntily and cockily Irish

—as I knew I was—the excuse is simple boorishness inborn in me—'tis a valid excuse really, tho' it doesn't look so—plus a heart perpetually sick over the failure and degradation of my country which I have loved as a religion.

I would like to add that the substance of this was written when (a fortnight before the event) I learned privately that the delegates to London had arranged a plot to rush the Dáil Cabinet into the allegiance position—what I then wrote to you I destroyed on reflecting that I could not be sure that they would actually carry out what I knew they had planned, and that I'd appear to be wasting your attention on futile heroics if they repented or found the English Cabinet too dour for even their own new tastes. (It is not, by the way, suggested that they acted from base motives, tho' their means certainly were base—trickery, deceit, machinerigging, a score of such arts. It is entirely believed that the motives were good—Collins war-weary and weary of bloodshed on one side and the other, and Griffith longing to see Ireland applying to her good the manifold schemes his admirable brain has been for 10 or 15 years inventing and preaching in his various weeklies.)

17

To E. R. DEBENHAM

COLLINS' HOTEL,
ENNISKERRY,
CO. WICKLOW,
[*beginning of January*, 1922].

DEAR MR. DEBENHAM,—Forgive me beginning with the abstract side of things :—*Firstly*, that letter [1]—whose applicability to the present situation astonishes me—was written a year and a quarter ago : things done and suffered during the year and more between its writing and the Truce did not create in this country any love for

[1] An earlier letter from MacKenna to Debenham.

England. No Englishman will ever understand how that year and more intensified hate—or made hate of what was mainly little more than a national sense of difference. A settlement very possible a year and a quarter ago has to my mind become quite impossible now.

But *secondly* :—Despite an occasional phrase (not misleading in the context, I think) it is made perfectly clear that the entire stress in my mind was on the calming and healing power of a measure *forced upon us :* I have underlined in the copy of my letter two or three passages which show clearly that this was in my mind and this only : " Sinn Fein, even moderate S. F., will never negotiate " (p. 1) ; " The day S. F. begins to negotiate it crumbles at once ; it loses the confidence of its own etc." (p. 3.)

S. F. did begin, after a year and more, to negotiate, and we have the " crumble." (I think it probable that the Dáil will ratify the treaty—but dishonestly ; there is scarcely one member of the ratifying party that dares to say he ratifies in the intent of abiding by it : even Wm. O'Brien, the ex-Redmondite M.P., urging ratification urges it as a weapon, as a half-way house, a means by which we become strong to cast [ourselves] out entirely from the British Empire.)

We have the crumble : I, for example, " crumble away " ; why ? because Sinn Fein has not merely accepted Dominion Home Rule as a thing forced upon it which it is not able to resist—in which I would agree with it—but has (as far as proposals and signatures of delegates go) declared Ireland to hold " status within the British Empire," " adherence to and membership of the British Empire." Immediately on reading the Griffith-Lloyd George proposals I wrote to the two National papers of Dublin a letter which both suppressed, saying that if this were forced upon us by English might, as Black and Tans, martial law etc. were, we might tacitly use it ; but that its acceptance in the name of Sinn Fein (which is in the name of Ireland) was a national abdication " unthinkable " to those who still cared for the freedom of Ireland. Of course I have been told that this is quibbling, hair-splitting etc. I'm utterly unable to see that : to me it is as vital as it is simple and self-evident. It is all the difference between accepting a personal wrong which one can't redress and approving, identifying oneself with, a wrong spreading widely—in this case affecting a whole possible nation. Under a forced scheme we would still be morally free : consenting to the scheme, merging ourselves (by the approved oath of members of the new parliament) into the British Empire, we have abdicated all right to future action, to private hope of a future nationhood. " Any form of constitution or formula of oath which left us without that stain might be accepted on its merits, this never " (the quotation is from a later letter of mine which both the National papers published on St. Stephen's Day, when they saw that there was at the very least a large minority not willing either honestly to sign away Ireland's right or to perjure themselves and their nation for the sake of more surely breaking away in the near future).

There is just one point, in my doctrine, in which I myself see myself open to the charge of " hairsplitting &c."—tho' of course something in my mind, something not definitely formulated, obliges me still to hold it : it is this :—I think that in practice if a scheme of Dominion Home Rule had been forced upon us (from above, regardless of our formal consent, as a purely English measure for the Government of Ireland), I think that in practice all would have worked out to long-lasting peace and, in a limited sense, amity. To my mind a terrible mistake has been made on both sides : our men should never have signed consentment to " adherence to and membership of . . ." and the like ; and yours should never have insisted upon it. It has been publicly said that Ll. George threatened " immediate and terrible war " upon Ireland if we didn't accept this : in that threat, and in the value set by the English negotiators upon the words, there appears at once the fact that the mere form is of vast significance : the English insist on our crawling into (or declaring our native membership of) the British Empire : they insist on our abdication of our hereditary affirmation of non-membership. We therefore must resist : but why need they have insisted ? It did not pass the wit of man to devise a formula of constitution which would leave the whole bitter question in abeyance. No one, or few, very few, expected the English to announce withdrawal of all claim over us ; but as few believed when the negotiations began that the English would insist on our formal pledged and perpetual adherence to and membership of. Anyone that knows the depth of Irish feeling knows that no permanent (or even any more than momentary) pacification is possible on such terms : a quarrel is best made up by simply ignoring the detail, even the principle, of the first dispute : it is not made up by John saying to Mark, " I forgive you and grant you these and those boons on your admitting my superiority," or even by Mark saying to John, " I recognise your superiority for the sake of the boons you offer—and (sotto voce) those boons will strengthen me for the day when I can show you what I really think of you."

Once more—the dominant point—those who are for ratifying are (a) those who never wanted the freedom of Ireland or were opposed to it (Indifferents, Unionists &c.), (b) those who ratify, immorally, as an anti-English and anti-British " step forward." There is no (c)—absolutely no signs yet of a party that did want the freedom of Ireland and that accepts this treaty as giving it. One of the Bishops did show a " c " tendency in one pronouncement, and followed it immediately (in a day or two) with second thoughts that put him slightly disguised among the " b's " : " the best we can hope for—strengthen the national resources—expanding freedom &c. &c." Of course there may be, must be, some true " c's "—people converted to Britonism by the Free State proposals—but they have not yet emerged ; they are not met, or read ; not at all.

Now can anyone think this is reconciliation ? Is it not honorable to protest ? Is it not absolutely compulsory on the conscience of anyone who, for a life-time, has held the theory I have held openly ? It happens that there is need, for the present at least, of all who can serve in any way to enforce the expression of honesty and nationality : the issue we can only leave to fate, but we must do the work and take the risk.

I do not see the hopelessness of the agitation : anyone, I myself, would have pronounced Sinn Fein a hopeless agitation ten years ago or less : I have learned that nothing that has an honest basis is hopeless : it wanted a very little difference in the position of the country, or in the personality of our Irish negotiators, to secure us peace without that unnecessary trailing of the coat in the clauses declaring the status of Canada and adherence to &c. Some of the most authoritative organs of the English press were already preaching abandonment of Ireland as an insoluble problem—Garvin was strong on leaving Ireland (extra-Ulster Ireland) " to stew in its own juice." It is not hopeless, though certainly difficult now, to create a situation in which we negotiate for peace and friendship (or at least friendly relations) on the distinct understanding that we be neither anti-British nor actually confessedly British. Probably if Lord Morley, younger, had been of the negotiators, Garvin, one or two others we could think of, had happened to be Cabinet Ministers, some such abeyance on the English side with tacit acceptance on the Irish side would have been to-day's fact. That or a similar situation may be yet produced.

Now I come to the purely personal side. Had I died, of illness, as I nearly did, after the publication of the first vol., had I been killed by stray bullets in Easter week or, like many, by irresponsible shooting on either side during the months of the Black and Tan régime—we'd have to bow to fate. If I feel now, as I do, that I'm morally obliged to serve in this cause, I'm simply in the position of nearly all the men of Europe called by their country's need in the long war to suspend all their other obligations —they by force majeure no doubt, but a force majeure whose sanction was in their sense of duty to their country. It is true of course that (for the present at least) there is no force majeure over me in this matter : but, once convinced in conscience of a duty, is it according to conscience to wait for that force m. ? (I do not see for a moment that my work on Plotinus is any service to Ireland, any at all.)

There remains the financial side. Here I feel horribly ashamed and was for a while horribly in doubt—I mean I suffered pain of doubt, very acute. Now I still feel the pain, but the doubt only intermittently. Without knowing the exact figures I took counsel on the principle involved. The advice I received coincided with my own feeling, that the situation was very awkward but that, admitting the country's need and call, the country's need and call was the dominant.

I will take further counsel : I'm not so committed that I could not (in view of my age and health and practical impotency if things get really hot), not so committed that I could not withdraw—though on the other hand if the Treaty Proposals are repudiated I may be already marked for jail or for other punishment. If the Treaty is ratified, the agitation will be literary and oratorical, and I need only take a limited part in it—something I must do even then, but of course it is at the start only that any one man would be very important—unless (which God forbid) it becomes a real civil war—I couldn't and wouldn't fight in such a horror (could not *fight* for any cause), but I'd again be marked more or less, and only chance would decide what I'd suffer. Assuming that " limited part," I'd still go on with Plotinus—I was working at it yesterday —only there'd be more delay than I like or had anticipated. Supposing the worst happened and the work was not pursued—I would owe you £900 plus its interest over the time, or, assuming some further sales, £900. It is a big sum, but my wife would certainly charge herself with it and if she lives long enough would pay it all off in time —would certainly pay annual instalments reducing it. She would do this for my honour's sake and because the greater part of what I received was taken solely for her sake and need, in her sickness. I am heir to a small property which would enable me if I lived (but could not for any reason finish the work) to pay all off in three or four years from the year of receiving the property. Here I feel that I am " bald and unsympathetic "—I found nothing such in the business part of your letter : how could I ?—it is certain that I ought never to have entered into any such place of tightness ; but, as I have said, when I began on the mischievous course I counted on fairly efficient physical conditions and had no doubt whatever that four volumes could appear in four years : I foresaw neither serious illness nor the nervous literary scruple amounting to inhibition.

I will reconsider this whole financial side—as well as the exact limit of my necessary participation in the practical work of the new Irish problem—and will write again ad hoc. I do not even re-read what I have written : I'm tired out by it : I leave it in the hope that whatever misleading flow of phrasing there be in it you will see the general point of view and, though not able to share that point of view, at least be able to recognise that I act on a personal compulsion from within.

All good wishes and lifelong thanks,

S. M. K.

I don't recall whether I made quite clear that, while I give full service for the urgent moment, I have no ambition or power of being a leader, but on the contrary—*taking full risks* at the necessary times—merely fill a gap, glad to retire, if may be, into utter silence, complete political inactivity, and Plotinus, as more competent workers come forward. If I see that the country is determined to Britonise, I'll probably go for good and all to the South of France and never see England or Ireland again : politically I feel " broken-hearted "—in the exaggerated phrase nearest to the truth—that the country should even dally with voluntary, declared, abdication of its ancient claim. Again, as a Pole to Russia—possibly associating with Russia, accepting or bowing to Russian rule, but utterly unable to merge.

18

TO E. R. DEBENHAM

COLLINS' HOTEL,
ENNISKERRY,
CO. WICKLOW,
[*beginning of January* 1922].

DEAR MR. DEBENHAM,—I'm wondering whether my huge letter of this morning made clear one all important matter :—that *I'm not hankering after any but the studious life, the Plotinus work.* I felt in honour bound to tell you that I felt in conscience bound to answer the immediate call for service, and therefore run a risk and am occupied as otherwise I should not be. If the country accepts the Proposals I shall probably leave it for ever—and Plotinize. If it repudiates, my present action will have been merely a slight addition to my bad name when in one way or another the troubles break out again : only a *slight* addition, because we shall all be passed through the sieve, and as I have always indicated I could under no circumstances take an oath of allegiance to England : I would be caught automatically by that.

The whole thing then is that I'm unable in conscience to refrain for the immediate present : the rest lies with the fates, with whatever God guides such things : my will towards Plotinus is as it ever was ; only, this temporary call is for the moment paramount, like a fit of illness. My service is purely literary—but there are times when the pen attracts the sword or invites the bullet in the barrack yard—it may very well prove, and very soon, that (Repudiation or Ratification) I have, in the first shock of the crisis, exaggerated the reaction of the crisis upon my own life and work. I was bound to tell you of my at least temporary emergence from the study.

Again all good wishes
S. M. K.

19

To E. R. DEBENHAM

COLLINS' HOTEL,
ENNISKERRY,
CO. WICKLOW,
[*January* 9*th*, 1922].

DEAR MR. DEBENHAM,—Just a word to say that the Dáil vote releases me from what I felt a most imperative call. I will not take part in anything that approaches to " civil war "—I bow, with shame and grief, to the country's decision. Of course this decision may yet be altered by a general election—but the fighting of that will be for politicians, not for antiquated Grecians. My call was for a moment when every little power might count most vitally : there will be no such urgency, such need of immediate full-strength action, as in the case of the Dáil decision.

I would have been happier—as things have turned out —had I simply taken my necessary action and said nothing to you : you would, as things have developed, never have known of my two or three weeks' truancy and risk. But I could not leave you in such ignorance, since you had always my assurance that I was not in what is called " politics "—to me not " politics " but something far higher—and since, in the event of repudiation, I would be in increased danger.

I have not yet decided whether I shall leave the dishonoured country—but leaving or staying, Plotinus resumes himself to the full of my available energy.

All my most cordial good wishes,

S. M. K.

20

To E. R. DEBENHAM

24, CHARLEVILLE ROAD,
RATHMINES,
DUBLIN [*September* 1922].

MY DEAR MR. DEBENHAM,—Your very deeply appreciated letter of kind enquiry reached me in the midst of alarms and perturbations. My wife ill again for the past two months : a consultation this week pronounces it a relapse into the old disorder : future not to be predicted, disease too obscure. A dreary prospect for the poor old lady, who thought till last May that she was completely cured.

Just before she began to fall ill again I was going to write to you on Plotinus : she dissuaded me (of course honestly in intention) but whether actually honestly I doubt now. I had reached a stage at which I simply could do no more. I wanted to go over and see you and try to show you that I ought to give it up, and to plan with you how we might arrange for the rest to be done (with all the help I could give) by someone else, preferably Eric Dodds. She persuaded me to take a long rest, try again after that, and then, if I found I could not go ahead, then only to broach the matter with you. Only for the fact that I am financially bound I would take this release : the obligation to the Plotinus public is to give them the good stuff, the echt, and if I couldn't do that, to arrange for someone able to do it ; as things are, i.e., in view of the financial obligation, I'm for the present unable to judge what is right. I may get again such a period as I had had fairly recently, all going very fairly well if slowly :

on the other hand the period of incapacity may go on : I have not dared to try yet—lest I should fall into the agonised despair which itself keeps me back for longer than if I took a long rest. There are weeks during which I can't hold the thread of an argument in my head at all. For the moment I ask only a suspension ; if my wife's illness doesn't reach the danger point again, I will try again in a little while.

I'm heartbroken over the country. I could never accept the Free State ; but I'm utterly unable to approve (on the point of expediency : I don't at all mean morally) the method of opposition adopted. The only expedient way is constitutional work for freedom, either by advocacy only or by " passive resistance " or some such devices : but there is no sign that such a thing may be. Poor Art O'Griovha,[1] a lifelong friend, had to my mind made such a chaos of Ireland as must cloud his eternity. The Republicans, my party, seem to have nothing but hopeless destruction, spreading frightful demoralisation, with which to meet that first disaster, the signing.

I'm ashamed before you over this ill-starred work, your work.

S. M. K.

21

TO E. R. DEBENHAM

SWEET MOUNT HOUSE,
DUNDRUM,
DUBLIN [*October* 30*th*, 1922].

DEAR MR. DEBENHAM,—Very good of you to write : my wife's address 3, Spencer Road, East Cliff, Bournemouth, and very East Cliffy she seems to find it, but then I believe 'tis bitter everywhere. I keep urging her to go to the S. France (tho' I also keep hoping she won't) : the puzzle is that if she fell as seriously ill in those remote parts as she did here she'd be in a sad plight and a distant place ;

[1] Arthur Griffith.

on tother hand the very sun might, ought to, be a flaming sword keeping the pains and their sad suite away. " Que faire, mon dieu, que faire—mystère."

I'm working hard and, I think, well : hope very soon to name days. Our Plotinus gets a princely praise in A. E's dedication of his new book to it : his *Interpreters*, which does (in its first chapter, all I've yet read), does interpret with magic and grandeur on the top of penetrating truth, does interpret the revolutionary or rebelly mind as we know it, or have known it till a year ago, in this torn land.

I remain by the way impenitently republican (as the last ditch of non-Britonism) but I like to say to everyone that I deplore and loathe, utterly ban and bar, the work now doing in the name of those high things, those true principles. I'm the sole Non-Military Anti-Britonist in my country : the mad military mind has us in tongs.

Always all good wishes and great admiration,

S. MACKENNA.

22

To E. R. DEBENHAM

3, SPENCER ROAD,
BOURNEMOUTH [*December* 28*th*, 1922].

DEAR MR. DEBENHAM,—Woes upon woes, and more hindrances to the work. My wife is deadly ill again, the doctors thought she must die on Christmas day ; she's a trifle better, but they hold out only faint hopes of recovery. If she dies I will go back at once and try to bury myself in my work, our work ; but she may be long on the borderland and I not able to leave her even for the few days required for the double journey to fetch over my books : I had to leave with a collar box on the urgent summons. It was most horrible, not only on account of my wife (my dearest friend) and her agony of disappointment over her health, but because I had been for the last month waiting for the death of an old aunt, one of two who were mothers to me. I had to fly from one death bed to another : a terrible time : but I care for nothing but my wife : if you saw her, a little withered old flushed face quite unrecognisable, a skull with a fiery skin stretched over it ; yet when we're not crying together, we are laughing ; she's the liveliest thing that ever lived ; the very bravest and brightest too : if you listen, you think she can never die ; if you look at her, you ask can she live a five little minutes.

If I can go over and get the books when she has turned the corner, I will never again be 12 hours away from her : her long sufferings and bitter disappointments have earned her all the help and comfort one human being can give another.

Kind regards,

S. M. K.

23

To EDMUND CURTIS

4, RANDOLPH ROAD,
BOSCOMBE CRESCENT,
BOURNEMOUTH [*early in* 1923].

D.E.[1]—. . . My story here is bad : every betterment is followed by a collapse. The vital powers seem to be all but exhausted ; such a white thin limp seaweed as there is now to see, it cuts to the heart : but most days the patient seems still full of quiet faith ; we talk much of the gorgeous life we're to have as soon as her strength returns —first here in the sunny Bournemouth in which there has not been one dry day since I arrived on Stephen's day, not one warm day, not one day which wouldn't make one vomit ; later in the S. France with music and gaiety etc. Sometimes the tears rise as she talks and I have to go to the fire or open the window to cover me and to get up force for the farce. All the medical side is hopeless, I mean doctors and nurses : I would be too, the weakness is so steadily overtaking her, but for the past experience :

[1] Dear Eamonn (Edmund). The beginning of this letter is lost.

Stephen and Marie MacKenna in their garden at Seaview Terrace.
From an oil painting by Mary Duncan.

she rose from among the dead before and therefore may again : I scarcely have faith, just a faint hope. She's very patient, very wise, sometimes still very entertaining—a great soul, really, under the appearance of wild-rose simplicity. When I look back over the years—21 this year—I see a native grandeur of character working steadily outward, so that in yet another 20 years of living and seeing and thinking she would be all-good and all-wise. I wish I saw any evidence that I grew this way : I feel myself getting odious as I olden : I love God, or my picture of It, more, but man less, and I'm filled with mean irritabilities : I thought that if one grew in love and aspiration towards the divine one would ray out, like a genial old Kruschen grandfather, on all humanity : I don't find it so : I love children more, but I grow Synge-like in a nasty scorn of all who tackle the problems of life and don't, da varr,[1] see as I do : this I think the lowest of human traits : I'd rather be a gross sinner than a sinner by contempt and irritation. In fact I think that is the gross sinning, bitterness and gloom and reserve : goodness is to shine as the sun on all things and men and ideas, all. Here endeth my confession.

Always most cordial good wishes.

S. M. K.

24

To ROBERT MACKENNA [2]

[*as from*] 24, CHARLEVILLE ROAD,
RATHMINES,
DUBLIN, 12*th April* [1923].

MY DEAR B.—I just learn from Mamma that two little packs of little books I've sent you have been sent to an old

[1] Irish, " for that reason."

[2] Stephen's brother. After serving in the Royal Marines, in the North-West Canada Mounted Police, and in the Boer War with the Imperial Yeomanry, he settled in New Zealand, where he was successively a farmer, a schoolmaster, and a clergyman of the English Church. He died in Australia, May 5, 1934.

address—an interminable bible of an address. My own wasn't in them, so there can be no return—you must raise Cain if you want the books. I have another little lot, a very few, which I will soon send off to the Garland address : I can't keep them, since my own movements are very uncertain.

Putiki and Warhake and various P.O.'s and School-houses and Islands and other things were in that bible ——

Little letters went at the same time as each instalment of books.

M[amma] seems ill and troubled : times are hard : I fear she's working like a general servant again, and she not young : I can do nothing : our expenses—my wife's and mine—are terrific in this long illness. " Terrific " means, for months past, exactly two and a half times the total of incoming money : one of the " Serious problems of Life ", eh ? But one thing I have : I never worry long : the worry presents itself : I study ways out ; if I find, I rejoice : if I see none, I say " well then there's no way ; let's see what happens ", and except for pure study (as unemotional as that of some problem of history or mathematics) I don't consider the matter again. I hasten to add that I don't think this is the noble way (the moral and virtuous are the worriers ; they more successfully do their duty than I) ; but it's very effective as a means of keeping the hair on the man. Wish you luck.

S. M. K.

25

To E. R. DEBENHAM

[*as from*] 24, CHARLEVILLE ROAD,
RATHMINES,
DUBLIN [*July 4th*, 1923].

MY DEAR MR. DEBENHAM,—My wife died today, 4th July : a merciful release. For 6 months she has been suffering more than one would imagine any justice would allow to be inflicted on one so innocent of harm to man or beast or flower ; a real good soul ; the soul of kindliness essential ; the gayest, chatteringest thing that ever walked I'd say.

In about a week I will be back in Ireland at the old address above, and hard at work trying to make up for lost time—which however one really can never do ; one can only try to show one's rectitude, the days are gone—pereunt et sometimes imputantur.

I will write from there as soon as I see where I stand. The past long time now has been a standstill nearly ; impossible, for me at least, to do anything with one's loved comrade gasping and moaning and visibly fading and in all but daily peril.

Sincerest good wishes,

S. M. K.

26

To RICHARD BEST

24, CHARLEVILLE ROAD,
RATHMINES,
[*August* 6*th*, 1923].

CHER AMI,—You were always pure gold—a thousand thanks. I'll cherish the book as the apple of my eye. I'm most grateful to you also for sending for the two from Germany : I enclose cheque for £1 to cover all expenses.

As for your lovely letter : my dear friend, there are things that cannot be thanked : no one showed any appreciation but you of what to me was the simple truth about my Old Lady : to me she was the most vividly lovely thing always that ever I knew or saw—a flashing life as a flashing eye, that after 22 [1] years made me still seek her company or neighbourhood, wherever we were, with the certainty of good entertainment : and you delighted me with the memory of the quaint in her : I was

[1] Apparently a slip for " 20."

always affectionately and admiringly amused by the things she wore, as by things she did and said : I think still of them with a smile, forgetting for the moment, in the amusement, that all that is over for ever and that no one knows will I ever know it again in any shape or form.

Again a thousand thanks : be at ease ; the book will be always out of all peril. Cordially,

S. M. K.

27

To E. R. DEBENHAM

24, CHARLEVILLE ROAD,
RATHMINES,
DUBLIN [*September* 1923].

DEAR MR. DEBENHAM,—I return your cheque with a hundred thousand thanks. I have enough to go on with and am making arrangements to sell out all our furniture, silver and things—by the way, if you know anyone that sincerely wants what to my mind is a most hideous bronze by Rodin, the Centauress,[1] I'd be glad to know of it. I was offered 100 guineas for it some years ago, but my wife to whom Rodin presented it cherished it, and now the offering man (—— —— in fact) is said not to be so well off and I don't like to offer him the thing again—he was burned out and robbed of motor car &c. &c., and in view of money tightness people don't get him to cut into them so much.[2] The bronze is now with Lady Handley Spicer, 8, Aubrey Walk, Campden Hill, who on a telephone appointment will show it to any connoisseur. W. Rothenstein is most kindly trying to find me a purchaser : like all Jews I've ever known he's the amiablest of creatures—as well as personally charming. But he reports

[1] Figured in Rodin-Gsell, *L'Art*, p. 134 Eng. edition ; R. M. Rilke, *Auguste Rodin*, no. 26 ; Judith Cladel, *Auguste Rodin*, p. 50.

[2] The prospective purchaser, whose name I have omitted, was a well-known surgeon.

that everyone is horrified with the thing, as I am, for its lack of sculptural quality. Personally I always wished it out of the house, but I'd imagine that the very line of it and bizarreness of it would attract collectors. His idea was the soul emerging from the brute.[1]

Please understand that I'm not asking you to do anything in the matter—just if you know anyone that collects these things. I add, impudently, that I would not sell it to you if you bent me the knee and begged for it.

Now Plotinus. I have been thinking of coming over to London to see you ; only not doing so because you are so good, so unfailingly good, that I have dreaded a further appearance of profiteering on your goodness.

Here is the whole ghastly fact : I can't say what time may do for me, but for the present the work is too much for me and my visit would have had the motive of asking you to allow me to make arrangements with Eric Dodds to finish the IIIrd. vol. and to do the IVth. and last.* * * * I torture myself trying to devise plans by which to clear myself of the financial obligation—the disappointment of your plans is beyond my cure, but I must be in your debt now for a huge sum, and, tho' I'm quite determined that if I live I will pay off much or all, the weight of this obligation crushes me : once I would have been happy (as I was, so long ago) to think of *my* Plotinus standing there printed to carry his mingled message of silliness and sublimity for the final gain of thinking—moral thinking, religious thinking, philosophical too—now my happiness, or sense of huge relief, would be when a better man was

[1] Gsell describes it as " an image of the soul, whose heavenly impulses rest miserably captive to the bodily clay." It is sometimes referred to by the title " Body and Soul."

doing that, and I, at my footy journalism, slowly paying off my debt of honour.

A propos de quoi I repeat pro forma, but with the most perfect assurance of my rightness within myself, that the whole disaster rose, not from calculation as to my advantage, but from miscalculation of my powers. I should have known my temperament better than to accept what bound me in honour (and even in law I suppose). I should have understood that what looked very nice and "all but ready" in MS. and in typescript would look appallingly unfinished, crude, "failured", when one was about to publish. It always seemed to me that all the final work could be done in a few slashes of the pen after a rapid rereading of the Greek : always I found myself full of uncertainties, fears, scruples of the literary and metaphysical and scholarly conscience : "Could not this page sing better?" "It is possible after all that so and so is right here, and my Grecity, or my sense of Plotinus' thought and manner, at fault?" that sort of question—keeping me weeks scraping at one little place, taking off and putting back and very often after the weeks leaving the thing, the place, as it had been in the MS. of years back.

I'm bitterly ashamed—even bitterly ashamed that I'm in a position forcing me to try and justify myself—I feel it a stain to be clearing, or trying to clear, my character.

If you say you would like me to come over and talk the matter through, I'll come : don't ask me to stay with you : I'm a boor and have no clothes and no manners ; at a little distance I'm all right but, close at hand—ah, zut !

If you say "No : go on" : why I'll do my honest best—but will not think you wise, or at least quite au fait with the facts, the facts of me and my brain etc.

Think, and at your leisure let me know your decision. Whatever it be, I will accept it to the full and work at it loyally : free of the work, and working otherwise to pay the debt ; or toiling at the work because, unwisely, you so wish it. * * * * Very cordially, S. M. K.

28

To ROBERT MACKENNA

24, CHARLEVILLE ROAD,
RATHMINES,
DUBLIN, *September* [10*th*?], [1923].

MY DEAR MAN,—I've not yet found here a clean clear complete *Iliad* worthy of you ; so as you seem pressed—and I understand that literary impatience very well—I've ordered one for you from a Cambridge bookseller. Myself I like of course to possess completes, and I think I have *every* Greek and Latin author so ; but I have a great desire too for pocket, tram-car, hedge-side, pack-in-your-week-end-valise separates—one play, one dialogue, one chunk, with notes. I like the elaboratest and childishest notes—I can skip what I don't need ; and such is the wobbly weakness of my Graeco-Latin mind that I often find myself referring with zest to some note which many times before I had disdained and not needed : I am capable of forgetting the imperfect of *τύπτω* or the ablative of munus : what I have done with Plotinus is a miracle, the miracle of persistent resteadying of a mind that dips and tosses and disappears like a cork on the waves of your Bay of Islands.

You've cheated me of a cheat I really tried to work on you : I disapprove a man that prefers the *Iliad* to the *Odyssey ;* such a one I'm sure God doesn't love ; I meant you to read the *Odyssey* through before I Iliadised you at all : when those separate books were a penny a-piece I thought God wouldn't love me unless I grabbed them for you, and so my plan ganged agley. The Sophocles by the way that you liked so lyrically in your last cost 3/6. Aeschylus and Vergil were 1d. each : I tried to get the two for 1½d. but the brute *wouldn't* climb down. The Ovid was the apex ; 8d. and 6d. refused with scorn—such dogs there be. You never send a word to little Lizzie ? A blessing to all.

S. M. K.

When I get at my stored books—soon now I hope—I'll probably send you several billions of odd copies, duplicates, tear-stained, underlined and blasphemously annotated veterans of my scholarly agonies. The postage is the mischief—generally more than such books would ever fetch or ever cost.

It's pleasant to give such pleasure : I thank you for giving me the chance. You ought to get the *Iliad* about a week after this : let me know ; and above all whether as I most strictly enjoined they sent a clear edition. Let me know at once of any very special desire : I think you as yet mentioned only the *Iliad* as pressing ?

29

TO E. R. DODDS

SWEET MOUNT HOUSE,
DUNDRUM,
CO. DUBLIN [*October 7th*, 1923].

A CHARA YIL,[1]—You don't give me much time with your " by return " : the English are corrupting you ; who ever heard of a decent man living at such a speed ?

I thought it was agreed that you were not to mention my name unless in actual bibliography, if there inevitably. I don't however care what you do—or anybody does—or anyhow bes done : only I never was nor my seven ancestors before me Mac*k*enna or McKenna or anything but yours faithfully S. MacKenna. Him what steals my capital K, may he never not never in churchyard lay.

Also you made a fatal mistake in asking me to Reading : I might come : I may have to be in London for my sins very soon ; but I could polish you off in a morning between two whackings and be back by tea time unless I misunderstand your distance—40 miles or 40 hours ? Oh the book : thanks : I love pocket vols. and look forward to profiting greatly. By the way anyone what says as my translation is free—God will not love him nor I. S. M. K.

[1] Irish, " My dear Friend."

30

To E. R. DEBENHAM

24, CHARLEVILLE ROAD,
RATHMINES,
DUBLIN [*October*, 1923].

MY DEAR FRIEND,—A present arrived for me from Droitwich. I suspect you, tho' I had a vague notion that Dr. lives in Essex—why I don't know.

I scarcely know what to say about the work. I'm in a dreadful state of incapacity : far better for you and for Plotinus had you released me : I peg away, but with a powerlessness to get things pleasingly right that tortures me : all my little literature seems to have deserted me save, most miserably, the sense of what should be and what must not be. I feel that I ought to be keeping pigs or sweeping floors.

By the end of next week I'll be sending the " finished " IV to be retyped, hoping that having it perfectly clean and (as now) sense-approved before me I'll be able to ram in the literary neatness which still seems far to seek.

As for the Vth which ought to go—must—with this fourth, the Sphinx alone knows when I shall feel even as far advanced with it as with this IVth.

By the way, I'll send you the IVth direct from the typist so that you may have it as it now is in case I get a bullet or a cold or anything of that sort. If, as is most likely, I don't get any such release—I feel most perfectly well—then the last revisal will go to the Medici people when I have the Vth nearly ready.

I'm really in a most awful mental fix : no religion or philosophy has any validity over my trouble, nothing gives any value to life : it is a fatal folly to be as attached to anyone as I was to my wife : I still weep daily, uncontrollably, and scarcely dare to go out lest I break down in public : the case seems to me to approach insanity, which I suppose includes emotional uncontrol as well as the intellectual. Music solaces me, but no reading and no thinking ; they on the contrary put me " wronger ". I find religion nothing : we know nothing : we can only guess, and our guess changes with our health and our environment : the one religion I have now is a longing to see my wife again, and like all other religions there's much more doubt than faith about it. I'm tortured too wondering would she want to see me : who can possibly tell what changes the habit of eternity may bring, supposing even, as on the whole I do, that we survive and know. Music, with one finger, and the calm beauty of fields and trees and the simplicity of children, these are the only things that keep me from the burst brain that at times seems to threaten—a sort of boiling in the brain pan with most singularly no sense of ill health, generally even no physical lassitude.

Doleful, this : I feel it due to you to report ; and if I wait—as indeed I have been waiting—for a better state, I'll be long in reporting.

Very cordial good wishes,

S. M. K.

I suppose there's nothing in all that Reunion of Christendom ? It's Catholicity would win in it ; for I believe, against nearly all the opinions, that Catholicity is doomed and that the victory will be to Judaism modernised, which is to say, to modern Protestantism, Judaism with the Lord Christ for a lovely Prophet : your people can slide out of your dogma, we can't out of ours. Of course the win would be temporary only : we would get a countenance which I believe (in the strong under-current) we are losing ; but in the long event religion must be free and not dogma-bound, an inspiration and a readying, not a creed. If Mahomet had been a trifle less Oriental his Koran would pretty well represent the religion of the future : 'tis Judaism with a beginning at least of the sense of the Lord Christ.

S. M. K.

31

To VIOLET MACKENNA (MRS. ROBERT MACKENNA)

24, CHARLEVILLE ROAD,
RATHMINES,
DUBLIN, *Xmas Eve*, 1923.

MY DEAR VIOLET,—It was very good of you to write to me : I wrote immediately to the child lest she be disappointed and chilled, and with the notion that maybe she would like an imposing-looking letter all to herself : a thing that pains me very much is the thought of a child suffering disappointment ; I remember my own sufferings in that kind, though I must say my experience of the babies of to-day is that, like us older ones, they don't care a rap over such things : probably I was morbidly sensitive.

I'm not bored by children ; on the contrary I'm charmed, spell-bound by them, though, to be honest, rather afraid of them until I know them well : I have village children—of Dundrum where I live, four miles outside the city—who halloo me from the cabins and offer me half-sucked sweets with grimy hands and trot down to the station or back from Mass with me, and I'm ravisht by their conversation, their pretty words, their queer phrases, their confidential trustfulness : one little green-cap girleen often walks the ten minutes with me, then can't be satisfied but to come in on the platform to keep up the talk till the train (always late) puffs in ; then she slides away just before the gate is slammed for the new arrivals to show their tickets. I accused her the other day of coming with me to keep me in the sweet-giving mania I have, but she denied, indignantly though very diplomatically : "The way it is : we like you, sweets and all !" She's an exceedingly bright childeen and never stops talking : you never have to prompt her, but she running along when I'm in a hurry hurriedly pouring out all the news of the family, breathlessly, with a slight stutter and the very prettiest little brogue you ever heard and incredibly beautiful words. " How's Andy-Joe ? " I asked, of a sick baby. " The child is but puny to-day," she answered ; and her " but puny " was said so thinly and finely that the baby seemed to melt away to a faint blue spot in the far distance, so infinitely puny was the long sound of the very word. I would like to adopt this child, but she has a dreadful mother and seven brothers and a ghoulish-looking grandmother, so the relationship would be too large and dreadful.

There are about six other children I'd like to steal—from the age of two to that of twelve—the richest talkers I have ever known : our people may have spoiled in many ways, and we're certainly dirty and in every way slovenly and shiftless, but by heavens we're eloquent : the beautiful words are a joy, and what is more remarkable still is the sense of conversation in the people : it is an exquisite art, practised with love and fury, and warmly appreciated by each in another. One meets it in all ages of the poor people ; in the tiny tot only just able to toddle and in the grizzled and stooped old people, a magnificent natural talent but one unfortunately that doesn't seem to bear cultivation : our educated classes are as dull as the English, except of course when you come to the point of real genius, the A. E.'s, W. B. Yeatses, James Stephens, etc. Nothing impressed me more over in England, during that tragic seven months while I was waiting on the death of my wife, than the dulness of all classes among those dignified mannerly and kindly people of that lovely western district : never a fresh phrase, never a newly coined combination of pleasant sound such as I hear all day long around me in my own Dundrum. (You see I live in the country, though for letters' sake I date from the permanent old address : impossible to live with the Aunt : suddenly, under stress of age and grief, she has changed pitifully, and, with still a kind enough intention, has grown bitter, inquisitorial, tyrannic : you must be in at nine; you must be in for every meal; she's afraid you are not executing your religious duties, are you reading doubtful books: and this though you are a warbattered world-rover of 50, with 30 years thinking and 22 years of marriage behind you.)

All this is meant, in my rambling way, merely to explain that I was glad to scrawl some nonsense to Bessie in answer to her very vivid and direct message: some of it she will understand, some of it you'll have to explain, in the total I hope it will have pleased her as a large and grown-up-looking communication to her very own self. It was necessarily in the void since I never saw the child and do not make myself any picture of your life or ways—a difficulty I have not to face here, where I see the Maggies and Mickies and Shawníns and Mary Theresas and Brideens and so get over my natural terror of the loveable little scalliwags. I have often wondered about you people so far away, whether your houses look like ours, whether—I can't even go on with the whethers, all is a fog to me: I have never seen a picture-house scene laid in New Zealand: I don't know where you are on the map: some one told me you were a series of islands but for all I know they may be islands 3000 miles long: the depth of my ignorance appals me; I once saw N.Z. troops over here and was told they were Maoris, very fine slim dark grave young men: one of my wife's dearest friends in one of her dreadful illnesses was a New Zealander born, of Irish origin, a Miss Killeen, who was torn between her two loves—Ireland so chill and so charming, New Zealand so lovely and so democratic and so hospitable and of so lovely a climate but still—not Ireland. What I owe to Miss Killeen! An angel in the house when we had a gorgeous flat over a lovely square and no servant that could cook a thing my wife, sick to death, could be induced to look at: she would come in and I in tears and the very sweet little incompetent girl we had in tears and my wife weak and distressed; and in five minutes she had everything in order, Marie smiling and I mixing eggs for an omelette, and in half an hour there'd be a lovely and varied meal and everything perfectly happy where all had been bleak and hopeless misery. Long after we got things fairly right Miss Killeen was still a fairy friend to us ; and in that time of the first chaos and horror, well it was an angel from heaven, or New Zealand. That's all I know of N.Z. but you see it's favourable knowledge as far as it goes.

By the way, until I write to Bob, tell him that I didn't clairvoy anything wrong with his Greek : tell him I acted merely on my own knowledge of my own : it runs so low that I periodically have to have recourse to the one infallible method of revival, that of back-translation : I take Greek-Latin, Greek-French, Greek-German texts, and translate (generally in the mind, sometimes in writing) from the Latin, French or German, and compare my results with the authentic text there before me : a few days of this, and I find the dialect or the particular author's style coming back to me (my memory is very bad), and I can then go on reading gaily, until after putting the author by for some time I find myself rusty, then the same trick again. I think I have read again and again everything in all Greek down to Byzantine times (and much of that too, as well as a great deal of the purely modern stuff, lives of Washington, of Rodin, etc. etc.), yet at no moment can I be sure of understanding a passage put suddenly before me : after all these years and all this devotion I do not know Greek : I add that I have personally met only one who did know Greek, and I would find it hard to believe that in any one decade in any one country there have been as yet more than ten people who do know it. Mainly a matter of proper teaching : teach ancient Greek as a living spoken language (a very possible thing) for the long beginnings, then carry on by the back-translation method, and we could all know it, we who care, just as we can learn French or Russian. It's the barbarously imbecile teaching by rules and exceptions, by comprehensive paradigmas, and by premature mixing of dialects, and with stupid choice of texts and stress on foolish notes—all that most cursed folly has stupefied us into inability, at my age, to hold Greek in our poor old weary skulls. I believe it is now being taught at Cambridge[1] in the modern graded conversational way, the modern modern-language way, and is succeeding. The editor of the *Freeman*, a good Grecian of my old style, told me that his daughter came back from three years of this school saying to him daily and all day in excellent fluent Greek, "Morning, old lad: like your eggs fried or boiled? Going to be cursed hot to-day, but thank Heaven I've nothing to do but grill (*ἡλιάζω*) on the lawn and smoke (*καπνίζω*) a handful of cigarettes (*σιγαρέττα* or *σιγαρέτια*) until it's time to go and jazz over at the O'Briens (*σκιρτεῖν* or *χοροπηδᾶν*) etc. etc.: all in Plato's or Xenophon's style and vocabulary, only borrowing from the modern language the few words necessary for purely 1920 things. As the editor of the *Freeman* is a bit of an artist, I don't guarantee all this to the foot of the letter, but something like it I have every reason to believe has been realised—and there's no earthly reason why it shouldn't. Mere matter of method, it is.

This I perceive is a chunk from my unwritten letter to Bob: my letter to Bessie contained, similarly, things for you two less important people: I'm afraid I'm an incorrigible mixer. Bob's, you'll see, will have chunks addressed to him but obviously meant for you. I have (since the subject has been wrongly raised) somewhere a book or magazine articles on these modern methods of ancient language teaching: if I find it I'll send it on. Sorry I haven't sent any books since the Homer: I have them out of store, and a friendly dweller here (a Col. Long,

[1] At the Perse School. MacKenna himself at one time collected materials for a "direct method" Greek primer, but did not finish it—probably because he found that he had been anticipated by Dr. Rouse.

grandson of old Long the scholar : Epictetus, Marcus Aurelius, Herodotus etc.) has made me splendid shelves round a stable in which I keep them ; but I haven't been able (or zealous) to get them sorted : I sort of shrink at the task : I feel sort of will-less, oppressed with a sense of futility and insecurity, and indisposed for any strain or stress of decision : I can't even go on regularly at my own work, my long overdue 3rd vol. : and there's a fourth after that : I'm ashamed, and the more ashamed I do be, the less I'm able to polish off. You must have patience and forgiveness.

This is a bad time of the year also : this time last year I was called over to the long deathbed of my wife, my only true friend in all the world (I mean of course in the sense of one closely at hand), and I'm foolish and grieve sadly. I had the great misfortune of dearly loving my wife : the loss of the double sense of being protected and of protecting, and of being amused and of amusing, the sense of an intimate comradeship absolutely unbroken, this makes me feel that life has nothing in it for me. But that's wrong : only that I haven't the courage to rewrite what's on the back of this, I'd tear the sheet up and leave out the weeps. I'm very strong on the theory of not telling (or even to oneself encouraging) one's griefs, but just grinning along : but theory isn't always sure to come out in practice : I start to tell people how I really don't care and I end in a howling sob.

Sob-Bob : that's the connection (it's always amusing to see how one's thoughts develop the one from its former) —I meant to tell you that while of course you hit the nail on the knob in telling me what a splendid being I am, you're also not far wrong in your judgment of what is sterling in Bob : often, contemplating other people's lives and doings and mutual reactions, I reflected that, while we two absolutely must have had bad times together as boys side by side, I don't remember any one such time. Among my other brothers—whose list is long, like the

Army List—I observed many ructions and remember them vividly, even some terrible hair-raising scenes ; but I absolutely cannot recall and never have been able to recall any scene between Bob and Meself, not even the coolness of an hour at a time : I remember bad half-hours even with the Aunts, even with the gentle little old Lizzie who usually was as putty and butter in our subtle fingers, but I don't remember the eighth of a second of more than casual frigidity with Bob : that I think must be a record of fraternal relationship ? I remember once, so noble a soul am I, nearly killing myself to save him from a peril of which he never knew : I remember innumerable trifles which it would be amusing to tell of some day : but I don't remember any quarrel. I remember once when he unjustly accused me, with cool disapproval, of a thing I didn't do—we must have both been very small : I remember the very shine and smell of streets down which we passed about 40 years ago together : I remember bowling hoops with him as fast as we could bowl, as close as we could just without murder brush by a decent old fool who was just after teaching us, or trying to, the dates of the Kings of England : I remember penny bags of gooseberries bought and eaten together, all sorts of absurd, infantile things like that : I remember my amazement at his taste in reading, and his contempt for mine (I couldn't read adventure stories, and he despised my taste for tales of little girls who didn't mend their gloves and so distressed their dear Mammas when the crime was discovered, at the teaparty, by the Vicar's wife)—a thousand such things I remember, and I can remember many disapprovals on his side and on mine, and I cannot remember one quarrel, one nasty reproach, I do not believe there could ever have been one solitary blow. Cold disapproval, instantaneously past, that is all I can remember: I remember one, no, two grave injustices in judgement he did me, and still feel them fairly vividly : I remember once loathing him for a contemptuous phrase he uttered over a very foolish but well-meant act of our Aunt Katie : but with all this—I repeat I can remember no quarrel, only the very faintest cloud of a moment.

The more I think of this the more I'm astonished : it is a great and glorious testimonial to the two of us—though as a matter of fact mainly to him, since though I was the older he was naturally much more of a leader than I, and might well have found it quite natural (in the nature of boys) to tyrannise over me and, I resisting as even the worrrum will turrun, a quarrel leaping up—and there never, in all my memory, was any such thing. One of my brothers hurled a lamp at my head and ordered me out of his house, so that I had to flee to Ireland from London immediately : others punched me, others called me appalling names ; others stuck knives in yet others (we sound like a gang of drunken criminals : but most boys are as bad as that). Hosts of such diabolical scenes enacted themselves round us, and one of my brothers for twenty years wouldn't speak of me or write to me, though I did him no wrong : but with all that hot blood around us and in us, and under the stress of close companionship and very different tastes and temperament, Bob and I never to all my memory had any scene at all : we appear to have behaved better to each other than two little nice old maiden ladies or than the terrible Colonel of the Lord Roberts story—you know it ? The dreadful blasphemous and obscene martinet, and Lord Roberts abhorring such conduct, and on a great field day before Lord Roberts, the trumpeter blowing " Disband " or " Retreat " instead of " Charrruge ! ", and the Colonel beginning " *You* . . . "—then, feeling the Roberts eye coldly upon him, continuing gently, " *naughty* trumpeter."

Thus we were : angelic beings, apparently : we couldn't really have been that, because though MacKennas we were human ; but we must have been remarkable, or some memory there would be of those dreadful things that are normal in the association of boys, especially where there was no big Old Man with a horsewhip to keep order by terror. Or was it perhaps precisely because there was no terror to wear upon our nerves, nothing but two quiet little old women (who by the way must have been almost babies at the time when they ruled us) ? Problem : puzzle : mystery : but I maintain it showed virtue in us also : and, remembering how very much more virile Bob was, and yet that I in a quiet way had as I have the pride of the devil himself, he certainly deserves some sort of bun.

This has been a long scrawl and perhaps incoherent (and illegible ?) : it's my way to go when I'm going : I never stand on the mat. So good-bye—thank you very much for beginning an acquaintance which I will not wish to cut short.

So my love to my sister.

S. M. K.

32

TO E. R. DEBENHAM

24, CHARLEVILLE ROAD,
RATHMINES,
DUBLIN [*January 27th*, 1924].

A CHARA YIL,—Yours crossing mine advocates what I had vaguely adumbrated as almost too good to be true. The very notion makes me younger.

To-morrow (Monday) I give one half of the IVth Ennd. to the typists and will send the clean script to you as soon as I have it checked. The rest will follow wad by wad : short of accident, three weeks ought to give you the complete IVth.

What I have read of the new stuff—nearly the entire half for the typists—strikes me as very good, far and far better that I had in my sick soul imagined it. Once already I wept for the sheer beauty of a passage—the Greek no doubt, yet adequately enough carried over into your language. It's true the passage was one I remember citing to my wife—ages and ages ago, as we rode between Magdeburg and Hanover on our route, Berlin-Amsterdam, on bicycles—such ages ago, was it ; in the good days gone. She loved the passage and we rode chanting it in an improvised translation, like the gay green fools we were. But, this memory apart, the thing is good—tender and large, like Casals on the 'cello.

All the stuff as far as I've gone strikes me as at least dignified and immaculately clear (to the willing and sufficiently instructed), and clearness is my Rachel, if that was the lady some Biblical gentleman toiled seventy years for and I think I remember didn't get in the end. It's a great gift of the gods, stupidity, if only time is added : a real bright fellow bes unclear by swiftness of insight ; I suffer so much by anything unclear that I delve and spin like Adam and Eve only to get clarity—the first jewel of literature to the likes of me.

I veritably believe this translation to be unique in its clarification of the most unclear writer that ever wrote. I'd be happy in death if they put on my tombstone : " He toiled for clarity and by gum he got it."

Many thanks for this most relieving thought and act.

Cordially,

S. M. K.

33

To ROBERT MACKENNA

24, CHARLEVILLE ROAD,
RATHMINES,
Saturday, 29*th or* 30*th* [*sic*] *Feb*., 1924.

MY DEAR BOB,—I can't write very much, but this tells you that Aunt Lizzie died to-day ; nearly 80 years : painlessly, as far as we could judge, from the very beginning of the graver condition to the very end, It was a lovely little soul : I think that it was a very fairly happy life as life goes : she was embittered towards the end—by the state of the world, the state of Ireland, her own financial decay and of course the sense of loneliness in her old age. But all this was mainly a matter of the surface : deep down I think she had found life pleasant, as hers was innocent and kindly and surrounded by affection : of course many, most, of her old friends were dead—she was lonely enough, but those that remained loved her. * * * *

Given the world as it is, the little old lady no doubt whatever served faithfully and usefully in it—gay and good, loving and calling out love and kindness in others —but why the world should be at all for anyone to help in it or to mar it, that's a mystery beyond all solution to any reason. As I watched the poor little old lady die I couldn't but smile to think how horrified she'd be if she knew what questions I was asking and I standing by her little bedroom altar where the blessed candles were lit, by the holy water stoup and the statuettes and the holy pictures and the sprig of last year's Palm. Just a day before the 8-or-9-days unconsciousness fell on her she begged me to take care of my dear soul—the poor little old lady. The last time I saw her up, it was in her little " drawing-room " she was, on her knees at a chair with a candle to light her prayer book. When she took to bed for the last spell and the eyes began to cloud over, she used to take her little old prayer book in the hands—blue and thin like a hen's claws—and pat the little book and cry. To me this life of prayer seems at once beautiful and silly : I can imagine, though with difficulty, a creator of infinite worlds who wants me at Dundrum and my Aunt at 24 Charleville Road to keep a law ; but that He should want me to say Holy Holy to Him, or need that I ask Him to keep me good—that I confess is impossible and almost repulsive to me. In fact life with or without religion seems to me equally to be disapproved : without religion it seems beastly or " dead " ; with, it seems slavish and unreasonable. I'm in the utterest fog. Have you any convictions ? The nearest I get to my own is a vague

Judaic Romishness : a doubtful feeling that there's one God and father, creator or immanent power of the worlds, plus a sentimental attachment to the forms and to the tradition of Old Rome. Sometimes I confess I think of living in England and becoming a vague Broad Church philosophical "Protestant"—but I hate the name of England and couldn't bear hymns about split Rocks and bloody Lambs.

Love,

S. M. K.

34

To E. R. DODDS

CHAMBERLAYNE'S MILL,
BERE REGIS,
DORSET,
[*August or September*, 1924].

MY DEAR CHARA,—Very good of you : I don't agree with you of course :[1] I couldn't accept anything from a society, or even from a Games, where the title or purpose is such as to play the old game of pretending that anything with any shreds of respectability flapping about its flanks is British or pro-British. The one pure spot in me is the passion for the purity of Ireland : I admire the English in England, I abhor them in Ireland ; and at no time in more than 30 years of my emotional life—alas I'm 53 now—would I ever have accepted anything from Royal Societies or Cawstles or anything with the smell of England on it. People think (I've received a shoal of abusive letters) that this is a new thing, a de Valeritis: 'taint nuffin of the kind, 'tis a life-long insanity, an old fever working in the blood : the mere news that I had been thus raped in my absence set the blood dancing with fury so that on the heights of Boscombe cliffs where I read it, I kinduneued[2] to fall

[1] I had written to expostulate on his refusal to accept the gold medal conferred on him by the Royal Irish Academy : see Memoir, p. 82 and letter 37A.

[2] ἐκινδύνευσα.

down into the sea with a tremble of rage and a blindness and giddiness of shame. Had I heard of this thing quietly beforehand I'd have simply written privately to decline : I don't love fights and publicities : but outraged as I slept I had no resource but to swot them one : as a matter of fact, everyone thinks I'm an ass. I've received only one
ive?
approbatory letter : people have emptied unnameable things on me poor old cranium—whereby I know that Ireland is doomed, dunged—sordes eius in pedibus eius and herself rejoicing in it.

I don't know what's happening to Plotinus : he's like the Republic, can't emerge.

I wish you the best things in life, you and yours—I'm afraid your mother'll never forgive me : no one ever does : I fled from all Ireland in a sick headache that was like a portable hell under my hat the last weeks, and everyone writes to me that at least I ought to have laid it aside and come to see him her or it : yet 45 times one him her or it is 45 ; that's a thing no one sees.

Very cordially,

S. M. K.

35

To ROBERT MACKENNA

[CHAMBERLAYNE'S MILL,
about September 1924.]

MY DEAR BOB,—I congratulate you and Madame on the new life opening before you. I don't quite clearly understand whether you will be at once a clergyman. I'm sorry I don't even know what a deacon is in the English church, and have only a hazy idea of it in our own ; a sort of vestmented holyman that sings the gospel I know, but his ecclesiastical station I don't know. You see how far I've drifted : I'm more in sympathy now with Judaism than with any of the (now) western forms of religion : though indeed (as I horrified a parson friend of mine by saying recently) the Book of Common Prayer, save for a mumbled creed and the frequent " Through our L.J.C.", is really Jewish religious service. I think the western world, in so far as it cleaves at all to the olden forms, will be increasingly Jewish : certainly the Anglicanism I observe, over great names, in the *Hibbert Journal* (to which for years I'm faithful) is Judaic, monotheistic, undogmatic except in its monotheism. I'm afraid our beautiful Roman mummeries—which I love with all my quivering heart—are doomed, damned by their dogma. Some of the practices of obligation too are odious ; the Confessional for instance (as an obligation) is a dirty interference with the sacred secrecy of the human conscience. As a non-obligatory advisory or consultative institution, it seems to me very valuable : as a compulsory rake-over of all one's sins or leanings to wrong, it seems to me to be psychologically the maddest folly ever invented ; it fastens morbidity on to the soul, fills the sinner with the very thoughts he should avoid like the devil, and is besides, as I have said, to my mind the most loathsome outrage on the dignity and self-guiding efficiency of the soul. If your Anglicanism excludes compulsory self-exposure, I'd approve it as a whole on that point alone : I mean, that one thing alone would make it better to me than R. Catholicism. I know an Anglican clergyman who in a London slum district heard confessions and thought it good : later he took a country living and added to his income by taking three boys as pupils, preparing for a military school (Sandhurst ? I think) : he told me he found it quite impossible to invite his boys to practise confession ; couldn't bear the thought. Has come to think with me that the confessional system is inhuman ; will gladly advise, will never no more not nohow listen to a set declaration of faults from any one at all, save on a deathbed. I delighted in this ; an exact confirmation of my own ideas. I'd like really if you have time (and if I'm not making an indiscreet request or suggestion) to know what you really do believe on the Gospel story, the old Bible, the sacramental system ; and whether you adopt this new thing with full intellectual adherence, or only (to my mind on the whole a very legitimate thing) only as a vehicle of spirituality without intellectual adherence to dogma.

Very cordial good wishes,

S. M. K.

36

To ROBERT MACKENNA

CHAMBERLAYNE'S MILL,
BERE REGIS,
DORSET [*October* 20*th*, 1924].

CHER AMI,—A confession : Mamma pressed me so hard to let her know what I knew about your move that, being utterly incapable alas of lying or even of deft concealment, I told her the truth, making her promise however not to pass it on, and not to let you know she knew. This last proviso I see to have been rather dishonest, so I write and confess : I always tell my friends to tell me no secrets, since I have no diplomacy, no arts by which, once suspected, to save me from betraying all I know. Anyhow I don't greatly see that it matters : I suppose you'll have to be—or are you now ?—Reverend (or Very or Rather or Almost Reverend in Sydney Smith's gradation) ; and your position is honourable. M. took the matter well enough : just O O O and then silence—and not a word since, except that after a while I said, " We must suppose him sincere : I know myself how subtly the conscience works." That was all, absolutely all. I might have told her that at one time I debated myself whether I might not do well to abandon the superstitions of Rome for those of Lambeth, as putting a less intolerable burden of dogma and observance on its people, and that I was saved, or perverted, mainly by the purely extraneous reason that I'm a furious nationalist in regard to Ireland and that Rome is the best trench against Buckingham Palace or Downing Street. Besides if I did make any conscientious change it would be to some non-hymn-singing Unitarianism or to a Modernist Judaism—that of one of the Montefiores (I forget his first name), who is a beautiful soul and has written lovely religious books and has founded a Modernist Synagogue etc.

Sometimes I think if I were young and felt *nationally* free (free as regards Ireland) I'd found (and be Pope and especially treasurer of) a new church which might be called the Exploratory Church : the rough idea; groups of Seekers with always a president or moderator and a vice-mod. and a deputy mod. and a vice-dep. mod., with a kind of grave debates preceded and followed by meditation and guided a little by variously chosen religious readings, of which the moderators, holy and learned men, would be the choosers, things from all religions, Buddhist not less than Jewish, the Koran next to Epictetus and Seneca, the poetry of all nations, the deeper, the enquiring, the awed poetry. Positivism, now dead apparently, would help us ; but we'd not go on the absurd, the monstrous Comte hypothesis or dogma (unless I'm wrong ; my memory is vile and it's long since I looked into Comte) that we do absolutely know ourselves doomed to eternal ignorance. In my own group I'm afraid there'd be a good deal of Plotinus, who if you accept (or simply ignore) his main assumption offers a fine religion of awe and straining and working. "The Awed Seekers" might be a name for the total of groups : they'd be absolutely free, except that they'd have always to be in close consultation with their Pope (and then—this is essential—remain free to snap their fingers at him if they so judged) ; and they'd have to stump up handsomely to keep me in my palace in books, gramophone records, musical instruments and motor bicycles. I veritably believe that the Religion of the future will be something like this, an awed seeking, an orientation towards the superhuman, the Power behind all ; with no permanent dogma, but the use of any and every dogma when, if only for a day, that dogma appears to be either true or a bridgeway towards truth or towards spiritual value, spiritual beauty.

I don't know much about the English Church, but it appears to me mechanical, repetitive, and utterly lacking in the magnificent magic of Rome : I find far more religion in a Mass, the lowest, with its silences and mystic gestures, or the highest with its gorgeously symbolic ceremonies and its majestic music—the Gregorian, liturgical I mean—and in a Benediction, which is a ceremonial hypnotism towards the Divine, than in all the Book of Common Prayer which (though beautiful, often, in literature) seems religiously quite numbed—quite outside the meaning of religion, the awed personal search. It seems to me smugly sure and at rest, where religion throws itself about in a kind of agony and must use magic. That magic is the difficulty of my own proposed Searchers : how are we going to get the creatures to be more than logic-choppers, a young man's debating society ? All I really see clearly is that first principle, that religion must be much more a search than a settled acquired body of literature. Of course within the English Church, with its recent freedom (Bishops who practically believe in nothing save God and virtue), a passionate searcher can inspire his people if he's orator and ascetic (or artistic : in some way highly sensitive and therefore moving) ; and it may be a good compromise. But perhaps you really believe all those quaint things ? I know, though I understand not at all, that many do.

Cordially,

S. M. K.

37A

From " A. E."

ROUNDWOOD PARK,
ROUNDWOOD,
CO. WICKLOW, 14 *Nov.* '24.

MY DEAR STEPHEN,—Miss Mitchell has forwarded me your letter but not the book. I am here for a week taking the last of my holidays. I do not envy you your Bournemouth. I walk in Autumn woods all day and sit on stumps of trees, and feel happy when I do not see a house : the thought of Bournemouth stupefies me. But you are so wild in your mind travelling over the universe that I think you like contemplating stolid comfortable citizens. You would not be one if you could, but it rests you to see a villa and a comfortable seat and a bandstand and pleasant unimaginative folk. It is nature's way to attract us by our opposites. No, I did not get the letter you speak of. I am sorry. I always delight in what you say, whether written or spoken. I have been wanting to write a letter about your Plotinus for some time, and when I get this last volume I shall do so. I am pleased you should think I would appreciate your Plotinus ; and I do. It is one of the books I take up again and again and read in my fashion, which is to take a sentence and brood and brood over it until I find the life behind it. It takes me a long while to read a real book, and your Plotinus is a real book. I hear that you were indignant that Yeats crowned the Plotinus at the Tailteann games. Alas, I was the culprit! I wrote that part of his speech referring to your translation. You must forgive me. Or perhaps you did not read the speech but only heard you were awarded a medal. Anyhow if I write myself I will not write as a member of anything " Royal," which I am not, or as a loyal subject of any State free or enslaved, which I am not, but as A. E. who is I hope always an anarchist in his soul and who feels like Omar about the world he lives in :

" Could you and I with Him conspire
To grasp this sorry scheme of things entire,
Would we not shatter it to bits and then
Remould it nearer to the heart's desire ? "

If I am not a Republican it is because no Republican has raised up a lordly image for me to worship, and I am simply an endurer of things until I find the scheme of things for which I can fight. It is heavenly in the woods here. The sun is white in the sky. The sky is blue. The trees are like jewels, the grass is frosty and the stillness is alive. I think after all I am a poet, nothing else really, and I am writing poems all this autumn. Here is one for you. I call it " Promise."

Be not so desolate
Because thy dreams are flown,
And the hall of the heart is empty
And silent as stone,
As Age left by children
Sad and alone.

Those delicate children,
Thy dreams, still endure.
All pure and lovely things
Wend to the Pure.
Sigh not, unto the fold
Their way was sure.

Thy gentlest dreams, thy frailest,
Even those that were
Born and lost in a heart beat,
Shall meet thee there.
They are become immortal
In shining air.

The unattainable beauty,
The thought of which was pain,
That flickered in eyes and on lips,
And vanished again,
That fugitive beauty
Thou shalt attain.

The lights innumerable
That led thee on and on,
The Masque of Time ended,
Shall glow into one.
It shall be with thee for ever
Thy travel done.

You see the things which are truly at the bottom of my mind all the time I have to write about economics and finance and education and government. I know I shall take none of these things to Paradise and I feel about them as Tagore felt when he cried "What shall I do with that which will not make me immortal?" But we have to provide for the wretched body, the wife and family, which things also have their meaning. Here is another of my meditations.

Sometimes when alone
At the dark close of day
Men meet an outlawed majesty
And hurry away.

They come to the lighted house;
They talk to their dear;
They crucify the mystery
With word of good cheer.

When love and life are over
And flight's at an end,
On the outcast majesty
They lean as a friend.

And here is a last and indignant protest about the darkness we live in which I call "Mutiny" and which is a mood continually with me.

That blazing galleon the sun,
This dusky coracle I guide,
Both under secret orders sail
And swim upon the selfsame tide.

The fleet of stars, my boat of soul,
By perilous magic mountains pass,

Or lie where no horizons gleam
Fainting upon a sea of glass.

Come, break the seals, and tell us now
Upon what enterprise we roam,
To storm what city of the gods,
Or—sail for the green fields of home.

I send you these that you may believe I am somewhere in my soul going along the same road as your philosopher, though a million aeons behind him, and that I will listen to any words of his you send me with passionate interest. Perhaps he will break the seals for me yet. I am sure you will find Ireland is your spiritual home and come back to it. I never pretended to be anything specially national but I would be in despair if I had to live outside Ireland. I take all its gombeen men and its gunmen and its dull politicals as the weights Heaven has attached to it to prevent too great injustice to the rest of the world. I am delighted to hear from you, my dear man, and am pleased and proud you should have sent me the last volume of the Plotinus. I hope you are getting good health over there in that dismal land you have chosen to live in.

Yours ever,

A. E.

37

To E. R. DEBENHAM

CHAMBERLAYNE'S MILL,
BERE REGIS,
[*November* 17*th*, 1924].

CHER AMI,—I don't know whether you or Mrs. Debenham care to read these things, e.g. A. E. on his own adventures with Plotinus : it may be something to you that a few such men value your offering. I got also a line from Compton MacKenzie the other day ; he writes that he got his IIId. Plotinus the day it came out : it was a stroke of luck that I was able to tell him in reply that with H. G. Wells he is the only English novelist I'm eager for, almost the only one I can read. Yeats, A. E., C. M. K., G. K. Ch., it's something that these few care—tho' all the time I think the less of them in so far as 'tis not Plotinus but the Pls. of S. M. K. they value.

In about a week I shall know about my new heaven : the nomad will pitch another tent, and contemplate near a tramline : you know of course that the tram was the invention of an Irishman, Irish American ; trams are " entirely holy things," linking the pig in the green field to Kreisler in the Winter Gardens : I can live neither without sight of my pig nor audience of my Kreisler, hence I reverence the immortal memory of the man whose name I forget.

I returned your Pauline, whose name I misremember, with great disrespect, and will soon send Mr. Alexander the Breviary—this before I peg my tent on that tram terminus. Wetstein [1] I retain, returning, tho', the Plotinus as soon as I can open my own cases.

Very cordially,

S. M. K.

A. E., like all great men, is a bit of an ass : I hurled Bournemouth at him as editor of the *Irish Statesman*, hoping he'd begin to think how sordidly inferior Dublin is : he chose to take it that I preferred " bandstands " to tree stumps—and himself living in a suburban slum—a noble poverty, but an ignoble contentment with civic inefficiency. Poets should sing but never speak : his philosophic indifference to environment leaves him a public peril, content with Dublin cities and free states.

[1] The Wetstein *New Testament*, which Debenham had lent him.

38

To E. R. DEBENHAM

WANDERLEA,
MOORDOWN,
B[OURNEMOUTH] [*February* 8*th*, 1925].

DEAR BOSS,—You needn't have worried over that rubbish—many thanks tho'.

I've been half hoping you'd be down again and take me en route : I really must be on your way from B. to Moor House : there's no commandment, " By Poole shalt thou go " : Wimborne, as Emerson said of the roses, exists with God to-day. Of course without a warning I might very well be out, but what then—you fare on.

I have had a bad week : after lumbago came on the old bad nervous symptoms, the physical weakness, the blurred brain, the utter despair. I all but wrote you to go and be dee'd : but, tho' I'm still unsteady, I have been able to begin work again. You would have had the four new tracts long since, by the way, but that my typewriteressina first flouted me as not able to say Bo to a goose, and then, by a vengeance, fell ill : she writes me that I'll have them by the end of next week : I'll send the duplicates, new and old, i.e. seven tractates of the 9, to Mr. Alexander. This is a measure of precaution against fire or my own extinction, which last seemed to me probable and desirable for about a week until 2 or 3 days ago, when it suddenly and irrationally began to appear less interesting to take Plots. by the beard and demand what the devil he meant by this and that. I have often wondered what P. would say to me if we ever meet. I'm sure he'd behave like a perfect gentleman, but I think he'd never understand how unnecessarily difficult he'd made himself and probably would be rather chilly over some of our renderings. The French translation, the new, E. Bréhier, strikes me as [more] lamentable the more I examine it : the junctures, especially, seem utterly ill-advised or not thought out at all [1]: my work is avowedly tentative, but France and Germany don't seem even to have tented anything at all, but to get down words as nearly representative as possible (i.e. as the dictionaries allow) of the words of Pls. : the connection of ideas seems scarcely to have troubled anyone : yet it is the only thing that can give Pls. value to-day. When my slaughterer arises he will slaughter me largely by the light I have given : I shall die rosily, so, and from my ashes a better Pls. will arise. These others, these silly cribs (some cribs are not silly), have never lived ; they shed no light but that of dictionaries. Of course one has to have them, to study them, if only to be sure they are naught.

I don't know why I meander on this way : glad, I suppose, to be quasi talking to you.

I hope you get—or is it possible ?—good news of Mrs. Debenham on her long pilgrimage of mercy.

Don't pay any attention—I mean don't reply—to this farrago.

Cordially,

S. M. K.

39

TO EDMUND CURTIS

"WANDERLEA,"
MOORDOWN,
BOURNEMOUTH [1924 *or* 1925].

CHER AMI,—I blame me for not having written to thank you for the splendid present and the shop-going act thereto : my excuse, that I have a certain amount of nerve trouble and a good deal of physical weakness, kind of flu feeling without the other signs. I find myself hoping every day that I'll wake up to find myself dead, which I take to be peace. This doesn't mean that I don't read Corkery : I do, slowly, with intense interest and sense of

[1] He qualified this judgement in another letter.

value, tho' the pathos of it is not the best tonic for the present languors : the old sad pull of Ireland at the heart-strings, quoi. Next to being a Jew I don't know anything more desolating than being of the Gael : if I had children I'd have planned to save them from that as from being English, I'd have worked miracles to make them French or Greek—torn up all life to bring them up in some continental or even American environment from the earliest. Ireland seems to me doomed : it will be pitifully British (feebly, torturedly, I mean : never coming quite to rest). I abhor the free state, but I don't know were I in Ireland would I vote for a Republican : I could never work either for the Britannisation of Ireland or for the renewal of its wound : I remain a Republican only in the sense that it seems to me (in so far as anything seems anything to my vague mentality) that one of the follies of history was the acceptance of that fatal treaty ; there I remain where I was that dismal Christmas. * * * *

I wonder has anyone heard of Jamesy Stephens, whether he likes America, succeeds as a lecturer, etc. : he looked to me very ill when he was here, tho' he talked with immense animation and showed every way vitality. I secretly feared the strain of travelling, grinning, roaring in halls, would be too much for him—tho' I notice he doesn't take eagerly what he has to take—he has nerve placidity with intellectual agitation, a very enviable conjunction. I know that were I intellectually eminent to the degree of being commissioned to lecture so, I'd rather live in a brown coat in a country teach na mbocht [1] (how would you say in Irish *a* house for *the* poor ? Tig or teach na mbocht seems to mean the particular house of these or those particular poors ? I s'pose left to our Gaelic selves we'd have given all these things quite other names—names caught from quite other angles).

Did you ever open a book on Motor Cycles or on making your own wireless set ? Open ; and see, the doom

[1] Irish, " poor-house."

of the Irish : more easy, far, to translate one of them into Homeric Greek than into Irish. The best attainable would be to paraphrase a booklet of 100 pp. one shilling into a tome of 550 pages 7/6 : Irish like Ireland is doomed; there is one God and Progress is his Prophet : be incapable of progress and you're damned by his law.

Which may you, tusa,[1] not be.

S. M. K.

40

To EDMUND CURTIS

"WANDERLEA,"
MOORDOWN,
BOURNEMOUTH [1924 *or* 1925].

MY DEAR EAMONN,—You say write soon and I write soon, touched. But what to write? You write me a letter of philosophy and sociology or anthropology and history and all sorts of things in which I'm utterly incompetent, hopelessly dense and dull, I the least capable in the entire human race of that generalisation which I know to be the only sign or source of wise action and wise judgement. Also it happens that I'm to write on a day of trouble; Seumas [2] has just left me, in rain and drearth : and I'm engaged in a row with my "landlady" who from being as kind as a mother of the cinemas has suddenly come on me with fantastic exactions : I tremble as I write.

I always loathed and intensely admired the gentleman of whom you write : the only generalisation of which I'm capable is that all Irish Ireland is abominable and admirable, gentle and savage, saintly and diabolic, generous beyond words and mean beyond all example, beautifully wise and most dangerously silly. I quite agree with St. John Ervine that the English are far the better people of the two, adding, against him, that we will never be half as good until we have them out of Ireland lock stock and

[1] Irish : =French "toi."

[2] James Stephens.

barrel and the very thought and memory of them, that at last we may elaborate our own character, working up our native virtues and working out our native or induced vices, which last are mainly the growth of a slavish irresponsibility and a slavish rebelliousness. Frankly, if I were you, I'd cut the whole thing : you served nobly, very magnificently, very heroically in the immense heroism of private service, of constant loyalty to an idea not so much resisted as sneered at, the witheringest opposition that can be encountered. I'd turn either into a benevolent careless old don or, if I felt young and fresh enough, go questing a good job in some warm and sunny untortured land. In England you'd probably groan over Ireland and for it, miss it and despise it : in South or North America or further Europe it would soon be as distant and faintly amusing as one's childhood's hopes and shames and rages and triumphs and fears.

As for B.'s[1] position, it seems to me quite fantastically untenable. Munster's temporary topdoggism is of course B.'s own triumph. But for the Fola texts I don't believe Munster would have held ground at all : if Connacht had printed those keys, learners and teachers alike would have gone to Connacht once the first legitimate O'Leary boom had faded out. I see nothing written in Munster Irish to-day or these Gaelic League years to justify the idea that you can think better in Munster : get a blue pencil and make two re-writings per page on P. O'Conaire's stuff, and you have the only thing of modern Ireland that could be written by a French a German a Russian a Swedish novelist or playwright or essayist. It is also a fact that if you explained to any nation the general phonetic system of Irish (as a Munster man would have to give it were he to be short) and then gave them an Irish text to read, they would produce automatically a Connacht pronunciation : an crann thall could not possibly be pronounced as " a crown howl," suaimhneas couldn't

[1] Prof. Osborn Bergin.

be "synus" or "síneas," etc. etc. For Connacht you have a reasonable all-Europe phoneticism, nearly comparable to the precise easiness of Greek and Italian and I'm told Russian; and you have in P. O'C. absolutely the only writing you could imagine a European reading, though what his final judgement would be is another question; P. is often grammatically careless and inconsistent, sometimes confused, a hundred faults: but he belongs to the European kind: compared with any Munster I know from O'Leary to to-day he stands about as a rather crackedy crotchetty university don to a schoolgirl: he is mature tho' faulty, he has range: the Munsterites are bright limited childishness.

I don't know one Munsterite that has any notion of literature whatever: their one idea is a racy phrasing, and even at that they don't mind a most unracy repetition. One of them, not it's true famous, showed me a script in which 16 consecutive sentences began with tá, vi or ni raiv,[1] and was amazed and angry when I pointed out that in no language could any raciness of single phrase excuse such a debauch. This was no doubt an exceptional case, but short of that extremity the thing is typical. The article by the way was an effort to show the overpowering charms of 18th century songs. The man was especially amazed when I said that it might do in the matter of the contents of an ironmongery store: tá 2000 saucepans—vi 2500—ni raiv ach 200 sales thereof, etc. etc. Munster has the sense of phrase but no notion of literary congruity, no sense of literary architecture or carpentry, no sense of dignity, no sense of depth or range, no notion of true observation or of significant selection; no spiritual emotion, no nothing that makes literature: above all I should have said they have no idea whatever of creating a phrase; they resent new coinage, which is precisely the mark of literature (on the purely technical side, of course I mean). P. O'C. is full of new phrase, new to Irish if not

[1] "(There) is (are)," "(There) was," "(There) was not."

so often new to the European languages on which (at first or at fifth hand, i.e. thro' translations or thro' English writers so influenced) he draws. Men who have every sense of these things, who coo over a new coinage in English (or an old that has gone out but is discovered in old writers, intelligible and charming), cry " haro : on me fait tort " when they find a novelty of idiom in Irish, even when the " novelty " is something that was in the literature but has been preserved only in a non-Munster district.

The whole truth is that Munster is more alive to jobs and jobbery, quicker in this world's quickness, than Connacht or Ulster ; and also because the native speaker of M. spoke better English they became teachers : they spoke better English because Irish was much nearer its death among them, tho' of course I admit that their Irish, quâ mere phrase, was on the whole richer as a rule. I maintain that with all P. O'C.'s little flaws he's such that an imaginary non-English-speaking Irishman steeped in him would be prepared for all European conversation and literature : no Munster writer prepares the mind for anything but a Munster cabin or old Irish story-life. With a very little patting, a man nourished on P. O'C. could translate into Irish from any European literature on any subject save science and the inner construction of motor cycles or wireless or aeroplanes : he'd have words and forms for all that deals with religion, with morals, with all normal human emotions : had he the " culture " or the humour, he could write Elian or Pateresque essays, Shaw plays, Dostoievsky stories. P. O'C., with flaws, and speaking not of his mental value but of his range and language, goes very close to Maupassant : Munster keeps to the aonach and to cro na muc.[1] Of course all this might be reversed in a day by a new thing, a Munster thing : then the honours would be equal, with only a C. priority. It would still remain the fact that M. could never deserve

[1] " The fair " and " the pigsty."

the Bergin Law (that M. is this or that, C. and U. only that other).

D'ye know I think that Máire, who is an Oinseach,[1] is alone enough to disprove the alleged law : I abhor her thinking, but her language states a thought and states it very dam well : it's an irrelevancy that the thinking is poor or to me wrong : Fr. Dinneen's thinking is of a poverty that fills one with disgust, yet the language is the appropriate language of thought. Don't by the way take him as M. : he to my mind has always represented the best standard we have ever had—for journalism and that sort of thing. It dates

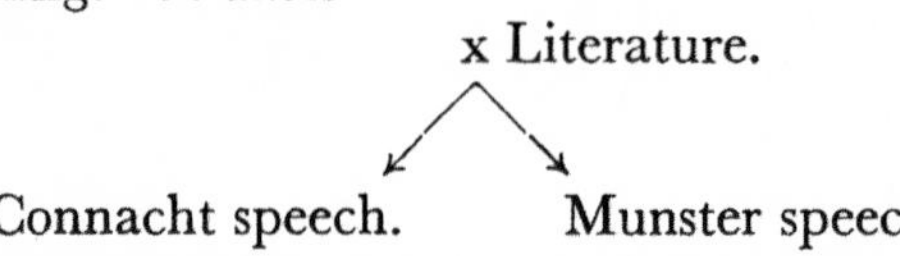

from the top of that triangle, and contains as much that is now exclusively C. as of what is exclusively M. If Dinneen had anything to say, or ever felt anything deeply, could think anything out, had any fire in his dim little blue-eyed soul, his stuff would be all we'd need : probably it would be demonstrably better than P. O'C's. It's a very great misfortune that he's a baby : did any cleric ever make literature, except as Bossuet in affairs of the métier ? Here again I think the Jews lead the world : their Cohens keep pawnshops and are Cohens only on the Sabbath : hence they're in touch with life, or were. You can't get Isaiah out of under a top hat or a clerical sloucher : Isaiah you may be sure lent money, or like St. Paul made beach tents for some Bournemouth. But this is wandering : I quite forget what I am to prove : " Quid erat demonstrandum " asked the boy at the end of the exam. paper : all I know is to Hell with O. G. B. and Munster, and up P. O'C. and the Republic and you and me.

You know of course that this (or even the other) side of

[1] " idiot."

idolatry I idolise B. : a noble-hearted gentleman and a gay scholar and an entirely scrumptious person if only he weren't a bloody Munster faction-fighter like every other dam Gael that ever lived. A lost race, Eamuino mio, a kind of pink-and-blue-faced monkey, God's grotesques and the devil's delight. To Hell with all Ireland and long may it live, the best little land at all, G. dam it. That is the uttermost wisdom, the Hegelian reconciliation of all the contraries, and I am your loving friend

S. M. K.

41

TO EDMUND CURTIS

"WANDERLEA,"
MOORDOWN,
BOURNEMOUTH [1925].

MY DEAR EAMONN,—Certainly you write a superb letter : grave fancy, pleasant cadence, powerful phrase, bright picture : Best (Dr. Dicky) used also : he and you I'd say the best I have known. I'm scrawling this late on Sunday night or Monday morning, to be sure not to let it interfere with to-morrow's work : there'll be nothing in it, therefore ; even if otherwise there could be. All you tell me of the house is sad gan auras,[1] but you'll be wise on that side of the thing : there are sorrows too big for me (so that very often still I long to be away for ever), but I'm far too big for those material things : they look up at me and I look down at them and they simply run shrieking to their dens. I believe that if I find myself in a year or so with no money to buy roof and table (as I may) I'll not care: Epictetus and Plotinus have at least taught me that. I'd suffer without books or music, but even that loss I think I could bear. This is not to suggest that you're not quite as wise a soul as I am : au contraire I recognise in your whole tone and tenour that, there too, you are one of Plutarch's men. * * * *

[1] Irish, "No doubt."

I have sent a small subscription to a new political thing—Col. Moore-Beislaoí-Milroy constitutional anti-free-state (as I understand from a scant notice in the *Independent*). It grieves me to see the old struggle afoot again ; but I can't bear the idea of an unchecked unmenaced Britonism so I jumps in waving my £1 note. God help us all : it was a foolish dream, but I have to dream it out for the rest of my life. If literature didn't exist we'd all I suppose be happy pigs with our feet and noses snug in the trough : I can't forget the poets or the dead. And I have the deepest, a kind of tender, feeling for Col. Moore who seems to me a very noble type, honest and gentle and determined and dreamful, all the things a good man must be. Nelly [1] gave me a pang also, a good soul : I wish I were half as good as so many we have known. I'm really sorry to find I can't go on : I'm as trachta tanarha [2] as a hunted hare : extraordinary how tired I get and I doing so little : better soon and thin than fat and never : I mean a thin screed on the spot better than a long and plummy letter a year too late. I yawn : I can no more : save to wish you well and to wish also that you with so fine a literary gift were writing real books (in one of two languages or in both) instead of judging on dead things : I suppose you make even the history readable : Dan Godfrey gave a prize for children's answering to papers he set on a course of musical lectures he gave in the winter here : one little girl wrote " Sir Dan told us that high class music gives us something to think about but I don't find it gives us anything to think about." I'm like that in history : I respect it and wish I knew a few yards of it : Irish Greek Roman and Med. and Mod. European : but alas I never could hold two facts of it clearly in my head : I praise it but I don't find it gives me anything to think about. Indeed nothing does but music and the eternal religious problem : I suppose I, still, think as hard and as determinedly perseveringly as

[1] Miss Nelly O'Brien. [2] Irish, " completely worn out."

any brain that ever turned the mill, and it all leads nowhere, leaves me the most ignorant, least convinced of human beings. I envy the ploughman who has a conviction and lives by it.

Twadddle, I do ; forgive—goodbye, good luck. Very good of you to have remembered me.

S. M. K.

42

To EDMUND CURTIS

"WANDERLEA,"
MOORDOWN,
BOURNEMOUTH [*Summer*, 1925].

DEAR YOUTH,—Many thanks : I find I can get most of those books from the admirable public library here : most grateful for the list : I ought even myself to have remembered the Bryce—God help me I even read it once and forgot every blessed and unblessed thing in it : I can't remember facts, only ideas, and them weakly because of their dam being-based-on-fax. I deserve great rewards for so continuously managing to escape detection; no one but myself dreams what an ass I am, my one intellectual title is that I am able to carry it off with a swagger and pass for an ordinarily reliable ratepayer.

Surely me son you mistake about " like Disraeli " : I may have said that as a rule I'd prefer such as Disraeli, but that must have been all on that head : what I have never been able to endewa is " *like Disraeli did* "—where *like* is not a conjunction or a past participle or something, but a preposition or an adverb or perhaps vice versa you know what I mean : *like* with a verb to me dams a man to hell : in fact is his hell : he doesn't have to go anywhere, he is in an unholy place ipso damo facto. I hold this abso-bloody-lutely, as a character in a novel said the tother day and I listning.

Probably the last novel I'll ever read : I find nothing half so stirring, now, as theology, and nothing half so pleasantly soothing as History—H. in the large—e.g. of Reformation, of Early Christian Church, of Rome—Greece I find too small and local, Munster waging war on Leinster, the Gresham Hotel on the Hammam.[1] I do think history the very foundation of all civilisation or rather all state-building, the natural dramatic humanly grippable introduction to nearly all the sciences, all that have to do with citizenship, touching as it does character and political economy and discovery and a hundred such things that you know better than I how to set forth. History for the big canvas of humanity, novels for the facts and types of daily life in our own times, poetry for the high style and the language of subtle emotion, that I think to be all that should be taught in schools until the "age of specialisation." The novel-reading school is my invention, but some day 'twill be discovered. Had I children it's so I'd educate 'em : history, novels, poetry and if they'd take it music : and of course the newspapers, i.e. modern history, modern sociology.

I'm leaving my lovely place—poverty hunting me. I'm going, after Jamesy's visit (in about 10 days for about 10) to unfurnisht rooms, very charming, where I'll boil my own shoes and shine my own egg. If you too can do these things perhaps you'll visit me on your way back from Austria : after Jamesy here I hope to have MacGreevy there, then you if you'll come. I'll feed you one cheap good meal out of doors ; the rest would be cold, self-made, sufficient, monastic : ham and pickles and tea sort of thing. Bournemouth is simply ravishing the last month : my own view would melt you to tears, does me.

S. M. K.

[1] Two Dublin hotels which faced each other across O'Connell Street.

43

To EDMUND CURTIS

"WILDS,"
GARFIELD ROAD,
ENSBURY, BOURNEMOUTH,
[*Autumn*, 1925].

D. C.—Lest you do things : once it gets definite—you to take house Blackrock [or] Bray [1]—I realise I couldn't live in Dublin, county or city. London or Bournemouth with 6 weeks in Ireland is the utmost.

I have had a brief all but fatal illness—a week of agony with horrible tho' comic symptoms, my nursing home (with shroud and all complete) actually dated—Monday the somethingth of something, October I think—and lo ye on the Monday I was, exhausted yes, but angelically cool and pink and painless. I had been the most frightening yellow green. Now I'm declared to be all right and quite supremely O.K. in about ten days.

MY DEAR YOUTH,—You made no blunder about AE—once you didn't get my letter you did nobly for me. Nor is it possible for me to be annoyed with AE—Good God, if I were editing a paper tho' it were only a paper of pins I'd expect to be the Gorrawmighty of the show and no one to pretend to contribute unless I liked him to do so. I couldn't quarrel with a man for not liking my writing stuff. I neither like nor respect it myself : to like my writing and wish for it is a most insolent flying in the teeth of my judgement, pure impudence.

Seen the Oldhams ? Margaret or Eithne Kelly ?

Flourish.

S. M. K.

Darrell [2] did well : little in his life so became him, poor

[1] Curtis had suggested that MacKenna should join him in taking a house near Dublin.

[2] Darrell Figgis, who committed suicide.

fellow : great gifts, I liked him well yet foresaw, much, this. I'm thinking of opening a shop to sell predictions. Twice I have secretly made the most astounding and lo they came true : I have never made a false one. Any man, and I to say of him you'll steal, you'll murder, you'll self-murder, he has got to watch out for he will. I add I know nothing against yourself.

44

To EDMUND CURTIS

"WILDS,"
GARFIELD ROAD,
ENSBURY, BOURNEMOUTH,
[*Autumn*, 1925].

D. E.—Your otherwise noble and Plutarchian character is marred I perceive by a pettifogging honesty. Who but you in the world would offer to send £2 for a forgotten borrowation. 'Tis what the Gaelic would say, The Rule of Borrowing is to Keep It. Keep it, so ; as a gift from the Lender who would I'm quite sure wish you to have what she liked to store with you.

Miss Patey [1] loves you duly but will not take you, or ever anyone at all not no more never : she obliged me that once ; not twice, not for gold or kisses. I struggled up from one disgusting illness into an illness not so plain-spoken and illbred but even more painful, muscular rheumatism ; 'tis nice to have a mentionable illness for drawingroom use, one fit for publication and portable through the mails. But it's deuced painful and besides foments nerve trouble so that for two days I couldn't see : all the world a mist and all its beauties missed ; the human face just a concurrent turnip, no distinctions you know. I don't feel a bit dead, and the doc who was has ceased to be worried, but I have prepared for my death

[1] MacKenna's landlady.

in many ways : the only thing that worries me is poor old Plotty who will go bocketty on 3½ legs when he should have 5. If I'm alive at Xmas I'll be delighted to see you —at the hotel, as you say—if not, why I don't care a dee.

Cordially,

my love to OB.[1] S. M. K.

Don't laugh : I re-open this coz why I suddenly relise (as Inez says) that you'll probably misconceive : shameful, yes, as the vile corpus is shameful, but not as the soul may be—my disease was the acute stage of a pee-ability that has intermittently haunted me for years, and I took to spouting blood from whence only innocent streams should flow and that in strict limit. It's more comic than shameful yet remains unquotable : there's a nice Greek name for it, something like I suppose urethrohaimatorrhea, but I'm not up to medical Greek at the best of times or any Greek most times (but that's a secret shared only by a few hundred of my most intimate friends and their circles of gossip and scandal).

What an infamy by the way that armistice smoke bomb business. I'll die a Republican, but I swear I think they ought all to be flogged first and shot afterwards and shat upon after that. I'm the only decent Republican I know, and I'm futile. If I were in Ireland I'd write to the papers (tho' they seldom used to print me) to protest against this murderous blackguardism, masquerading as holy freedom. Let you tell it abroad. Especially to Republicans if any.

Ask at any Dublin bookshop or of any classic friend for the *third* vol. clean and cheap of the Didot Greek Anthology. di ever tell you I got the Wetstein New Testament, noble vols, for £3 : some *amadán*[2] told another, I think yourself, they'd be £20.

Good Luck.

S. M. K.

[1] Osborn Bergin. [2] Irish, " fool."

45

To ROBERT MACKENNA

THE WILDS,
GARFIELD ROAD,
ENSBURY, BOURNEMOUTH,
[*about November* 3, 1925].

DEAR BOB,—To-day (about 3 Nov.) left this house to you-ward the little kegeen of books. I kept them long, hunting for 4 I remembered : two of those I found ; one, alas, and alas one of the most useful, I don't find, can't and won't. It was the first vol. of a 4-language Old Testament, Hebrew Latin Greek (Vulg. and Sept.) and German (Luther) ; you have only 2 out of the 3 [volumes]. The other missing volume was a little pocket New Testament in Hebrew, used for the perversion of the Jews, and a mighty good way of learning Hebrew. This I'll send if it turns up, but no more packets or gross vols : the Post Office has me hairs grey with their restrictions and fussifications. The books looked a dismal raggedy crew as they got into their places for their long journey : sort of Dr. Barnardo Boys going off to live a new life in a new land, and they not fresh and clean and elegant at all at all. One of them had no breeches to his bottom, and several or nearly all were otherwise disreputable : I'm hoping you'll get this warning before the kegín arrives, so that you'll not be disappointed.

I wonder what you thought of the Hibbert (if you don't know it) : it was less religious than usual : astonishing, the Broad article, very unsatisfactory to my mind, though I'm too lazy to attempt to reduce my objections to any attempt at demonstration—I mean even in my own mind. Try as I will I can't not believe in a God : I thought also that this had gone out of fashion. But the whole age is upset : in England everyone seems interested in religion, but the protestant Churches seem to be down and out, living only on music and stolen shreds of Roman Catholicism : even in Ireland Catholicism appears (as in other Catholic countries) to be at last dying dismally, but it's flourishing like old boots in England : sometimes I think it will just be a swap : all Catholics becoming Protestants (as a dignified form of bare One-Godism) and all Protestants becoming Catholics by the need of the Protestant mind for clear-cut systems, and also by reason of something slavish I can't help seeing in the English : the things the people here suffer, grumblingly but resignedly, astonish me ; things which in Ireland from time immemorial even to to-day have meant gun work.

Of course I don't know how much Hebrew you know, but from my own experience I say that to me Arnold's 1st. Book with key, supplemented by Bythner's Psalms (many transliterated in the Voice), makes the best kit for one either beginning or wishing to revive. I wish I had time to go on with this 'Brew. I liked it well : I like the very sounds of the words and the turn of the idiom. That old duchessy book, by the way, is a pure codd : there never wasn't no such duchess.

Good luck ; let me know when the keg arrives.

S. M. K.

46

To EDMUND CURTIS

WILDS,
GARFIELD ROAD,
ENSBURY, BOURNEMOUTH,
[*Spring*, 1926].

DEAR E.—Yes I got the book : stiff, much too stiff, the price but good to me to have : between the *Imitation*, O'Gallaher, and an occasional page of O'Conaire, I read my Irish 5 to 10 pp. nearly, all but, every day : God knows why I don't let the Irish die in me but I don't, can't : I always have—for one thing—the idea, which would make Bergin snort, of one day quite suddenly and gan fhios dom fhéin [1] blossoming out into a Irish Essayist. Anyhow this bee has built his nest in my bonnet and nil leiyeas agam air.[2] No fool like an old Gael.

I'm delighted you spoke of me to Dr. Purser—he's a dear good lad. Which reminds me what a dishonest old fellow that O'Gallaher was and, tho' I maintain writing a most admirably useful Irish, what an utter imbecile. In nearly the height of the heroic Penal days those Donegal peasants were all pouring hourly, screaming, into hell : " the very sacrament of penance instituted to save sinners " their devilish iniquity " turned into the poison of their souls " : I wonder all Donegal didn't go forth in procession to their Bishop and solemnly cut their throats in his presence : I suppose they didn't take him seriously : I take it he was mad : all good writers of Irish are.—28 out of all T. C. D. doesn't seem a huge Iresian congregation ?

The man of the house is ill, writhing and groaning in my front room, with sleepkilling rheumatisms—we're not able to test the squeejee : 'twill need retuning and the bellows recasing, as it's weak on the outpull : I haven't been able to take it to the orse piddle yet : been well but not very well. My book finisht all but to correct the last typesheets which the typist won't emit : I have engaged a menial to correct the proofs ; a job below my jenius, so I've already begun on the ouf volume, i.e. the last.

If you ever be on Grafton St. thank the Harris boy for me : I liked him well tho' I had some bitterness against him I forget what. I find I like all Jews and they invariably love me and run about picking up my pocket handkerchief. " Hear o Israel," I suppose. Poor dear Daniell, who's one of the mellowest wisdoms in Dublin and the affectionatest loyallest heart, is bitterly grieved over my apostasy ; writes me like a father, or more like a mother

[1] Irish, " unbeknownst to myself."

[2] Irish, " I have no cure for it.

and aunt ; it never occurs to a Catholic that one changes not of a lamentable devilry and deliberate malice but out of a stern conviction. And they'd all far rather you became a mere awful " free-thinker " than attached yourself to any full-blooded religion : I suppose, to do them justice, they know by experience that many unattached free-thinkers yell for the priest as soon as they get a pain in their belly, whereas if you're attached you're for ever beyond priest or prayer. But then, to do them an injustice, they never reflect that the intermediate space between the apostasy and the final pain of the belly was spent, presumably, in the contact, or on the fringes, of the Divine ; whereas the other dog has sat like a politician on the fence impartially spitting on all the spiritualities. All those who deplore a change of religious profession are thinking of religion not as a devotion but as a magic : it's obvious that to change implies a devotion, tho' of course there are many devout that need no change.

Well, youth, be young and gay—as I say to John, who likes the phrase and corrects me vigorously when I say " young and strong."

S. M. K.

47

To LIAM O'RINN

VINECOT,
WALLIS DOWN,
BOURNEMOUTH,
[*October* 15*th*, 1926].

MY DEAR LIAM,—I'm wondering will you ever forgive me. I've been in heaps of trouble and worry and affairs. My new vol. is out : I buried my mother a fortnight ago : I have been flat with lumbago : I have been trying to settle in a new house—a mud cottage really but very pretty—which I'm hoping you'll perhaps visit for a week in the Spring or Summer—in a new mud cottage which won't settle itself; and in 20001 other ways have been driven off my chump. I have written to no one at all save to some 600 (amongst them I hope and believe yourself) to say that I can't write but will. Yours is the first letter, if it turns out to be one—I'm cold and tired and old to-night—which I will have written in the dear knows how long. Yours to me unfortunately is for the moment mislaid—all my books and toys are still in a chaos: Plato glad to rest amid a pile of American detective magazines, and the A.D.M.'s trying to look as if they enjoyed this Highbrow Companionship. Of yours I remember for the moment—besides its friendliness and the pleasure it gave me—only that you asked for a book—whose title I forget but I know the one, an interleaved vol. giving Anglo-Saxon equivalents for Latin-root English words—and that you honoured me with a question as to style. The book is mislaid like the 1999 other sheep which are lost but will certainly one day come home carrying their tales behind 'em: you'll have it.

On the style question, I can't imagine anyone asking himself shall he Keatingise or O'Learyise or Liam O'R-ise: one must Liam O'R-ise: there's no other way: but as Plotty says, a Man is a Multitude: one must choose within that multitude the particular L. O'R. whose style is most suited to the subject matter. There's the L. O'R. who makes a joke with his babe, and the L' O'R. who beats his breast before his God, and the L. O'R. who talks betimes, perhaps with entire reverence perhaps with a touch of irony, to the great (or greater) ones of the earth; there is the *L. O'R. perhaps of grave public speaking.* And many more. Among all these one chooses first the one generally adapted to the subject of writing, and secondly those (as they suit) that play in and around this main one; they are to vary the L. O'R. of the chosen general style lest he become a solemn old bore if he's generally to be solemn, or a nauseatingly slangy jaunty cheapjacky buffoon if the general theme is light.

But all style must be modern : Plato was modern to Plato, the Bible to the prophets and narrators ; and the Lord Christ spoke the Aramaic of those cornfields and lakesides and of the fishermen by his lakes. Any " archaism " is to be spewed out of the mouth or the —— : a horror, a folly, all the stuff in which all the Jebbs " translate "—go vforraiye dia orainn [1]—Sophocles. The " Thou wottedst notedst " style is not forgiven in heaven or on earth, and no fires will purge it. If your stuff is high and fine, read a page of Ruskin every day before working : think in your own Irish in that mood of care and of rhythm, and you'll produce an Irish style worthy of your theme : if your matter is light, read a page of Shaw, *then* think your own Irish to your stuff ; you'll be clear and fresh. I knew a good writer of English, Vance Thompson, a dear good drunken brilliant friend of mine, who always read a half an hour in French before writing a page of English : he chose his French stuff in the general line not of his stuff but of the *mood* of the stuff. Perhaps even better than Ruskin (as above) would be a good page or two of Wordsworth, the Sonnets (sublime) or chunks from the *Prelude*—intoned ; aloud ; or rather softly voiced : that's a superb style, nearly all utterly simple and utterly grand. In general if I were able to write Irish, the only linguistic effort I'd make (supposing I had a rich vocabulary of familiar words—we must only very rarely use unfamiliar, and then only in a careful context to explain them), the only thing I'd do by way of burnishing my style would be to aim at all the terseness which the ordinary use of the language to-day would still leave clearly and quickly intelligible. * * * * Terseness and the avoidance of friction on the readers' minds, these and a general plan of drawing on the L. O'R. whose mood is most nearly that of the subject matter—that's to my mind the only planning one wants for the dressing of a book. I'd use old Irish authors, never as models of general style or for

[1] Irish, " God help us."

words, but *simply to suggest to me methods of phrasing which by analogy ought to be in* the language of to-day, which, that is, are sufficiently carried and explained by things still in the language : even here of course one must be careful : it's as bad to be too ancient in phrase-mould as in actual word ; or, not only too ancient, but too persistently terse and laboured ; the great rule is I suppose this : " with a dignity adequate to the subject and its mood to *avoid* (or minimise) *friction*"—H. Spencer's great contribution to the question of style.

I'm afraid there isn't much help in this, but 'tis the best a cold brain on a wet and fireless night provides. Perhaps, to be very practical, a good method would be to say to oneself " Here I'm to address a public meeting : I'm not to be too trivial, I'm not to be too pompous : I'm to be grave, yet not heavy or obscure, I'm to *hold* my audience in so far as it consists of people up to the level of this given theme."

You ought to get someone to buy the new Epictetus in the Loeb Library and to put it from the English into Irish : admirable stuff of a very Irish type to my mind. Long ago I hoped to put it into Irish myself from the Greek ; but alas my Irish was always below all the belows, the supreme joke of the universe and I toiling for it as few men for virtue ; had I but served my God half as faithfully as I served the Irish that left me with a *ton* in a *poll* [1] as the result. . . .

Dear Liam I continue to think of you with every tenderness.

S. M. K.

Have you any official address ? Permanent and easy ? I never can remember your road or gardens. Give me, always, something quite simple—Leinster House ?

[1] Irish, " backside in a bog-hole."

48

TO E. R. DEBENHAM

VINECOT,
WALLIS DOWN,
BOURNEMOUTH [*October*, 1926].

DEAR BOSS,—The A. E. article in the I. S.[1] may amuse and encourage you, as it did me both. A. E. is incapable, for any affection, of paltering with his standards of style ; but I suppose his amazing paeans are really for the glamour of the name Plots., deluding him into the belief that the stuff is in that high quality of English. One of the comicalities is that at least part of his second extract is a thing over which I sweated and wepted and cursed, and finally gave up to stand as it stands, saying to me " Lo : man is of few days and I can't give this bit the 10 or 15 years it requires to trim it properly for public promenading." Another little encouragement : Yeats, a friend tells me, came to London, glided into a bookshop and dreamily asked for the new Plotinus, began to read there and then, and read on and on till he'd finished (he has really a colossal brain, you know), and now is preaching Plotinus to all his train of attendant duchesses : he told my friend he meant to give the winter in Dublin to Plotinus. To catch two such fish—no cods—at one throw is wondrously bucking-up.

For the rest all is ill news : the brilliant promises and actual unreliability of the English have me in a mess : they make holes in my walls on a Tuesday, a window or door to follow on Wednesday : on the Wednesday-6-months there's still a hole and a mud heap, but divil a door or window. They promise that a week will see ~~Plotinus~~ my book-shelves ~~out~~ up, and 2 months pass and I'm still unable to pick out Plato from a nest of American detective magazines : pantry shelves are to be ; but, weeks after, I'm

[1] *Irish Statesman.*

still poking my tea with clarinets, unable to find on the non-existent shelves the tea spoons that aren't there. Worse still, I have had languors and ferocious headaches : progress there has been, but very slight. God help me, I'd be wishing I were dead, and only for fear of Plots. I think I would be : it scares me to think what he'll say to me if we ever meet.

I see that A. E. Taylor, of whom I spoke to you re Plots., is one of the collaborators in a new book with a title something like "Catholicism & Criticism," an Anglo-Catholic apologetic (or defining) work just issued. A superb brain and an immense knowledge : yet there are still people who think, or say, that it takes an ignorant and an imbecile to make a Christian. It's true this is no argument for Xtianness : it merely disposes of the notion that Xtianity is for children and savages : no argument for Xtianity, since Conan Doyle in his own sphere is certainly highly intelligent, and yet the things he believes —I never see his name now without loathing.

About three weeks ago I buried my mother : a certain considerable upset, tho', to be quite frank, an emotional indifference, blank : I'm amazed and horrified to see how little or nothing such a death has been, compared to the devastating effect of others lately that ought by all the canons to have been of much less grief : a wife I suppose should not count like a mother, still less aunts who are ever matter for comedy. This change, releasing me from a slight financial obligation, again complicates the Plotinus accounts : there's another matter too, just risen, which may make a difference : I begin to hope I'll finish, if I can work at all, without any subsidy. I'll talk of all this when we next meet : but do not send for me yet awhile : I'm quite unwell, quite lifeless and reeling, again. Nothing like as bad as I have been, but incompetent, muddled, nervous ; ferocious headaches, besides headaches not so ferocious but constant (which is worse I find). I wonder can you read this scrawl : I loathe bad writing myself: but I can't find or disinter my typer and so venture the scribble.

Cordially,

S. M. K.

49

To MRS. A. F. DODDS

VINECOT,
WALLIS DOWN,
BOURNEMOUTH,
[*December* 31*st*, 1926].

DEAR MRS. DODDS,—It was good indeed of you to think of me and send me those pleasant greetings and I far away so long. Heaven send, by the way, that I find your card before my death. I have no memory for addresses or for the place where I file things so carefully away, in what seems always at the time the ideally memorable place and always turns out to be the most indiscoverable: I think I shall venture 41 if I don't find the real thing, the document. I'm still moving, tho' I'm in this place since the summer: one chest of urgently needed books I did in a flash of genius put to itself: all the rest is the most discouraging huddle: a man needs at least one wife to keep him straight, and I have none. But a lovely place—I look actually on a sunset 40 miles off (I'm told 40: make it 30 if you like) from my verandah windows—on which the putty marks still blur the view. On the other side I look on my own ½ acre, desolate for January but still haunted by birds of all sorts and some others, the divils they even woke me at some preposterous hour in the morning to-day, the last of the year; a sunray that lied to them and told them 'twas Spring, and they praised God and set me blaspheming.

I like Bournemouth—a delightful 3 miles walk away—'tis a meditative place, all green quiet 3½ seconds at any spot from the hubbub, which doesn't hubble or bubble much at its hubblebubblest. Except of course in the summer when we decent residents hide in our gardens and damn the trippers—whose ways in sooth are noisy, being as they mostly come from the North of England whose accent is not soft like ours and whose eye not calm. The accent and eye here often remind me sadly of Ireland—even the face—and I mentally pack myself and go now : but I always wake up in Bournemouth, and here I imagine I shall die, perhaps never seeing Ireland again save from beyond the flaming walls—tho' indeed often I hope 'tis all rest, from all seeing and hearing and striving. I hasten to add that on the whole I don't believe 'tis so, but think we shall still be pegging on : I make my only, now, act of faith or rather of trust that somehow all is a good story with a happy ending, some celestial marriage bells for all of us somehow thro' all the failure and folly and farce—3 f's, I observe : I suppose a lot of our thinking, as we think it, is sheer verbality, alliterations and personifications and—sorry, I can't think of the last term of my trinity : I suppose because I have given up trinitising the divine and yell Allah is one and we're all of us his prophet. Aráméis,[1] all this : yes, but a thank offering if you can read it—no one can I find, but I daren't typewrite this to you and besides my Corona is wheel-less since I don't know how to stick the new wheel on and I have no man to show me.

A thousand good wishes and most cordial thanks,

S. M. K.

50

To MRS. A. F. DODDS

VINECOT, WALLIS DOWN,
BOURNEMOUTH,
[? *January* 1927].

DEAR MRS. DODDS,—I wouldn't inflict myself on you so soon again but for the zeal of the neophyte. I still feel

[1] Irish, " rubbish."

obliged when questioned to give my answer on my Unitarianism. MacRiovaig [1] my good friend was of course quite right: I am it and hope to live it and die in it and if necessary be damned for it: if it isn't sound, it ought to be, since 'tis the foundation of all religion and the entire substance of many religions, or systems of approach to the divine, from the time of Plato and Plotinus and before them and after them, and is the entire substance of Judaism, bar the *Torah*, and of Buddhism plus only, chez nous, a more obvious God. I want to convert no one to it who has already any deeply felt religion, however absurd that particular form may seem to me, tho' I do greatly wish that everyone that has no religious attachment but has the religious sense or feels the religious need would listen to its pure and simple tale: no fairy tales, I mean by that "simple": just one God, a just and fatherly. I miss, sickly, the gorgeousness and symbolical depths of the Roman Rite but could not, in intellect and in conscience, listen to its minute cocksureness or accept its practical tyranny or even respect its minor devotions, made so important. I greatly dislike, with all respect, any talk of "taking one's chance" and the like: religion, always very deep indeed with me, has never (in all my waverings and half certainties and rewaverings and now final satisfaction) has never been an insurance against peril in this world or another—but simply an intense desire after goodness in myself and in others, and also a craving, morbid at times, for something like union with the divine in whose personality—or some super-correspondent to personality—I have always believed. This union not at all in the sense of the mystic achievement: that doesn't tempt me one red cent's worth; but in the sense of being worthy, being high so to speak; in fact I don't know how to speak—just I suppose as certain heroic souls have wanted to serve their country, artists their art, hobby-imbeciles their imbecile hobby. I want also every-

[1] Thos. McGreevy.

one to be good, not under compulsion and not in any yellowfaced gloom, but by sheer delight in the beauty of goodness and with the clear understanding that part of goodness is being quite freely gay and using quite freely, quite enthusiastically, all the arts and devices of gaiety—beer for those who like it and abundance of jazz, and in fact everyone to his taste, only he she or it to keep one eye on the divine, not in fear or in frowning but in all good-timing.

I don't pretend of course to approfondir my religion here, only to utter my little credo like a little gengkleman, as I'd do at the stake if need were, crying "My children let yous all practise your little superstitions if they console you or keep you fairly decent : I cannot : but there's one God, and every man may be and should be his gay prophet."

You ask kindly after my work : 'tis my heartscald, would God it would be my death. 'Tis too hard and high for me : gin I but grind at it two hours, I get a headache like a slow furnace and reel like one that has quaffed off the winecup—I doubt will I ever finish it, tho' most unhappily I'm so situated, on many grave counts, that I have to keep pegging on, trying until my brain frys and I long to be quietly dead. Otherwise my life is happy here : I seem to have given you a false impression ; no grandeurs : but space and peace and freedom and delightful meditative walking, all round my mudcot (save where the villagers pile their dreadful heaps of dead salmon tins and broken glass and leaky kettles and Daily Mails—by choice just at my shrubbery gates).

Herewith, then my confession and thanks. Your card turned up—lovely : in all my half century of turning over pictures and pictures I never fell on that most decorative swell on his noble steed—the fresco of Simone Martini, if you remember your own bounties.

Most sincere good wishes,

S. M. K.

51

To W. K. MAGEE

[VINECOT,
April 5, 1927.]

DEAR BROTHER,—If you can't get your W. L.[1] in time for your soul's peace, I'll send it to you on the wind of the word for return at your convenience. I wish you would (and hope you will) do the *Odyssey* here. It has never been done: that bastard stuff of Lang and somebody is an abortion—may a bastard be an abortion?—and Butler's is irritating. I don't know about the Brook[2]; it didn't flow so wondrously to me; but all classics should be translated in absolutely up to date word and rhythm—the best of course, the most nobly appropriate—one of my dreams is to do a New Testament as true to the very nobly-appropriatest style of to-day as I suppose the Authorised was to its date. Such a thing as 20 years ago a man would do who had soaked in his Pater and Arnold and Ruskin and Meredith; and to-day—but I don't know modern authors. . . .

I'd love you to be sweating at the *Odyssey* and I reading after you: I've always browsed off and on there, and would like to know it line by line, word by word, before I'm called to Homer's bosom. Really very funny to think that if things are true they tell us, there really is an identifiable Homer beyond the Flammantia Moenia? I often wonder is there a real Plotinus and he lowering at me. Dreadful eternity for you and me, being chased by infuriated originals through the corridors of Heaven for all eternity "Let me at him, the dog; the ass; the —— ! !" A purely and merely original writer of course has the best of it: critics and translators will be the hunted.

This is not for a reply unless you need *The Enemy*. I find that others made the mistake[3]: yesterday I read an

[1] *The Enemy*, by Wyndham Lewis. [2] *The Brook Kerith?*

[3] Of confusing the two Wyndham Lewises.

introductory article in which W. L. castigates his namesake for not forsaking his name and for being confounded by idiots with the only real W. L. Only a week ago a man asked me how I managed to write my novels so far from the life I depicted so brilliantly—as if I *looked* like a novelist, and I with the innocent mug of a village parson and frequently seen on the roads patting a baby on the cheek with an oil can in one hand and a new kettle in the other and a parcel of butter and tea and sugar hanging by a string from my teeth. But some people have no imagination—any more than I have any teeth—a man wrenched mine out one day [and] charged me 11 guineas for a new set which I can't wear them and so have had practically to give up playing the clarinet which like the only true Church will not be ministered unto by any maimed person—or for some curious reason which I forget by the son of a butcher, yet Wolsey was a Cardinal and the son of a b.? I must have mixed my drinks.

Well—Goodbye,

S. M. K.

52

TO LIAM O'RINN

VINECOT,
WALLIS DOWN,
BOURNEMOUTH, *September* 1927.

MY DEAR LIAM,—I'm often wondering why we never have words now. A fat packet from Dublin to-day looked like your fist, but turned out to be a very different wad of stuff; it serves however to produce these few, probably, words which hope very much that you'll reply to them as of old. I have little to say, and am rather hoping that you will make the correspondence which it would cost me to lose. * * * *

I was astonished at the strength of Devalerism at the polls; what it really means I can't imagine; if it implies that the people are not wholly resigned to Britonism I can't but rejoice, tho' on hearing of the oath-taking, after all the blood and wreckage and bitterness, I registered the sentiment that we are for ever a race of brutes, dishonest in the bone and brain, unworthy of any place in the world of earnest truthful men. Had they taken the oath in the beginning I'd have felt it bitter but understandable and possibly pardonable ; but now. . . . Yet as I say, to know, or to have some plausible indication, that we are not for ever sunk and swept away from the ancient hopeful tradition is a mild joy.

I'd like to know what appears to you the probable issue of this curious state, first of the popular mind and secondly of the parties. Are the people, the huge Republican voting strength, really in earnest as against the Prince-of-Walesification of politics ? would they stand for more trouble—which I confess I don't want, but shrink from like a Quaker—or do they merely register an academic protest, a declaration of faith felt to entail no consequences ? And what can be expected to happen ? can any government be formed that can actually perform ?

Glad to hear also how you all get on, you and the whole little teileach [1] (however you spell it) ; also of the Language—does it move, does it linger, does it die ? I still read at her nearly daily ; an act of homage, academic, since three thousand to one I'll never hear her spoken again.

Well, God be with you, my dear Liam, now and for ever more.

S. M. K.

53

To EDMUND CURTIS

VINECOT, WALLIS DOWN,
BOURNEMOUTH, *September* 1927.

DEAR YOUTH,—This is a bare line to thank you ; yours was a relief ; I have nothing worth while to say, but I grieve when I feel my very few friends are slipping away

[1] Irish, " family."

and so I write desperately out of my dumbness. My brother[1] is getting much better; perhaps I'll soon be able to ask you to give me a week; if he finds he can't stand the cold he'll probably winter in warm islands with the idea of toning up for work again; he is strong of brain but feels unhappy unless up to the eyebrows in ores and machines and jungles with lions and boaconstrictors in them. His idea of a passable life is to roar, scientifically, at niggers from dawn to dusk then to eat a large dinner with good wine then to bed till the next dawn; of course men who do this sort of thing do a great deal of thinking as well; but that is incidental; they don't understand a life of which dreaming or thinking is the staple; they call it footling; which perhaps it is.

I told you I couldn't write: 'tis a cold night after a day of the most radiant sunshine, during which I felt it a sin to do a stroke of work and G. saved me from falling into that, but now I'm exhausted de varr mo[2] Virtue and hang it yes I will go to bed the only true Refuge of Christians and even Unit-Arians—but I waste my jests on you. You don't know the Litany of the Blessed Bergin[3] and don't know a Unit-Arian from a Cabáiste[4]; a man should become a Papist in order to understand my jokes of the First Period and then be converted to the only Truth to grasp them of the Second. To-morrow I MUST work; so I fear this is all you'll get for my penny, or 3 halfs, unless I find an idea for five lines between slices of Plotty, who goes on not producing himself tho', most days, I toil at him as better men at the guitar. I'm quite honest by the way and quite unconvertible on that point. I'll tremolo melodies on it till the day I die, fondle it, love honour but not obey it; I'll never again play the simplest piece written for it, unpieceful pieces they all are and I an old man with his soul to make. G. be w.y.

S. M. K.

[1] John MacKenna, a mining engineer, who had come home on sick leave from Africa.

[2] Irish, "by reason of my." [3] Prof. Osborn Bergin. [4] Irish, "cabbage."

54

To STEPHEN MCKENNA [1]

VINECOT,
WALLIS DOWN,
BOURNEMOUTH [*October* 1927].

DEAR STEPHEN MCKENNA,—It is written that I'm to be a nuisance to you. I don't quite know why—reluctant to appear to force myself upon you—I feel obliged to let you know that Mr. Aylmer Maude has a rod in pickle for you. Which rod should be pickled for me. AE in the Irish Statesman [2] mentioned a story about Tolstoi—seen en gentilhomme in his woods but opening his door much later en moujik—I wrote as "*M,*" saying this was so, that Michael Davitt and myself were the observers, the waiters at the door.[3] Mr. Maude challenged AE—who with my permission gave him my name, the unhappy name, cause of all our woe : Mr. M. now writes AE that he'll talk to you about it at the next committee meeting of the Authors' Society. A very odd thing—not relevant but very odd surely—is that Tolstoi told me on a second visit about two years after the massacre at the Winter Palace—that you had visited him not long before. It is written.

I think I'll write myself to Mr. Maude to clear the matter up—as regards your perfect innocence—but I'm ill and loathe controversy and perhaps will not find the courage.

Don't worry about this letter : the sole idea is to prepare you : probably you are friends anyhow and will laugh together, or swear together, at me. Of course the facts are as I gave them, be the explanation what it may be.

Long life in glory to you.

S. M. K.

[1] The novelist.

[2] October 1, 1927, under the pseudonym of "Y. O."

[3] See Memoir, p. 24.

I suppose at the back of my mind is the idea of apologising to you : I do really feel ashamed that you should, not once or twice, be whacked for my sins : the funniest fact about our nearness of name (I can't spell homonymity (?) with any certainty) is one you'll never know : that ought to tantalise the imagination of a novelist. The scene was Vienna. I think you ought to put us in a story.

55

From STEPHEN MCKENNA

HONEYS,
WALTHAM ST. LAWRENCE,
BERKSHIRE, 28*th October*, 1927.

MY DEAR STEPHEN MACKENNA,—I welcome these misunderstandings that bring me a letter from you, as I rejoice in the great underlying delusion that I am or could ever be capable of translating Plotinus. From the confusion that periodically arises, it is I who get the ha'pence, you the kicks. To rise, between novels, to philosophy is accounted to me for grace ; but to lapse from philosophy to novel-writing can be doing your reputation no good. I should like to think that there are material solaces and that you receive volumes of poetry from voracious novel-readers ; one such reached me this summer, inscribed with the name of " the brilliant translator of Plotinus."

The Tolstoi story is delicious ; and I hope devoutly that " AE " has not overdone his part of peace-maker. I should love to be rated by Aylmer Maude when—for once—my conscience is clear. I expect to be meeting him in ten days' time ; and, if he does not introduce the subject, I think I must.

I am very sorry to hear that you are ill ; but I should like to think that, as you are now in England, there was a chance of our meeting. I shall be spending my week-ends here and my mid-weeks in Lincoln's Inn until the New

Year, when I have to go south ; and it would give me very great pleasure if you said that you would have a meal with me sometime. Tantalizing as is the untold tale of Vienna, this rare exchange of letters is more tantalizing still.

Alas, you give me no details of my visit to Tolstoi ! If I knew what part I had played, I would play it again for Maude's benefit. I suppose you are a fluent Russian scholar ? Have you ever considered what a fortune awaits the man who will translate the worst English novels into that language ? They would all be translated back into English and their authors would win fame and wealth.

With every good wish,

I remain,

Most cordially yours,

STEPHEN MCKENNA

56

To STEPHEN MCKENNA

VINECOT,
WALLIS DOWN,
BOURNEMOUTH [*October* 29*th*, 1927].

A CHARA YIL,—Mr. Maude, for whom I (at a distance) have always had the hugest respect, appears now (by what AE tells me) to believe my story and simply says there must be some explanation of it, a thing I never denied. You'll probably get off fairly lightly. If he doesn't raise the matter, I'd be inclined to ask you not to. But of course please your soul.

I gather from your letter (dimly, for I'm immeasurably dull and uncertain and see most things, including Plotinus, through a glass darkly though I don't drink at all) that you didn't call on Tolstoi : this is the comble of this unending farce—a sort of 50 years Chinese Play—T. evidently mistook me for myself, and I mistook myself for you. We're quite too impossible to go into a book : that (really " delicious ") Vienna story, quite unprintable, unspeakable, soiling the soul in the very thought of it, a series of things that no decent person would even understand, alas it must die : and the other thing, quite drably decent but comic, that happened in Pembridge Gardens Bayswater—perhaps we'll meet in heaven or hell (I think you've cut Purgatory out of the scheme of your life ?) and tell all and laugh. Lincoln's Inn sounds nearer, but it really isn't : I value the genial kindness of you, but I'm far more likely to meet you in other and foreigner parts : I'm a nervous wreck, as I fear my handwriting shows (and bad luck to it I'm too nervous either to repair my broken down typewriter or to take it to be mended), and London seems to me far more awesome than Eternity and Infinity and Heaven and Hell. About these I sort of know my way : London is a howling wilderness full of wild beasts. It's true the first lot change their geography and flora and fauna : they used to be Roman Catholics, but they have become Unitarian (if you know what that means)—drabber but a good deal more plausibler like—still either way more friendlier than London. I invite you to a great colloguing in our next life : there there'll be no name mess : star differeth from star in glory : we'll be known only by our souls, our sins and our virtues, as they have toned into some fixed colour, quite distinguishing.

Alas I can't undertake to translate the worst novel of the English language into Russian : Irish if you like : my Russian was first-rate for drosky and beefsteak work but wisely stopped at those essentials. Jamesy Stephens and W. B. Yeats once hired a Frenchman to teach them French together : he began with a quarter of an hour on the rules for the agreement of past participles : Jamesy at last broke in " Excuse me, M. Dupont, what is meant by the agreement of the past participle ? ", and W. B. said " I was just going to ask you, Monnshure, what is a past participle ? " So was my Russian : I hired a teacher cum interpreter and learned many phrases from him, but when he began to talk to me about the 17th conjugation or declension or something I cashiered him and swaggered about very successfully on the phrases.

Your letter warms my heart—may you never grow cold.

S. M. K.

57

To STEPHEN MCKENNA

VINECOT,
WALLIS DOWN,
BOURNEMOUTH [*October* 31*st*, 1927].

MY DEAR ST. MCKENNA,—Many thanks : I take your implied permission and jab your letter into an envelope for AE. There's no doubt of T[olstoi]. I went with Michael Davitt, who knew T. well from former visits made at a time when T. and M. were both cracked over some mysterious " Single Tax " advocated by some " George " or other. Michael was grieved for days over the quick-change trick.

My good friend Clement Shorter once sent me a par. he had publisht in his weekly, joking about the two Stephens sons of Enna, and among other things accusing us of having both been in Russia. I'm glad to know you are not guilty, for behold a new fun :—on the second visit I was at first refused at the door, then by dint of sheer cheek and vulgar wontgoawayness saw a son (Lyoff I think) and learned from him that T. had *taken a violent dislike* to a Stephen MacKenna, a newspaper man, who had visited him a few months before : as my former visit had been much earlier, and as I reasoned that no one could possibly take a dislike to me, I concluded it was you. Of course I didn't betray you : simply persuaded the son that it must have been some low dog of a Chicago MacKenna ; and had a 2 or 3 hours triumphant talk with T. * * * *

I imagine you've done with the business for ever ; but for goodness sake don't, not never, betray my address :

the Tol. society is furious and they'd march in armies to conspuer me.

Entire good wishes.

S. M. K.

58

To W. K. MAGEE

VINECOT,
WALLIS DOWN,
BOURNEMOUTH [1927].

MY DEAR B. IN T.[1]—(1) The sumptuous kindness of your letter awes me. Dear brother, there is no such matter, I have no such gift. My one gift is that of loving solitude, and mellowing I think in it, and trying (most desperately though not without pleasure) to behave very sweetly and gaily and friendly when cast among the brethren.

(2) I have no mission : my one great conviction (now that Ireland is rolled away) is one so obvious that I can't communicate it : you are not heard after your second announcement that 2 hapnies make a penny or that one God makes one and is worth all a man's passionate attention. For all the rest I'm a blank, and merely play as prettily as may be with the ideas that others toss me.

(3) With very great disrespect, I too think Tolstoi a great man—though not, I admit, a great solutionist, since I don't think his ethic or whatever you'd call it works : therefore perhaps rather a great spirit, a great moodiness, than a great man. The very great disrespect is for the idea that a great man or a great spirit is necessarily or possibly above all fall, sure as the stars, swift as the sun in a bee line to the g.b.t.[2] There's a speck on everybody's vermine. You note how Maude, as I quoted to you,

[1] "Brother in Thucydides." MacKenna had invented a Society for the Study of Thucydides, of which he and Magee were joint presidents. There were no members.

[2] goal beyond time ?

thought he observed one on T.'s : he was born to be a faithful disciple : there are such men : I have always, with immeasurable tender love for the human thing, a good dash of the cynicism which goes with the O's and Macs : I'm not Roman enough to want my saints all saintly all the time, fleckless in life and miracle-working for 2000 years after death. Such is the rumness deeply infixed in the universe that not long ago, on another subject, I had to tell AE that he's too much of a Jesus-Xtian for me ; and now I must tell you that you are too much of a bloody papist. There is only one God, and not even Tolstoi is quite up to that one's quality.

(4) The sumptuous charity of you took in, I remember, not only my old-age loneliness but my health also. Youth, what does it matter ? Awkward no doubt to be quite alone if I fall gravely ill, as has threatened twice : but I'd simply shut the placeen and go off and be nursed by lovely ladies at a few guineas a week. As for the ill health that ends in death, that's the best health at all : I'm utterly tired, have been for years and years, and at any time would rejoice to hear the " Quick Marrrrch ! " The Quickest March I ever made would be in response to that sharp order. I consider myself quite a gay old bird, but this is my deepest desire—if it were (which it isn't) only for one thing, that an ill-healthy old age requires vast monies, and that my income is so small that when quite unable to work, or pretend, and draw pay, I'd have to eat quite literally dry bread in a self-tended mud cot. Which same mud cot has vastly improved itself since you saw it : everybody says it's the cutest little place at all—of course it's full of unfinisht corners, gimcrack makeshifts; but the loftier a man spiritually artistically etc. etc., the more fervently he'd say " 'tis a cute little place." I take immense pleasure in it, more than in books or music or virtue. From my veranda I look through glowing chrysanthemums over 30 miles of sunset and moonrise and star-beam and growing things, including children whose

smile is to me the sunniest and beamiest of all—and bless God for peace in the soul.

I praise you S. M. K.

59

To EDMUND CURTIS

VINECOT, WALLIS DOWN,
BOURNEMOUTH [*Autumn*, 1927].

DEAR YOUTH,—Thinking of you I was, intending to write and among other things praise you on Inspired Scribblings, when I get Paddy O'Sofokles.[1] A thousand thanks—just the very thing, my pet play in my pet language. At the first smack it looks a little literal, but I'll go over it line by line and probably learn from it some Irish and some Greek. May you live as long as Sof. and A. and all good men and things. Not that I want that for myself: nothing surprises me more in all the world than to realise, from much reading of theological and devotional works, how deeply the (apparently) vast majority want to live for ever. "Dogs, do you want to live for ever?" cried King Canute V (I think) when he led the fragments of the Garde Impériale against the Tartars at the Battle of Fontenoy. And the answer is We do, which astonies me for I don't: of course when I found myself nonexistent I might change my mind, but envisaging the matter coldly in life I simply don't know why people want to, any more'n I know why people want to have a yacht in the Mediterranean or 3 wives or revenge or the world's record for motoring on Drayton Beach. I'd swap all these things for a natural life without money worry to end peacefully like the sardine tins at the gate of my cot—did I tell you of the fine fat fragrant rubbish heap the neighbours are compiling at my entry? I'm in quarrel with Lord Wimborne whose land abuts on mine about it, trying to get him to allow me to put a paling to force the sardine

[1] A translation of Sophocles' *Antigone* into Irish by Father Patrick Browne.

tins a few yards further on. The oddest thing is that the people who do this nasty nuisance are really, all things considered, the decentest people I have ever had to do with : they simply don't see anything unpleasant in a dead sardine tin at my gate. They call me Mr. Kenny with the softest greeting, till I'm embarrassed at so much genuinely tender liking, and then they visit me with these tins. I read a society dame complaining that after a ball at her house she found 55 cigarette buts ground into her best carpet, 233 half buried in her flower pots, 496 crushed into little ledges under the Raphaels and Titians of her parlour, and so forth : 'tis the English way. I don't think our people live on tinned foods ? or we'd do the same I suppose. The whole moor is a mass of gorse and broken bottles (and pots, many of a quite improper nature) : I don't think we have such pots in Ireland ? Have you studied the pots of Ireland ? We're not sufficiently trained in observation and you'll meet many a man who'll tell you exactly why Julius Caesar marched against Clovis or why Pope John XXVIII assassinated (or procured the assassination of) the Emperor Theodosius and yet they don't know whether there are tin pots in the cabins of Drumdreary. But this doesn't matter much perhaps : the main thing is that I'm very thankful to you and hope on investigation to be equally ditto to Dr. Paddy. Did I ever tell you that I did myself a large chunk of this same play into pseudo-Irish ? *Antig.* and the *Dissertations* of Epictetus, I dabbled with them both, long and long. These things should be done—Plato too. I hope P. B. will go on and give us Euripides and all. A Gaelic Loeb would be a good little start for Irish. In that way we'd come in time perhaps to be able to translate even a book on wireless made simple or on motor cycles : those two I have, the man that would put them into Irish would be God.

J. Stephens comes to me for a week to-morrow.

Cordially thank you.

S. M. K.

60

TO E. R. DODDS

VINECOT, WALLIS DOWN,
BOURNEMOUTH [? *date*].

DEAR YOUTH AND MASTER,—I'm greatly touched by your kindness : alas I'm too poor and old and sick to travel. My one hope of getting my work finisht is to sit here like a Yogi man waiting on the divine breath : out of four workless, unwork-able, days there bees perhaps one on which I can work : to lose that were sin and shame : the four by the way don't represent won't-work days but no-can-produce days : I sit with splitting head agonising to tears and either I understand nothing or can reproduce nothing : after from 1 to 2 hours session I curse God and rise and play the guitar or clarinet or mandola or mandoline or mandocello or domra or squeejee and recover my native sweetness of universal love : so to bed, and next day and next may be the same : then comes *the* day and Plotinus pegs on an inch and is almighty pleased with himself (till there comes a killing Professor and nips him in the Bud, saying " dog : look at Fiddle and Fot.[1] See Greek Accidents p. 3,956 footnote "). Those Greek accidents that never happen to me ! I most cordially wish Greek accidents had never happened and that Greek were as Hittite and Irish dead and damned : then I'd be a thoroughly sweet-natured and happy man beating my domra and praising God like little Theokrite, or passing like Pippa, you know in the play—all's right with the world since Greek's in its hell. I hate Greek : I hate culchaw and all things but summer days and vast incomes and the thought of God. Plotinus, if some [one] else construed him for me (and I could skip the dull proofs that don't prove and don't matter if they did), would be my friend instead of my fiend. As it is, a thousand honest thanks to yourself and your good bean-a-tiye,[2] but you must see it can't be. Very cordially,

S. M. K.

[1] Liddell and Scott's *Greek Lexicon*. [2] Irish, " lady of the house."

61

To HENRY HALL

THE BRIDGES,
RINGWOOD,
HANTS, *Sept.* 1928.

MY DEAR MR. HALL,—Very good of you to write ; believe it or not, I rose this morning with the idea fixed and urgent that I must surely write and get your news. I had an awful night of perpetual dreaming broken only by sudden wakings ; this is to say that I'll not (in this letter) be bright or even cheerful, despite the wonderful weather. That last I love, but I find it makes little difference by side of the mental or moral state ; in rain and cold, suffering physically, I'm often gay, or as gay as I can ever be; in this long succession of glorious days I'm sad, sad to death. You alone are not responsible, though you are in it for some considerable part. Several things have gone wrong, within and without ; among others, my house [1] will not sell himself, and, above all, that *cursed old man of the sea sits heavy* and refuses to go into decent English ; this last is a disgrace, a dishonour, though as far as I can see the fault is not mine save in that, most innocently if arrogantly, I undertook a task far above my powers, linguistic and intellectual ; I doubt if there are agonies, this side crime or perhaps cancer, more cruel than that of literary and intellectual effort that will not work out to achievement. My case is made the worse in that there is no escape ; I am not permitted, as in the case of some short work that proves too hard, to chuck it and try something else, something in a lighter style or of another order, little essays or sweeping a street. I'm tied till death or publication.

But it is cruel to worry you—though why should it ?—with my griefs and grievances when, as your letter indicates, you are not feeling too glorious yourself? Probably

[1] Vinecot.

that is a mood ; *your punishment, richly deserved,* for leaving us where you had honour and affection and the sense—had you but looked rightly at things—that you were doing a work which according to your ideas was as useful as it certainly was successful. But this should strengthen you ; I understand that you worked up the Ringwood effects out of material as unpromising or nearly so as that you find to hand at Trowbridge, wherever that may be or think it is. As you get to know your new people your extraordinary power will come into play ; knowing you socially they'll come to hear you professionally (avocationally) and you'll build up another stronghold of heresy. It is certainly a pity that your mind has not, and as I guess never could have, the Papistic twist ; there's no doubt that a believing and energetic Roman priest has all the material of a very happy life, happy (noble, rather) I mean in the sense of feeling his work alive and effectual ; Romanism produces in those that do believe—how they can, Heaven knows—a warmth of practice that must rejoice the heart of an enthusiastic prophet. But, do you know, that fact—which I intend someday to ponder out as a very curious problem and body of implications—seems to me to annul the very idea of organised religion ; if absurdities and inhuman grovellings produce the very most effective organisation, communities, individuals, then the religious idea is condemned—except of course as a purely personal thing, varying from man to man and from day to day in any one man.

I'm myself, in the midst of my gloom, working out a living religion for my own strengthening ; I told you that your departure was having that effect ; *I have not been to the Chapel since you left and scarcely expect to go again.* It took all your spiritual power—and, allow me, personal charm—to bring me to swallow the too minute and dictatorial prayers and the slushy-wushy sloppy-poppy hymns ; with an illiterate uninspired vulgarian in the pulpit there's every holy and wise reason to not go. Even with a good man aloft I probably would not go; I have to make my own religion now ; it will be a religion of waiting and preparation, of the best action I can conceive, lighted by the earnestest meditation : I cannot believe in a Godless world, but neither am I in a hurry to believe that God has any particular need of me or care for me or desire for my interests or even for my good and assistance ; the prayers in which we tell G. what he is to do for the sick and the evil and the Kings and Cabinets and the antiGamblingers and the Anti-Wine-and-Whiskeyers and all that sort of thing are to me revolting—silly and blasphemous, *an offence against the mystery of the kosmos and the majesty of God.* I believe I shall join Dean Inge, though he hates my sacred nation and spits upon my Irish gaberdine, in a kind of Neoplatonism-cum-Quakerism with of course a dash of Buddhism and a jolly humour from Epictetus ; if you like I'll initiate you for a small fee, and ordain you as the first missionary of the Faith ; I want to find a good long Greek term that would mean Waiterism—I must really learn a little Greek—and teach people under that slogan to—I really think the derided maxim or nickname preaches a great truth—to make the very " best of both worlds," to live with self-controlled gaiety and service here, tasting in innocence the best of this world but always ready to cry Adsum to a clear call from God. I suppose an enemy would say I have here simply the old Quietism ; I hate these easy namings ; but if it prove so, what harm? We are all too cocksure in face of the mystery, too ready to impose our ideas upon God and tell him to watch out and get busy our way. The difficulty would be to induce the people to come to me with the essential halfcrowns to hear every Sunday that they have nothing to do ; any suggestion against this difficulty will be welcome.

As regards Trowbridge, if it is, I think I must practise my Waiterism for the moment ; I'll hope to come when I'm feeling less depressed and less depressing and also can escape without fear of missing a sell of my house ; you have to catch your man and get him to sign before he repents of his folly; here Waiterism breaks down—except of course for the misguided buyer. In a fortnight the man now nibbling will decide himself; if against me, then I put the thing up to auction and at any loss cease to be a landowner of the County of Dorset.

Good fortune go with you now and always :—

S. M. K.

62

To HENRY HALL

THE BRIDGES,
RINGWOOD,
HANTS [*Autumn,*] 1928.

A CHARA YIL AND O BELTISTE,[1]—It was a sort of sad pleasure to hear from Mrs. Nunn that you had spoken of me and of my visit to Troughbridge as something to be hoped as it were a good. Alas, youth, this world and its hopes are as Plotinus reveals one huge codd. There is only one good, and that is not to be bought with money or held when caught. I cannot entroughbridge myself; if I said I would, the Grey Eternal Ironies ogled each other, more shame to them, and to Mr. Hardy. * * * * I'm obliged to go into retreat and am slowly letting my friends know it; Plotinus sticks; marching a little of late, his very movement makes him realise that he sticks; he is ashamed; also rude people are poking him up from behind: he is ashamed: therefore he has decided to rise early (at 8 no less) every morning, work all day and couch himself early like the other dickybirds till he'll be in fine form for the next day; unless for Christmas week, say your coming (promised) or Curtis's, he'll keep to this so help him the Powers till he's done brown. He finds also that he has an enormous amount of reading to do, rereading all the commentaries as if he had never opened

[1] Irish and Greek, " My dear Friend and worthy Sir."

one of them before, in the hope of arriving at some dim knowledge of what the he thinks he means. Hence, in view of the little energy of the man, no alarums and especially no excursions ; the eye glued on the One : that's the ticket. He is quite decided that this is the only thing to do, though it cost him all his friends and all his joy and all his health and all his life ; slow to make up his mind, he's the very devil when he does. If he ever publishes himself he'll maybe kick up his old legs a bit ; till then, nixie.

Our reporter found you looking fairly well and fairly pleasantly established ; so much to the good ; perhaps you'll get the habit of the trough into which you flung yourself, no man wishing it but the devil possessing you. In any case you are of a quality to do superb work in the thing in which you believe, the thing in which by the way I no longer believe even with the poor little spark of belief I half had. I'm definitely out of it ; I begin to think that all organised religions are the death of religion ; to me it seems that one is hypnotising oneself against the first act of religion, which is thinking on the mystery of life and on the mystery that may (of course in one sense must) be behind it ; I think (reserving to myself the right to rethink to-morrow, though the conviction for the present grows unhesitatingly) I think it immoral to go myself or to encourage others to go where Prayers and Hymns and Liturgies and all the environment announce and enforce a certainty which cannot be truly founded. Even if all were as Papist Lutheran or Unitarian would say, do say, I think that the saying is immoral for us, since we cannot know that all is so or anything so ; once more I'm a Waiter with no one to wait on and no meats to present (and no tips to receive). I detect in myself also, a thing I'd almost apologise for uttering to you, a growing hate for the very name of the founder (?) of the religions of the western present ; I think he or the thing that gathered round him has been a misfortune almost from the beginning ; the good associated with that movement would I think have grown (did I think grow) out of the growing or changing temperament of humanity ; the evil it has done in checking thought, setting rigid standards to morals and to extra-moral thinking, creating evil passions masquerading as obedience to the Revealed Will of God, a hundred such things—this evil has far more than made up for any good the system contained or could impart.

I'm become, re-become, a sceptic : with however a deepened spiritual sense, more of a Listener, a deeper sense of the possibilities of something stirring, emerging, from There Back-of-things. You had something, not a little, to do with this ; I deeply respect your sense of the values of these things, while your statement of them, (however, as they certainly are, however finely, I mean delicately, unbrutally expressed) your statement of them no longer would help me, however it might, would certainly, move me. That moving is the mischief ; I don't think we have any of us, after childhood or babyhood, any right to allow ourselves to be infected with certainties which tend inevitably to become rooted, to the utter repelling of any new light ; the new light, even if it were objectively spurious, would always be subjectively the best, the guide ; if the Power behind gives us no light or a spurious light, that is only a part of the general mystery ; that Power certainly has done so or let things be so done in the matter of physics, social systems, religions ; hence the output of books, all dead failures to my mind, seeking to answer in the Christian sense the question Was the Lord Christ A Failure. Quite obviously, incontrovertibly, it has not yet been meant that all men of goodwill should hold any one religion, even any one sense of what is right and what wrong. I forget where I read the other day—perhaps in an old *Hibbert*—that there is still a religion wherein it is grossly immoral (as lowering the standard of manly courage etc.) to marry a girl to a youth who cannot bring to the wedding ceremony the freshly bleeding head of a tribal enemy slain with his own honest hands ; you, I think, would not approve ?

Enough ; why this, Heaven knows ; 'tis only that I always had the habit of talking freely to you ; often I reproached myself therewith, kicked myself ; one hasn't much right to talk of things grave on which one has no intensely convinced and apparently-lasting-unchangeable views ; thus I never vote ; yet I prattle, which is perhaps still more deadly ; thus one is inconsistent and damnable.

The main thing is to explain why I don't alarum and excurse, and to wish you very well always, and to hope if any of us is alive to see you at Christmas.

Very cordially,

STEPHEN MACKENNA

63

To HENRY HALL

C/O JAMES STEPHENS,
EVERSLEIGH : QUEEN'S WALK,
KINGSBURY,
LONDON, N.W. [1929].

DEAR MAN,—Isn't it well I didn't what I almost did, go out to see you those last few days. I'd have got more kicks than ½d's. You frighten me when you tell me how you're working—remember what the Good Book says, " What profit shall a man get from his work : have ye not all eternity to work in ? " (*Hell* : 6.9.4-5). Also you frighten me when you tell of tears plashing over my departure : I guess I'm like the once notorious Mona Caird of whom it was written " Mona Caird for nobody and nobody cared for she." Plash, plash, let 'em splash ; I be d——d if I care a dash. Tisn't that I haven't deep admirations, deep regards, cordialest good wishes ; but I can't splash worth a cent. As for the London suburbs, there'll be a cow and a tree in mine : it will be very far out—probably about St. Albans. Where, given London busery, I'll be as near in time to big centres as I was in Ringwood to a little one. I found myself getting cranky at Ringwood ; too narrow : I began to hate everyone, from the day you took your hate to us all and your hat in your hand and your departure to your Trough. You ruined me. I'd have had my chapel transferred to a sunny hill facing to Christchurch had you loved us still.

As soon as I have a permanent address I'll give you it—meantime as above (C/o Jamesy etc.) : should you come to L. you must let me know ; we must meet again. 'Tis from a room close to J. S. I'll be hunting for the new heaven and the new earth—on a bicycle.

There are things I really want to talk over with you—grave matters of my life.

Very cordially,

S. M. K.

64

To HENRY HALL

12, QUEEN'S WALK,
KINGSBURY,
LONDON N.W., *July* '29.

DEAR MR. HALL,—I've been hoping to hear that you may be coming to London : that I may find you a room near by, so that at least when your business is done I may see you of evenings and occasionally show you some of the lovely walks at these doors. I hope soon to hear that I have bought a houseen for myself, but that's no hindrance to your being my guest for a week here ; I'd probably not move in for a month. Let me know about this.

But here's the real matter :—

A girl (14-15) I'm interested in ; her parents want to send her out as a servant girl immediately if they find the job : I want her to have a chance in life ; I want to send her for *just one year* to a goodish school ; this both to give her another year's childhood with sports and irresponsibility, and in the hope that she may qualify for something more promising than the career of the pail and broom ; she's a bricklayer's daughter, which is a deadly crime. Now do you in your greater knowledge of the world and of this funny little country of yours know any way out? Any school that takes Pariahs, scum, ungilded Images of God? I'm willing to go—this between ourselves—in all—i.e. for schooling, boarding, sports, dressing etc.,—just £100 (I'd prefer less). I could of course get the child into a French or Belgian convent, even into an Irish : but I doubt if the parents or child would be willing, and I'd have scruples about the religious teaching ; besides, these foreign holes would not really prepare her for life in this little country (friendships, knowledge of chances etc.).

If there were a school, liberal, well-staffed, non-snob, that prepares for office work, for teaching, or for some one of a hundred callings of which I know nothing, I'd be glad to hear of it. Or would it, think you, be possible to unearth some charming, liberal-minded motherly lady who for that sum would sort of generally educate the child in her (the motherly old Dame's) house? If I were a really motherly old lady myself, I'd be inclined to accept such a chance of making an honest penny ; would I advertise in the Inquirer for such an old person? Have you an idea in your nut? I can't bear the thought of that little thing (Heaven forgive me for not sufficiently recognising the bricks on which she is based) being set to scrub at alien doors, at the age of 14 & ½, when all children should be playing the guitar, learning how many's twice two's four, and how you parley voo. Later if she prefers, or can no other, to scrub floors and babies and doorsteps, tray beeang, I'll have done my best and bit, and that's that. But this particular Bricklayerina seems to me to be quite unusually perceptive, sensitive, intelligent, charming—all commercial assets, and as I'm first and foremost a business man I can't see money's worth go unrealised. Think, consult, advise.

I bought Rhada-Krishnan's Indian Philosophy, first vol.; you'd be interested in it; it's rather over-written and distinctly propagandist, pro-Indian and damn-the-foolish-West, but is taken to be very sufficiently authoritative and is very fairly easy reading even to my muddy poor brain.

Hope you're keeping well and happy and holy and rich.

Of course I bind myself as yet to nothing: seriously enquiring, that's all for the moment! [1]

Cordially,

S. M. K.

65

TO MARGARET NUNN

ELDENE,
PRESTON ROAD,
NEAR HARROW [*New Year*, 1930].

MY DEAR PEGGY,—How are you all for this New Year? Especially your mother? I greatly hope to hear that she is better than when you were in London. I know you're all busy about this time, but in a few days you must make time to let me know. The merest scrawl will do, if you are capable of such a thing. I am. Though as a matter of fact I scrawled no single letter for Christmas or New year save, if 'tis a save, this alone. On Christmas Day I went to chapel like a good Christian or rather unitarian, ate a dinner of cold potatoes with two raw eggs and a pot of tea, and then went to bed and read detective stories out of a bundle of 3*dy* Yank Magazines till next morning, my own Stephen's day you know. The ran the ran, the king of all birrrrrrds, On St. Stephenses day he was caught in the furrrrrrze. This I'm afraid is a digression, though as

[1] It appears from a subsequent letter that the offer was eventually made —and declined. Cf. letter 70.

there was nothing afoot 'twere hard to digress. In fact I have nothing whatever to say ; I write only out of the beauty of my nature—to greet you and wish you every good thing, all the desire of your heart for the new year and hundreds of years to come. You on your side are expected to wish me the end of my woes, i.e. of that Frightful Old Man,[1] and that I may soon go to heaven and there learn at last to play the guitar, the only thing in the world worth doing and the sole legitimate justification for (or of?) its creation. I have myself given it up for ever and for the 500th time ; yesterday having no zest in work, a miracle but miracles do happen, and after all work is a very ambiguous or triguous term, I worked like a nigger at the old squeegee and produced cascades of lovely sounds, in other words the devil of a din, the whole day long, swearing every five minutes that this is the only life. I wonder will I ever be forgiven for having given up the noble squeegee ; had I but served it as faithfully as I served that abominable and lovely fraud of a guitar I'd be master of it now and be sure of a living outside of the pubs for my old age. They call it busking, I learned the other day ; " he isn't no busker," I overheard ; and asking what it meant—thinking I might have a new word for Plotty, who needs a lot of freshening to make him palatable like an aged egg—I was told it meant one what makes a living playing the concertina outside of the pubs and often they makes a pound of a saturday night ; it didn't seem to fit in Plotinus, at least not in the part I'm at now ; but it was something gained. Plotty haunts my mind or the place where that ought to be ; to-day, the newest of days, I read in a paper how Dickens went to see Wordsworth and being asked how he liked him said " Like him? I didn't ; DREADFUL OLD ASS " ; I leaped up at once saying " O yes ; Plotinus ; I must get on with that." It's true I'd say the same of Dickens ; never have I understood how anyone can read Dickens ; I think they don't

[1] Plotinus.

(how could they ?) ; what they do is read Dickens Calendars, the way good people know Shakespeare.

In general I think we all read too much, or pretend. I'm always glad to meet people who with fresh personality, some interest in life, have read nothing and thought the more ; you can watch the very beginnings of human life and thought in such people ; were I to begin life again I'd give literature the go-by utter, and plump for science and hard abstract thought ; all the pretty fancies of the literature people seem to me child's play without the grace of childishness ; facts, facts, and hard thinking on them ; there's nothing so nourishing or so pleasant as a fact. Literature seems to me nothing but a falsification of values, a pretty-pretty reading of life, even when it seeks the ugly ; 'tis always aiming at the pretty, and by a sick desire of novelty makes the ugly into the pretty. Veritably I believe man is here to saw wood and fry beefsteaks, thinking the while. Though why that should be I don't know ; can't conceive ; the beauty of the world with its fundamental absurdity, meaninglessness (dreadful word, dreadful language the English ?), this has me tortured.

An infinite lot of I in this tappery [1] ; forgive me ; it's only meant to draw you out that you may send me a line.

Cordialest good wishes for the New Year :—

S. M. K.

66

To E. R. DODDS

"ELDENE,"
PRESTON ROAD,
NEAR HARROW [*about January*, 1930].

DEAR AND DREADFUL CARA,[2]—When you have time (in a week or two) will you give me counsel, I in return promising not to follow it unless it pleases me ? Here the

[1] This letter is typed. [2] Irish, " Friend."

matter :—Do you think the famous Flight of the Alone to the Alone [1] is right ? To me it doesn't seem to be in the Greek or to have been in Pltns his mind (or his substitute for a mind). I think it should be the Flight (or Escape ?) of Solitary to (or towards) Solitary. *τί λέγεις* ;

Of course I baulk a biteen at the mere refusal of what has entered deeply into the romantic thought of the world (English, tho') ; do you think, even supposing I'm right in my S. to S., that that is a consideration to halt me ?

Again, supposing I'm right in objecting to the A. to the A., have you any better word to present me with than S. ?

To me, Solitary to Solitary has a longdrawn sigh in it quite as touching as the lo-lo-ness of the traditional.

Advise me like a good lad and may you live long in power and glory :—

[No signature.]

67

TO E. R. DEBENHAM

"ELDENE,"
PRESTON ROAD,
NEAR HARROW [*February*, 1930].

DEAR BOSS,—A line to announce the End. All mine is in now. The stuff—thanks of course in large part to Mr. Page—ought to be described as highly competent, almost unfailingly neat (not quite ; that would take several decades more), at times quite beautiful—as in most of the sublime last Tractate, sent in to-day (where however I have left two, I think, weaknesses that must wait to be tonicked up in proof). I'm going into retreat for a week, to have all the poor old teeth yanked out ; after that I'll perhaps invite you to invite me to a poached egg, or offer you one, two even if you're hungry.

I'd very much have liked to see Mrs. Debenham : I

[1] *φυγὴ μόνου πρὸς μόνον*, the last words of the *Enneads*.

often almost went ; always got afraid ; seems as if she couldn't want my nervous babble and she surrounded with friends. But I do hope she is strong or strengthening, able to see the little first signs of Spring in that lovely and loved garden of yours.

Mr. Page I understand is almost ready, his job has delayed him ; Plotinus is not the sort of Old Lad that can ever be hurried. Cordialest good wishes :—

S. M. K.

68

To E. R. DODDS

"ELDENE,"
PRESTON ROAD,
NEAR HARROW [*Spring*, 1930].

MY DEAR YOUTH AND MASTER,—Infinitely good of you : I'm honoured and touched : alas, it can't be. I went the other day to see a man and he sat me, friendly like, in a chair and without a word tore every bloody tooth out of my bloody jaw : since then I'm a bloody wound, swelling and yelling at every touch of wind. On Wednesday, precisely, he has invited me again—he left a bloody stump and is determined to get it tho' I die in the attempt. I'm a dreadful spectacle and a mass of pain and wish I were dead and in heaven playing the guitar where there's neither teething nor extracting of teeth. By Whitsuntide if I survive, perhaps you'll speak again—come and see me to a cold tongue and a bottle of wine—my little place, tho' still raw, faute d'argent, begins to look quite tolerable; the corner is pretty.

Your idea that I toil over Plotty ! There's an innocence about scholars ! I'm so happy to have shuffled him off on B.S.P.[1] that I never look at him : I have done the best that is in me, a bad best, and I don't mess with him any more. My ideal of reading Plotty one day, the sole object

[1] B. S. Page.

I had in translating, or trying to, him, will never be realised. I can bear him no longer and will with my will never hear his name again. It was all a gharstly blunder as well as a crime, my illicit connection with this tempter of youth and innocence : fortunately I'm no longer young or innocent and I have risen like—oh excuse. (I honour Plots.—note—but henceforth at a huge distance. Never think I don't : I do, so there.)

Don't quarrel with me for seeming to make little of your kindness in thinking of me : indeed I'm touched and will hope for your conversation in the better days to come.

Please offer all my good wishes to your Mother : later on I'll hope to call on her with permission.

So once more a thousand thanks—long life in luck to you.

S. M. K.

69

TO R. P. AUSTIN

ELDENE,
PRESTON ROAD,
NEAR HARROW [? 1930].

MY DEAR SIR,—Professor Dodds tells me of your impasse.[1] I hope to find and send you later some little aid : I found —— of London quite absurdly useless in my attempts to get Mod. Greek, so too the —— of Paris. This is negative : positive is that a Greek Consul or even a Greek tobacconist would generally be delighted to help : there must be both at Birmingham ? A Greek priest is good : all Greeks are friendly kindly patriotic and boosty by nature, i.e. they like to boost their land before the stranger.

Here too is a positive : I have a very small and raggedy collection of mixed modern Greek stuff—grammars, dictionaries, silly stories, poems, etc. : some 3 little shelves:

[1] I had mentioned to MacKenna that Austin (who was a complete stranger to him) wanted modern Greek books and found it impossible to procure any in England.

you can have them all if you care to come here any day or night and take them : how I don't know : you'd need a motor car ? Not that they're many, but that I'm 25 mins. from station. Some few of the books of course are quite good. (3 book parcels go with this.)

I should never want them again : I have suddenly but finally given up all Greek, Ancient, Modern and future, as a sin and a folly. I was going to offer the stuff to the Hellenic Society here, but would greatly prefer to make it over to one person who might conceivably browse now and again.

If there isn't a Greek Consul in Birmingham, a letter to the Greek Consulate in London would almost certainly bring you the names and addresses : so also, as a second resource, to

The Right Reverend the Archimandrite,
Greek Orthodox Church Presbytery,
Moscow Road,
London, W.

You may think I ought to do these things : alas I'm under a spell (or a permanence) of aboulie. I can only tell people what to do ; that I do, I ? *μὴ γένοιτο*.

If you should think the few volumes worth fetching give me one day's notice and arrive : Preston Road Station (Metro from Baker St.) and then march march towards *Kenton* till Eldene dawns on you at a far corner.

All good wishes.
S. M. K.

Of course whatever little stuff I send to-day or to-morrow is sent for keeps.

Please tell Sir Harry [2] I'll write to him very soon : I have a headache and no less than two things to do to-day, and can't for the moment thank him.

I have a few modern Greek gramophone records (songs and church music) which you could also have if you wished. . . .

[1] E. R. Dodds.

70

To MARGARET NUNN

ELDENE,
PRESTON ROAD,
NEAR HARROW, *August* 1930.

MY DEAR PEGGY,—I mean Miss Peggy or Miss Nunn. Bad news that your Mother is laid up again ; she certainly has been tried as in a fire—you too, of course. That unconquerable spirit is a superb asset to you both : I take it that the source is something in the order of religion, which if it brings evil brings also good. I haven't much myself, but do hold—as an article of faith not a demonstrated certainty—that there must be a purpose behind the universe and that that purpose, personal or not, is good. (I suppose were I forced to it by a logician I'd have to admit that " good plus purpose equals a Person," in other words that there is a good God with all entailed by that ; huge things are so entailed.) If I didn't on the whole believe in that good purpose covering us all, I'd certainly think it were better I had never stepped out of the blank, the warm nothingness, into consciousness with its struggles and pains : and I think I'd hold it far better that not only I but all human beings from Adams and Eves downward had there remained. In the hands of a good Purpose I suppose we are all secure, and I can well believe that the agonies of this life are nothing but a toothache or a childish punishment in the corner when considered as mere moments of discipline in our eternity. Of course too the idea that I'm eternal strikes me as funny. I can't quite take myself so seriously : perhaps it's optional or merited : in either case I'm out of it—I won't choose it and I'm not likely to have earned it. Some Buddhist sects, I believe, hold that not only have all human beings the Buddha Nature but that all *must* one day attain to Buddhahood ; but this is an awful and awesome teaching—you have to climb some 30,000,000 stairways, each a life. Better never to be born than to sit in glory after such a pilgrimage. Of course, it's wisdom to say If it must be, be it—in other words to grin and bear it, the largest and most broadcast grin one can pull off (or put on)—and again of course all is really covered by the assumption of the good Purpose, and if one starts each of one's 30 million lives quite fresh and young and lovely their total is really just one life, just as if you add to a box its space and its height and its depth and the air in it and the sides that make it and its prettiness and its usefulness and its age and origin and so on of the 30 million qualities you could find in it—I guarantee that, tho' I won't work the 30 million out here—why it's still one box. Starting fresh each time, the incidents of any two such times of mine are as remote from each other as the joy or sorrow of some Chinese babe is to me to-day. As a matter of fact I don't believe in any such reincarnation, or serial rebirth incarnate or otherwise : I neither believe nor disbelieve—with a stronger tendency to disbelieve. I pray only that if such things exist I may be pronounced a failure and let pass out into the nothingness, or the non-discriminated all, out of which I disastrously emerged.

I'm sort of rambling on, contradicting myself doubtless at every turn : these are matters so vague and vast that few can see their way among them—and those few don't agree and can't communicate their vision. It all comes then to my pet Waiterism, Margaret (?) Fuller's " I accept the Universe " : to which Carlyle snorted " God, she'd better."

What a pity you didn't come to London to a tête a tête lunch with me when my roses were softly blooming quite Spohrishly ; followed by hundreds of really sumptuous poppies they were : but alas the poppies have all popped out, the roses are few and ragged, weeds triumph, with a few big daisies and nasturchurums to egay the scene. The greenhouse is a browny yellow house, everything withered save a few ferns : I think I'll turn it into a mere sunny sitting room and let flowers go to ——. I did have an idea of fish, aquarium style of thing—but I s'pose they'd die on me too—probably turn into pebbles or something. Inside, the little house gets shapeful : in a few years it'll be almost fit to live in. If you hear of any music you want—songs or guitar or other—you'll let me know like a good little thing—I mean like a Q. Tol. Yg. Prsn.[1] I'm wondering will you be able to read a word of this : I was feeling too hot to type it and I know my handwriting gets awfuller and awfuller. I read to-day that someone said to Tennyson of one of T.'s poems, " That's an awfully fine stanza," and T. said, " Don't say awfully fine, say bloody fine." But you are wrong about your own : it's awfully clear—not to my mind exhibiting your character, sort of flightier : perhaps you never write save in your artistic moods : I'd like to see a letter of yours to a lawyer or a stockbroker or a collyflower man, to see do you show solider, solidsenser, in such hard writings. (I wonder do you mind being put under the microscope and your pretty wings stuck down with glue on a specimen card.)

Definitely I shall not be coming West : nothing can be done for my little friend [2] : she'll have to drift about in chance-got jobs—sometimes of course such things lead to a solid settlement. The child is very intelligent, but isn't encouraged to concentrate against her own indecision. I'm grieved over it all, for I did hope to put her on the way of a good livelihood. I have to accept the Universe and the English temperament. They are a shiftless lot.

I was wondering did you hear the Brahms songs on the wireless last week or the week before—a man—not very good, I thought. My wireless is very good indeed for English stations—the best set I have yet heard—but since the power changes were made I don't get France and Germany at all well, seldom free from London. If I find I can afford it I'll try next year for something that will cure that for me. I agree that the English stuff is better in most

[1] Quite tolerable young person. [2] See letter 64.

ways and most times but every now and then I read the announcement of French talks or German concerts that tempt me. I do listen most mornings to the French news from 8 to 8½, and that's good to keep my French simmering, but isn't otherwise interesting. My German, always poor, is I'm afraid gone beyond recall, save of course that if I need it (to steal from commentators or translators in matters Grecian) I can still do the trick perfectly well—with the Greek to help me.

Well, child, I wish you well and will always be glad of your news—tell me some day whether you can or can't read my fist : if you said no I'd always typewrite.

All joy to you,

S. M. K.

71

To MARGARET NUNN

ELDENE,
PRESTON ROAD,
NEAR HARROW, *October* 30*th*, [1930].

MY DEAR PEGGY,—In your desolation you're probably happier than you know just for having all that worry and strain and doubt over the selling up, and the problematic resettlement. On all these matters of course I have neither the information nor the standing to offer any opinion : I'd only suggest, deferentially, very, that while independence is both a duty and a right it may be achieved in various ways and sometimes, often, by stages which include a certain amount of in-independence, non-off-ones-own-batism, a period of living with others and watching how the world proposes to wag. Independence right out may mean only a dreadful loneliness and discouragement and an avoidance of the very openings which secure its permanent reality. I'd in your case jump into the arms of any one that was able and willing to give harbour and solace and some acceptable occupation : one is always free to do a bunk at the appropriate moment ; a large part of the craft of life—in which alas I'm no master but only a teacher—is to *fit oneself snug with a prepared get-away*. 'Nother words take the goods the gods provide, with an agreement between you and them that you chuck all up when you damn well like. A true friend accepts this, honouring the personality of the friend and not sulking over points of difference, I mean not exacting all sorts of eternities of fellowship. (I know what I mean, but I doubt whether you will—unless by an intuition.)

As regards the religious question, I'm handicapped by the fact that I myself have none—unless, as I do personally think, the sense of mystery is the essence of it, leading as it does to temporary beliefs and practices. Of course I think that anything in the nature of a definitely-adopted-as-for-life religion can never depend upon anything but a deep intellectual conviction : any other adhesion is merely cowardice—often very pardonable but never meritorious—or slovenliness, slothfulness—same remark.

I am assuming, in this very hasty and casual, chancy scrawl, the full recognition of the huge difference between morality and religion. I think it not merely legitimate but imperative to hesitate and waver over strictly religious matters—in fact I admire men, of whom I'm one, with a very different " religion " from Monday to Tuesday and from October to November and from 1930 to 1931 : but morality can't so easily or safely wait upon our moods. If by religion people, as often, mean really morality, an organised set of principles by which to guide living, I think a sort of shifting permanence is essential : a sort of permanence and powerfulness, because otherwise we are merely animals and cannot live with others in any mutually satisfactory way nor get for ourselves the true good of life and the world, but on the contrary wreck all peace and all true pleasure and all fine things for ourselves and others ; yet a sort of shiftingness because morality doesn't ask reasons but acts on facts, and facts are always changing.

When I say morality doesn't ask reasons I say a foolishness: it does, its essence is to do so; but they are not such reasons and reasonings as people give in the name of religion: morality's reasons are for me simply on the question—not of Who if anyone or What if anything made the world, if it was made, and what that Maker or Cause or Standby of the Universe requires us to do—but simply on the question what in the existing state of the things with which I now am to deal—the persons, their needs and states—what am I to do, or to refrain from, to be human and not animal. These things, the answers to these questions, must vary much from century to century, from A to B, from one order of mind or of wealth or of standing to another: I can't myself conceive a morality valid for 1000 years ago being valid, of necessity, to-day; and I think things immoral yesterday may well in a changed to-day be legitimate or praiseworthy or imperative, and again reprehensible in a changed to-morrow. I think as a matter of fact that one of the great immoralities of the world's history has been the effort to crystallise morals—as has been done by all the religions (or attempted I should say) and tried also by organised society everywhere. Of course morality requires a law: but it must be a very free law, like the laws of literature or of verse or of music: it must be a law I think—or think I think—not of sacrifice but of expedience and of expression: it is to be based on the idea of the humanness of man, i.e. that man is not solely or essentially an animal, can't contentedly be one, can't healthily be one, can't express his best and procure his firm and honourable happiness if he lives by grab and greed and cruelty and impulse uncontrolled as an animal mainly does. Tho' perhaps animals are seldom cruel: I think they seldom kill for sport or wound one another's little feelings as men do: I'm sure no nice animal does. But they do appear to live mainly by impulse and instinct: man must listen to these; that is a duty; but he has also a cold reasoning power: to express humanness and not animalness in his life, his act, he must bring cold reason to examine and modulate impulse and instinct—even to modulate or repress impulses and instincts that somehow seem to him good (this often : thus I always give, for the first time, to any beggar ; but this is I know immoral, a bad impulse, a bad instinct ; the virtuous thing (I'm quite serious) is to address the whining tramp in a few appropriate words about the dignity of labour and the existence of beds and bowls of gruel in casual wards), and so many, very many, instincts which have a spurious air of goodness.

Morality applies reason to facts, and it judges them in the light of existing humanity and of humanity as it may come to be. The only moral law I could permanently accept—the only " you must " at all—would be, is, that I must do that which expresses me not as animal but as man and helps others so to express themselves (or, since this is really too much to enforce, at least does not unnecessarily hinder others from so expressing themselves). A sacrifice for any other than this motive seems to me not a virtuous act but an immorality, as unnecessarily hindering the self-expression which is a human instinct and a part, a large one, of the movability, progressability, of the world.

I think that the supposedly moral hindering of the arts and pleasures, gaieties and whims of the world, has been a gross immorality : I think the forcible preaching of sacrifice and of asceticism (save as temporary means of ensuring a healthy control, a human thoughtfulness, over thought and act) has been a gross immorality, far grosser than most of the deeds which bear that name : those others are temporary, personal : the forced " Puritanisms " have been long-lasting and of huge scope over lives, thoughts, arts, all the movement and machinery of life. I admire with some hesitation people who on principle and permanently suppress themselves, but have a horror of those bent on forcibly reforming others, unless where the simple necessities of communal life make it, as often, regrettably unavoidable. In the last case it is simply matter of police ; and there, while I'd make the prison walls high and barbed and the prison bed very far from downy, I'd often give no moral blame whatever : the criminal may often be a reformer before his time and without the necessary public opinion to make him a " plausible proposition " and a moral agent.

I find I could scribble on, ineffectively, for several hours or years : but I haven't these at my disposal : in a word my own sense of morality is intuitional or in your word " based on imagination " : but I think it is an intuition that would appeal, at least as a valid minimum, to the vast majority of fairly decent humanity, say children, that we must act not as merely animal but as reflecting animals, and that on reflection we would always approve that which expressed a human self with no touch of harm to other selves and [led] to expression as far as possible of those other selves : Humanness plus the great principle of Ahimsa—harmlessness—that would be a very generally valid and generally acceptable guiding principle. Religion is either morality or it is just an interesting study like the science with which it is so amazingly set in opposition. "Let there be darkness," says I, and there was darkness.

A thousand good wishes—

S. M. K.

P.S. It is ridiculous to be important about my own religion, but conscience will not let me end, as I inadvertently did, leaving the notion that there is no basic religion in me : I have no lasting cot : I float on doubts : but I have just one plank that never leaves me. I know nothing for or against God the Creator, God the Revealer (direct evangelist of man) ; but I do hold to a something more, far higher than the actual human, something to which it is human to aspire and to seek to translate into life individual and communal ; this something translates itself to me best as the Holy Spirit, and if I ever pray it is never otherwise than in the *Veniat Sanctus Spiritus*—" May the Holy Spirit Come "—which seems for me not the law but the foundation of any law I could feel binding. With this H. S. I don't personally seek the mystic communion—whose reality I neither affirm nor deny—but the sense of its brooding in or over mankind is constant with me, and I have often quoted to myself as a spiritual Couéism, " Grieve not the Spirit." Waiterism or Expectationism or — or — or — is only the waiting upon this H. S., being always ready to hear and act should it speak or order. This is the only true religion : I invented it myself and can recommend it as a solid wearing article, always suitable, never remarkable, warm and washable and very cheap.

Always,

S. M. K.

72

To MARGARET NUNN

ELDENE,
PRESTON ROAD,
NEAR HARROW [? *early in* 1931].

DEAR X.—Delightful to hear of you and of your forthcoming visit ; fix your day, writing or 'foning, and arrive : I still have that cold tongue and can of peaches—peaches to the peach you know. My garden is a norrible I saw, but I have four thingmabobs growing in bowls and not one of them threatens those insulting carrots : [1] also I have a new Lord Buddha or two. You can surely pass a pleasant afternoon looking at these wonderful things—even my new electric stoves have a melancholy interest : I bought them fervently, burned them joyfully, for the first time in my life was really warm, the way we'll be in

[1] MacKenna had alleged that whatever seeds he sowed turned into carrots. " My garden," he writes about this time to O'Rinn, " looks still like a pigsty with the pig dead—i.e. mud and nothing."

the next world, and began dimly to form a sort of dreamy drowsy half-thought that life might be worth living, when by an accident I learned my bill for exactly one month, i.e. £3 . 10 . 0—enough to keep an army warm on icebergs for several years. I have fallen back on coal, and this very minute have black hands from lighting a fire which won't. That I think is all the news : don't roar at me that 'tisn't exciting : the wise man excites himself over little things, failing the big, lest he get stupid and resigned and generally a nuisance. As J. S.[1] has said, you simply can't have corned beef and cabbage every day. He's flying last Saturday, so I suppose is flown, to Paris—for why so you suppose ? Because a Russian told him of a shop in Paris where music was (is and will be) to be sold, arranged from the 7-string Russian guitar for the Spanish and Ringwoodian 6-stringer : he has stax of guitarities that no one could ever play—even with all due respect yourself—and yet . . .

Lord deliver us from poets and from being poets. Which reminds me (I have forgotten that this letter is finisht) would you like me, if he's back with his Bolshy stuff, to have him here for you and that cold tongue and can of peaches ? He might play you something : for tone he's a jewel—a rambling meditativeness, a subtlety of summer breezes, a vision of a vague Heaven (the kind Heavens do be) ; also he sometimes talks. Did you know he has publisht a poem to me, "Theme and Variations" ?[2] He might read it to us and I blushing in the corner. (I would wear my red silk neckchiff to be sure of the blush, which is apt to come difficult at an age at which one has looked upon much and heard many things.) Let me know would you like this : he'll be back in a week * * * *

S. M. K.

[1] James Stephens. [2] *Strict Joy*, p. 25 ff.

73

To E. R. DODDS

ELDENE,
PRESTON ROAD,
NEAR HARROW [*January*, 1931].

DEAR YOUTH AND MASTER,—Very few things in my life gave me more pleasure or at any rate more of a certain trembling emotion than your letter of this frosty morning : I still tremble over it as I scribble. Such generosity is of classic quality—Roman . . . que sais-je. Only the other day I was telling Page that rereading my Plotty—with the queerest mixing or variations of disgust and admiration—I had found myself horror-stricken with the thought that I had never publicly given you an eighth of the thanks and acknowledgement due for your constant generous help over passages that utterly baffled me.[1] Over and over again I remembered agonies—often even tears, actual physical, globular, liquid tears : sometimes the planning of the Reasoned Exit [2] via Veronal or the Irish Sea—in places where Greek Latin French German all meant equally nothing to me and a word from you had clarified.

I shall never write my silly life,[3] but if I were to I'd say that : I'm ashamed (tho' it was not, strangely was not, present to me at the time) that I never said half enough in thanks to you. I have not seen Squire,[4] and unless some-one sends him to me (as people sometimes do, I don't know why, such things) I probably never will : I'm become of a torpor, an uninitiative that would be sublime if it were not simply stupid.

Yet I have rebegun on Plotty. Dr. Page has asked for it for Loeb : he wants apparently to publish it tel quel : this I have intimated delicately seems to me immoral : I

[1] Such help as I gave was in fact very fully acknowledged.

[2] Plotinus, *Ennead I.*, ix.

[3] I had suggested an autobiography.

[4] Squire's review in *The Observer* of the completed Plotinus.

propose to redo the whole thing : to undo some of my crimes under the heads of (1) Greek, (2) English, (3) Metaphysics—the Unholy Trinity of my diabolism. And I a good Unitarian, the only living Unitarian (5 people at the Sunday of Golders Green a highly posh suburb and most of them young girls of a religious eroticism I divine and the rest aged colonels and repentant Manufacturers of China Ware with a sprinkling among the five of old ladies of a bossy temperament several of whom have tried to pat me on the cheeks as a promising youth snatched or snatchable from the evil life of my compeers—such a disgusting set of imbeciles gathered under the divinest banner. . . .)

But I don't know will I be let go on : the Medici edition might suffer if Loeb came out with a less abominable mess-up : and the Noble Heart Patron to whom all is due (save my crimes) can't bear the thought that his Plotinus is one of the colossal frauds of the century or the millenium for which we should both be stripped and flogged and dungheaped—difficulties everywhere.

But not this but that—as we used to say in Irish—I was for weeks writing to you at the University nearly every morning and I in bed planning my day, to beg your London address that I might induce you to come see my little place—and never did the letter get written—next time you're in London won't you write and tell me you'll sup with me ? My little house is really getting quite pretty and snug and as I write I look over miles of snowy fields with real horses eating snow on them and ravens and seagulls aspiring to the One in great circles, fleeing from Matter πρὸς τὸ ἄνω.[1]

May the One bless you and keep you and feed you and fatten you.

S. M. K.

[1] "to the heights."

74

To E. R. DODDS

[*Eldene*,
January, 1931].

DEAR Y AND M,—Please let me have just one word, Yes or no—very sorry to trouble you—don't you agree with me that it'd be immoral to republish the thing as it stands ? All these Eminences make me ill : the work was useful since no one else would do it, but it must be-ristle with belunders : I see some myself : the E.'s don't take the trouble to compare one tract with the Greek or think of all the side-allusions and echoes I have missed. Myself I feel I'd be guilty of fraud in not doing a reasonable best in the way of revision : I'd much rather, too, rob a bank than consciously rob the millions of the Perfect Plotty they have a right to (I wish I knew how to rob a bank : the way my accounts stand you'd think they robbed me).

Just Yes or no : I don't think I'd do it even if you advised it, but I'd reconsider ; but I can't believe you'd advise deliberately putting forth damaged goods, stuff one can better by a year's work (the reprinting of the Medici thing seems to me O K : this is in quite another pussy-gory ?).

Forgive : cordially,

S. M. K.

75

To E. R. DODDS

ELDENE,
PRESTON ROAD,
NEAR HARROW [*January*, 1931].

MY DEAR YOUTH,—You're surely the generousest fellow. I have written declining the Loeb thing, suggesting that they pay for a proper text and honour me by using my version as the basis of one more correct.

I have not refused to allow a cheap edition of the Medici as it stands, but have urged, here too, a revision by some competent person removing the really howling among the howlers. I feel I ought never to have touched Plotinus, and am afraid of going into eternity with that sin on my soul. My excuse was that I couldn't read him in the Greek and there was no English or even Irish in which I could.

I shall hope to feed you out of my tincans some day soon.

Most courteous thanks for all your so long goodness and helpfulness.

S. M. K.

76

To LIAM O'RINN

ELDENE,
PRESTON ROAD,
NEAR HARROW [*May* 17*th*, 1931].

MY DEAR LIAM,—A grave scandal and me without writing all this time. But I have been down in the dumps—wherever them bes—and didn't find it in me to take up pen, lest also I inflict my dismalities on the young and gay. I read your book, the last Gaelic I think I'll read ever. I want to learn a little Greek before I die—which I would God would send * * * *

I have the greatest respect for anyone that writes anything out of his own stuaim,[1] and I unable to do aught but feebly retell some old Plotinus's story. I have by the way given up the old gentleman entirely: I began on an ordered book of selections, but found I'd have to re-work every page to meet my sick conscience, and I really couldn't bear that agony—so I lose a good deal of money and am now only hoping I'll disappear into the void before the last penny of my capital does so. I implore you to take the good of my experience and, at all costs at all

[1] Irish, "genius."

possible, make provision for yourself and your little lot against the time when you'll be too faded to write—unless of course your job entitles you to a retiring pension ; and even then there's the family to be thought of? I imagine that £2 a week would do wonders at your age in securing such a standby for the wearier years. Of course Marie and I had such a provision (laid up from my European earnings) but it all went in her 7-years illness and operations. Forgive this advising : 'tis the privilege of years to preach what one hasn't practised—as it is of babyhood to smile at the dotage.

I daresay you'll be over in London again this year? You know there's a key for you here. A week of book-hunting would freshen you up, and you could write a *Turus go London* [1] and make a penny?

I'm still dull and find nothing to write this sad but beautiful day—all green and grey and gloom, curious Japanesy colour effect, with awe on the birds who chirp faintly, asking " Is it the end of the world? what's on at all, at all? " A small boy playing in my greenhouse just said, " It's ghostly to-day, like sometimes you play on your guitar." A great compliment, by the way, because I never yet did play on my guitar but only with it—it's like virtue : I can never achieve it, and never cease to strive at it.

God be good to you.

Always most cordially,

S. M. K.

77

To MARGARET NUNN

[ELDENE]

Sunday, October [25], 1931.

X.—Just a line to thank you for your gracious visit and kind help. I hope you will make as good a guitarist as

[1] Irish, " Tour to London." O'Rinn had written such a book in Irish about Paris.

you are a sandwichist : I wish I hadn't been too cold and old to watch you make them : I'm afraid it will be door-steps when I have to make them myself—granite blocks or crums idle crums. Next time you come you must show me.

I hate to press you to come, but you know the sun and the roses and large incomes and vast mugs of tea without too much milk but plenty of shugar aren't more welcome than you : and that it's not only me but all, all blessing you when you will come and ——ing you when no.

S. M. K.

78

To LIAM O'RINN

ELDENE,
PRESTON ROAD,
NR. HARROW [*December* 1931].

MY DEAR LIAM,—You're certainly the forgivingest of humans, to write me that delightful letter while I go on being silent. But this very sheet proves that I'm not utterly damned or damnable ; so determined I not to be beaten in any virtue by the likes of you that I type, me that loathes it ; can't write failing my hands, torn, one of them and the best, in a motor (or pram [1]) accident—a fellow on a motorcycle that ran into me and threw himself, I sitting like a lord in my chair as he lay in the dust. I was pleased with this, charmed with myself for taking it so calmly, and delighted to realise that you may have many an accident and no great harm done ; in this case all that arrived was that the fellow got a spill, tore his clothes, lost a footrest for which he refused my offer to pay, and that I lost a bolt (jarred out of my mudguard) and found what was good compensation for the loss, that I have still nerve enough in moments of crisis. I took of course great care to go out the very next day for fear of

[1] The " pram " is MacKenna's motor tricycle.

fear ; it is all long ago now, some ten days, but the hand which he tore with his handlebars won't wholly heal : thus (every story has a moral you know) I'm proved very noble in tapping this to you ; every tap is pain and virtue and merit and proof of decency and an entirely holy thing.

As for your article it curiously touched, very well if you'll forgive me saying so, on a subject much in my thoughts : I have impeached the Divine on many points, but on none with more utter perplexity than that of dulness : the tragedy of life—its agonies, its vices, crimes—fill me with wonder, question : but the supreme mystery to me is just that strange dulness over human things : in a setting so splendid, so majestic, natural occurrences so awesome, that the total of life to almost the total of humans should be so petty, so no-whither, sordid houses, sordid streets, sordid cities, sordid days—this is the miracle, the production of these out of such power, such sublimity; how, why, the Sublimity planned, or permitted and therefore perpetrated, such a sordor, such a pitifulness, this meanest of pettinesses ; voilà de quoi il s'agit in my mind depuis longtemps. The saddest and mysteriousest of all is that the little humans seem to have no need of anything other ; they're happy nearly all in the beginning, and they're still unwondering towards the end. I thought of you as I drove, timidly, thro' the traffic of Ealing to-day—those bigger suburbs have for their shorter length a traffic as thick and nasty as that of Oxford Street—and saw an errand boy on a bike in front of me dodging in and out so gaily, so utterly happy in his skill and his ten shillings a week or so, his pals and his picture palace on payday, perhaps his girl in the offing, a couple of years off but dawning on him radiantly. Pleasant to see him so gay—that's a good in itself—but tragic that what's supposed to be an immortal soul born out of eternity for eternity should be gay over so little, satisfied, exultant even, over such nothings.

This is one of the things that give me my constant sense of the tragedy of being born woman ; the Jew daily prayer thanks God " that I was born a male " ; a woman's life so kitchened, and stewpanned, and cleanupish, seems the very negation of the splendour of the Creator ; one is baffled utterly by the thought of the Sublimity that planned the Sun and the Seasons and the calm beauty of grass and trees excogitating a form of being so futile so petty so sordid. You don't think I mean that woman is f.p.s. ? I mean that woman's way, enforced, of life is so, so utterly so, so unvaried unegayed, that even more than the equally dull male she seems to negate the idea of any plan producing at such cost so miserable an issue. Yet the dulness, futility, seems somehow too elaborate, too farfetched, to be chanceriz ; here's the mystery. AE has a splendid poem touching this : but his solution is of faith ; all is a masquerade of Gods ; but why we Gods should make such bloody fools of ourselves as to play this ugly game of makebelieve, or how the idea of the pettiness and ugliness came into being at all for us to entertain, approve, consent—that of course the faith cure doesn't explain.

Enough ; besides, my wounded paw cries and I'm letting my fire go out and am cold and tired and would build um up and take a book and bask. A thousand thanks and good wishes. You say nothing of Dante,[1] whether he finds Galway gall him or gay him. I'll never return to Ireland ; I may move from here ; unless I can make money I should : I think vaguely of setting,[2] or selling up, and settling perhaps in a workman's cottage, in Cornwall perhaps, where on what is left of my little means I could live in my simple fashion until I die naturally ; on the present scale of living, simple tho' it be, I'd be forced to die unnaturally in about 5 years, faute de quoi vivre.

[1] George Thomson.

[2] *i.e.* letting (a Middle English use which has survived in Ireland).

I have said nothing about your Irish talk : were one still interested in Irish that were a most interesting set of ideas. Also I am rapidly forgetting my German which was simply a tool of my trade ; I'm drifting into a marvellous ignorance, forgetting as well as refusing to learn.

Goodbye Youth,

All Xmases to you all. S. M. K.

79

To MARGARET NUNN

RESKADINNICK,
CAMBORNE,
CORNWALL.
Mid April or something.
[*April* 12*th*, 1932.]

x.—I'm unable, unequipped I mean, yet to write to anyone : workmen, huddled tables, impossibility of finding anything, still less of not losing it again (IT means the thing I didn't find).

Sheer shame and I thinking of your lovely letter drives me to write and tell you I can't. But THAT I WILL, sooner or later. Only one thing occurs to me, to my flighty unestablished mind.

A :—That I have never succeeded like you and J. S.[1] in taking Yoga so seriously, as an approach to the divine ; in fact I don't think we ought : I agree with the word—not the meaning—of Plotty when he said It is for the Gods to come to me.[2] I can't think it desirable, even decent, in us to go hunting God : I'm a waiter : if He exists, in the ordinary sense, and wants me, He must yell for my services at his table. Not only the young but even the senilely decayed, in others words both X and SMK, are wasting their time and doing wrong in seeking to know any God, or be a God, or conciliate or serve a God ; it's

[1] James Stephens. [2] Porphyry, *Life of Plotinus*, c. 10.

our present business, short of a clear call, to have and give as good times as may be, to be I mean, and make others, as happy as we can in all ways which our true deep instincts or our sense of wisdom, good sense, approve, or in all ways which neither instinct nor judgement condemns. I remember fighting apparently the other side at Ringwood once ; but 'twas Apparently : 'twas against those that refuse to consider the fact—a fact like a tree, a cow and a guitar and a day and death and dogs and bread and butter—that there are sick souls whose activity seems to them a peril to the world or to their own sense of the right, people too whose deep instinct tells them rightly or wrongly that they should serve in that way a God whom they feel calling them. I add that I think in most cases this is the kind of people whose presence or absence doesn't matter a damn. They think they're seeking or serving God, and are seeking or serving their own uselessness. I think of Y. only as a mental discipline, the very queen of all ; one that certainly does give power ; a power that can be used as effectively to doing wrong as to doing right ; helps you keep your hair on when the plumber refuses to plumb, helps you to murder and rob an old rich man in a dark lane and get away with it, smiling ; many useful things like that.

II : But I forget what the IInd was ??????? Or did I only promise you ONE ? G. help me, I haven't the brain of a pig ; not a very good advertisement of his Yoga, says you. But you forget when you make those unkind remarks that I've been at it only about 40 years ; it hasn't had time to get its really fine work done ; come 20 years hence.

Just a memorandum, then, of me—
A thousand good wishes.

S. M. K.

P.S.—Please understand that all this is dead serious, my very finalest decision.

P.S.er.—I open this to add, ridiculously, that in this

very hasty tappery I omitted what is to me the all important thing—a thing to which all those notes of mine in the margins refer—that it is a proved and invaluable method of (*a*) realising what one really wants to be and do (for good or for bad, " bad " which is one's real good to one's own true mind) ; and of (*b*) slowly (and not so d—— slowly) making, shaping oneself to that wish, to the more permanent wish as against the temporary, the momentary whim.

I add, again, ridiculously,—as if my notions mattered, so indigest as they are !—that it's my personal belief and experience that by this concentration and divining oneself one will always arrive at an ideal standard far higher (or at least far nearer to the conventional approvals) than by a policy of drift : one drifts into evil, thinking almost always points towards good : very few of us really want to rob that rich fat old man in the dark lane and smile it off successfully : we all, or nearly all, want to see him guzzle turtle soup and us chew innocent crusts out of his dustbins.

80

TO MARGARET NUNN

RESKADINNICK,
CAMBORNE,
CORNWALL, 11 *May*, 1932.

X.—Your letter warmed my old heart : one phrase touched me all but, no lie, all but to tears ; I wonder would you guess which. Dreadfully sorry for all examinees ; the one great joy of senile decay is that no one dares examine one ; it's assumed that one is either too wise or too doddery, neither of which can ever pass anything ; suits me because I never did be able to remember anything when anyone wanted to know it. What's the capital of the World ? Only when the examiner had marked me black, and I'd gone forth in disgrace and tears, would the keyword DUBLIN enter my head. Besides the mere fact that someone would some day be hurling the question at me would prevent me getting the thing into the poor head or the place where the head ought to be. A kind of subconscious protectivity I s'pose the psychologists would call it. I can learn anything, except of course the guitar and the path to Heaven, so long as I needn't to ; make me and I'm d u n done.

So I hope you'll pass yours all right, and attain such grades and dignities and wealths that you can snap your pretty fingers at all fossilised professors and matrons and earnest people of all kinds and settle down to the wise good-timing which *I assure you* is the will of the Powers for you at your age. The older I grow (and somehow I can't help growing it every day) the more utterly pagan I become ; if it's pagan to believe in this world, this life, these (apparent) realities, leaving it to any powers there be to give that loud call they're very well able to if they have need of any one of us. Wisdom not virtue I pray for, or rather think for ; common sense to deal with ALL the facts or apparent facts as they appear. Smarrafak I equate Wisdom (or Common Sense) with Virtue, don't see that there is any Virtue whatever in laying down, especially for others, laws based upon supernatural things or appearances, when all we, the most of us, have to deal with, can deal with, is the natural order around us, pressing us from within and from without ; all I'd ever order upon young people, babes or adolescents or adults, is to seek out what they *really* wish permanently to be and, as you very wisely say, shape themselves to that ; the way to this is a desupernaturalised Yoga : as for the supernatural, it is by definition over nature, need not therefore be worried about while we are in nature, and is well able, being Over, to stick its finger in the pie and pull out any plum it has a mind to.

Nothing by the way was ever better said than yours about the pill and the cloggy sweet ; I hope you keep a

Stephen MacKenna at 60. From a photograph.

note book and write down such things when they come to you : you'd have a splendid book of aphorisms in a few score years ; for that's not an epigram (which always drives me off my chump with rage) but a THOUGHT, and, as you also say elsewhere, B l o o d y well stated.

I venture to think, thus I wander in mind over your plummy letter, that the cure for the sad machinery trouble is that we all take a hand ; that kind of work for say two hours a day would do us all good ; 'tis the 8-hourness of it that's vile, inhuman, dehumanising : two hours severe and if possible monotonously meditative work a day, with infinite leisure after, is the very ideal, provided always that people, all, be educated not in the capital of the world and the rivers of Persia and Peru but in the art and joy of thinking : 'nother words, Y O G A.

Cornwall : ah one'd have to be an artist to tell it. Wonderful. Rather horrible at first sight : immensely, almost oppressively beautiful very soon ; utterly beyond me to tell it ; only don't let anyone imagine it a Riviera ; its subtropicality is a joke : but I'd have to be very serious to write about Cornwall : I will say, however, that it suits me so well that I'm annoyed I ever didn't go thither straight from Ringwood : my own little place is enchanting ; everyone says too that young and lovely as I was when I arrived, I'm ten or twenty years younger and lovelier after these few months ; in fact I feel so, and admire myself in the glass every day, seeing new streaks of a rich brown on my plump cheeks and a new radiance of combined benevolence and youthfulness in my beaming lamps. I'm like that old thing in Yeats' play, " Did ye see an old withered hag limping down the road ? No, but I saw a fine young queen " : or words to that effect.

Which reminds me, what's that about the distinguished traitor of Plotinus ? I seldom read press notices, but that interests me because of a thing that happened : I was approached unofficially, Would I honour the official republican organ with articles and reviews upon current

Gaelic writing : I replied that I'd honour it like old boots, for love or money whichever they preferred, but felt in honour bound to point out that my double apostasy—from the only true church and the only decent country—would tend to discredit the republican organ, since even in Ireland there are low dogs, and some of them might use me as an offensive weapon against the whole movement : since then I heard nothing : could any echo of this have reached London ? But it seems like asking was there a stop press on the streets to announce how yesterday I cleaned my entire orchard of a noxious weed, ten feet high, which in justice I add was like all weeds exceedingly lovely only a good deal too much of him ; the orchard looks hideous thus bared, but it appears I have deserved well of the community and also will eat apples and pears otherwise lost in the dense undergrowth ; what the devil I'm to do with all the apples and pears I can't guess : feed them to the pigs ? But I don't keep pigs. To the wasps ? But I don't love them. Hopeless problem.

Apples, pears, children : that's the progression : NO, I have no children here ; the houseen is silent, my grief ; I have to content myself with smiling at the dots on the road : but it's a fact that Cornwall is not a smiling country ; the people *all* give you a grave greeting—generally How do you do ?—but seldom smile before the 10th year of the acquaintance. I have just two friends : to both I'm teaching the guitar, or rather teaching them how to teach themselves ; 2 brothers, both very dear to me, one totally uneducated, save that he has a genius for 2 things which are also very dear to me, the radio and motor machinery ; he has built me a superb wireless set and has taken my pram to pieces and made it *pull* like a team of twenty horses, so that I roll quite roycely up the Cornish hills. Surely this is to be very highly educated ? If I learned out of books matters as difficult I'd be counted a learned man ? Also he reads books that frighten me :

terrible books full of figgers and diagrams by the side of which Greek roots are as luscious as canned peaches; how is this not education? My grief that I live in a world where such absurd ideas reign and keep people back in honour and in riches. The other is a small boy, 14, but more like 40, very grave, very musical, frightening his mother and his big brother, who visibly adores him, by talk of the futility of life and the advantages and methods of suicide, a boy who at 13 took (and came out first in Cornwall) an examination supposed to be for youths of 15, and is withal very kindly, very affectionate, very stately in manner; nothing, you see, like the darling rogues of boys and girls I had the good fortune to gather around my senility at Eldene. Over these I grieve still; my sorrow that I ever knew them, the devils; I feel them from me every day, as the Irish says.

You, by the way, are the only one save the Dago Nobleman and one little rogue—one Peter whom you didn't meet I think—the only ones, then, that remember that I ever existed; the D. N. wrote me that he had been ill and had been unable to write to you, but had luxurified himself in Portugal back to something like health and written at last; goodness the admiration or affection he expressed: perhaps one should marry him and go live in Lisbon? One would have to become a Catholic though: he always quotes to me the collect of the day, "I hope you noticed the lovely words, so rhythmical, so dark blue, of to-day, *Lux mea Tu es, domine: in te spes mea semper.*" You'd have to learn Latin, of course; but there are worse things; Latin, Russian and Irish are the 3 great glories of the human race, achievements, splendours, stars; orchards; symphonies.

On which I stop (I don't know why) save to say that I'm touched to . . . I said it before, by your friendliness to poor old me, and that with all my heart I wish you infinite happiness and will hope for all the years to come to hear from you to my joy and my gain.

I have spoken of friends : I have one funny acquaintance : an old man as old as me, and he came to see me the other day and told me his griefs with these memorable words, " To think of all the affection and devotion I have given my wife, and now I'd like to bash her nose in—." Fortunately I didn't laugh then, tho' I do now.

S. M. K.

81

To MARGARET NUNN

RESKADINNICK,
CAMBORNE,
CORNWALL [*July 8th*, 1932].

x.—So you're started in life : long joy to you. It's best so : you'll touch the real thing, be introduced to yourself, know the world, fight the real fight. Better than a suburban coziness with all that stodgy kindliness. Alas the poor of this world are worse off than animals, shapelesser (so well I recognise the type in your drawing, which by the way strikes me as clever), iller, slavedrivener, respectabler, duller : as I grow mouldy and ouldy I become a non-statistical socialist or bolshevist or something like that. Non-statistical because I haven't the least idea of the figures, i.e. of the working of economic laws—or whether even there really do be such things. I pray for a smash in our time O Lord that, yet so as by chaos, there come, perchance, a better living for our brethren and sistern, now so ugly and sordidly plodding, who once were children and therefore gay and quick and sparkling, free in mind. Of course, I think part of the fault is with the poor themselves—save that that very themselves was made by an environment which they didn't make—they seem to me so dismally unrebellious and inadventurous : Camborne, e.g., is tragic with miners and farm labourers standing whole days on the main street, drawing of course on what I understand it's untrue to call the Dole : anyhow, just subsisting, but with much less dignity than a lost dog : " Hello, Bill : Seen Jim ? Going to keep fine ? Hullo, Jim : Seen Bill ? Going to rain ? ". I have been 40 miles on my pram and returning seen the same Jims and Bills on the same spot mumbling every 10 minutes the same sillinesses. A lost dog would at least snoop about for a hospitable dustbin, find an occasional find, rejoice, gleam at the eyes, wag a tail, fight with another dog, live. I hate, as you know, to talk about Ireland, but I remember when there was not a dole but a Poor Law Assistance or something and our people didn't take it, except the very old : the young went by the hundreds of thousands to far countries, to America, to Australia, and gradually brought out brothers and sisters, mothers and fathers and cousins and aunts.

I know the world is closed now ; but the same spirit would invent something else, perhaps a general massacre of the likes of me, idlers, fatted capitalists riding prams to the public peril ! In any case what happens isn't human —I spoke so to a young fellow on the dole, quite happy on 15/- a week : he repented, and to my great loss and grief has entered the police : did you know policemen are made out of ordinary human boys ? He now gets 55/6d. a week (and he still in training) : an idea, why not make all those Dolemen policemen at 55/6d. a week ? Perhaps it wouldn't work ?

I don't like your old man at all : he doesn't sound human. I don't know a thing with no paws and an imperial. He seems to be interesting ; but had you had the decency to come to Cornwall I would have learned up a few stories for your entertainment. I do know a few already—Puss in Boots, Little Red Ridinghood, Cinderella, and one about a bad boy whose mother told him not to play in the garden : this is rather sad for a while, coz he did go and play and fell in the stream and was drownded : but there is a bright bit : they fisht him out just in time to confess to a priest who came up in the very old Nick of time, and so he was absolved from this sin and died immediately and went to heaven or at least to purgatory where he'll be prepared by a few thousand years of burning to enter eternal bliss, there to live in bags of vaseline and vests of halo. You see you needn't go to pawless imperialistic gnomes for stories. I could several more tails unfold that would freeze your young blood —I forget the rest (see Shakespeare or Milton or someone).

I was angry when you said you wouldn't look for a job here : I was in difficulties over stringing a guitar—do you know what a guitar is ? a kind of banjo, played with a plectrum after from 20 to 200 years practice—stringing one of them and wishing for some mechanical sort of person to do it for me. I can't imagine why I should have to string my guitars—and besides I can't ; they never keep in tune for me. I perceive I'm trying to be funny and can't : it doesn't comport with my years ; but I'll never attain to dignity ; the mouldier I grow, the foolisher ; yet I'm direfully sober at heart, sombre ; my feeble little jokes are protective, as I believe the New Psychology has it : deep down there is a gnaw—please pronounce the g : one reason I hate the British Empire is because people say a dog " naws " a bone and even—go vfoiri dia orainn [1]—that the bowwows of an aged tree are, go vfoiri dia orainn—" narled ". Where's the twist, I ask ? " G-narled " : there is twistiness. O how I hate some things in this world. " A nat naws a nome ! " " A nomic utterance ! " " Gnomic " has a deepness, a darkness, a gloom—not a loom—as of eternity !

Well, as we were saying, deep down there does be a g-naw : what the devil is the whole thing faw ? Why I ? But such thoughts are not for youth and beauty and power: senile : save :—save that a wise youth and beauty and power keeps just a twinkle of that thought in the faroffness of its self, that there may be, with the gaiety and

[1] Irish, " God save us."

grace and fun, just a saving dash of serviceableness : the thought that the apparent futility of the world as it is given us calls for an activity of thought and of deed, towards making it a ween more tolerable to its masses—nothing sure beyond, therefore mould the actual to some meaning and beauty and gaiety. God forbid we " go about doing Good "—dreadful presumption, horrible tyranny—but I have made a great discovery which I pass on to you for nothing : it is loathsome to try to do good to any single person, but most noble and necessary to consider the Good of the Totality : the problem is to leave the individual free, untouched by all our meddlesome goodness, and yet to reshape human life. Think of that for only a few years (till you understand it more clearly than I do), and you'll see there is something in it—or perhaps isn't ! So, Good Luck and Great Success.

S. M. K.

Dear Peggy : I do wish you well.

S.

82

TO E. R. DODDS

RESKADINNICK,
CAMBORNE,
CORNWALL, *October*, 1932.

D Y AND M :—Sorry you have had all this trouble : very much obliged : of course your reply to Dr. Rouse was exactly as it should be ; I said much the same, save that I was probably severer on my own crimes against my own text.

Infinitely kind of you to think for me : but Maecenas (who owns the copyright, of course) is dead set on the Loebisation.[1] Also I'd have to re-write nearly every line —I mean quite apart from matters of Grecity or Plotin-

[1] Cf. letters 73-5.

icity : re-write the English, which revolts me : me being utterly unable to understand how anyone can read it without vomiting which I could never do myself thanks be to God, me having some idea of what neat English is, what I don't like myself, preferring Irish or Latin tho' not pretending to know either not quite through my own fault which an old blighter got hold of me in my youth and innocence and no one knows what I've been through drudging and toiling and no one to help me or at least very kind friends but still in the long run you have to do it all yourself and you not up to it at all. But thanks be all is over : I have put away the things of this darkness : I'm forgetting Greek and English : I play the concertina and touch the guitar and watch birds hophophopping and bobbobbobing about my placeen and wonder why the devil I'm in it or ever was.

Dear Youth and Master I'm always wondering, too, why I never fully realised, or sought to return, what I owed to you, right through all those agonised years—your unfailing, most generous, most valuable help.

Long may you live : your Proclus I wish him well ; I shall not know him : I read nothing now but Irish and French—English only for news of murders and what little light may dawn in me as to the dreadful social problem—à propos de which, were I young I'd go forth as a militant and bombous socialist or bolshevist or something of that sort, with (I add for silly conscience' sake) a very powerful nationalist dash. Man's world such a putrid horror set against such a non-human loveliness—slums and sordor against the rising and the setting of the sun and moon and spring and autumn—not forgetting the sadder but delicate beauty of the winter.

Well, God keep you, or at least all good be with you now and for ever amen.

S. M. K.

83

TO "A. E."

RESKADINNICK,
CAMBORNE,
CORNWALL [? 1932].

MY DEAR AE,—Impossible not to be moved, deeply, by your letter with its so flattering insistence [1]—to say nothing for the moment of the confidential manner of it and the lovely poem.

For the friendly insistence—'tis in vain. I gave you the dominant reason—that I'm unfit : not of that rank : not a creator, no imaginer, constructor, thinker ; as for style I'm so ashamed of my Plotinus that, quite tired of life, I'd yet wish to be 40 again to rewrite the whole thing —not from the point of view of accuracy (to the Greek or to the thought) but for the style : I began on a vol. of extracts—a Plotty made easy or Plums from Plotty sort of thing—and I writhed over the loathsome things I found I had done.

Thus I class myself doubly not of the rank. But there are other reasons which it didn't seem necessary to give in a sort of official screed. One : that all my life long I have hated publicity and all distinction : I'd not have signed Plotty had I had my way. Another : I wish well to English letters in Ireland and am proud of AE and JS and WB and Shaw and, more mildly, of Moore, and I'm glad to see a whack made at the ignobility and immorality of the Censorship ; but I don't wish to associate myself with an Irish Academy—by the way I loathe the name Academy (French Academy or that kept at the corner of the street by Miss Amelia Birchington ?)—with an I. A. that is mainly English. As I grow older and old, I vastly admire and greatly love the English, but more and more I don't want hoof of them or smell of them in

[1] "A. E." had written urging MacKenna to change his mind and accept nomination to the Irish Academy.

Ireland : I grow furiouser and furiouser at what they have done and will do. The only Irish Academy I'd belong to would be one that won't take me, couldn't : it'd be one entirely Irish, Gaelic, not political but simply unable to understand subordinating Ireland to England or Irish letters to English. I have little faith or hope, though a fervent charity, in the matter of reviving Irish—though if that be done I'd say Ireland would surely enrich the world—but I simply could'nt take part in an only " Academy " not concerned mainly about that : " When the last Pope says the last Mass without an acolyte ", you remember—so " When the last Gael says his last curse without anyone that understands ", then I'll join an English society. I wonder is it possible to make it plain that I'm not whacking at anyone, or even at the Academy: I bless the Academy ; mildly wish it well—simply can't be of it—something in me, something quite independent of reason (above reason or below it, what matter ?) simply won't.

Dear AE, I'm sorry if this seems censorious, seems to judge any of you, all my betters, all more useful far to Ireland : I see myself that I'm ridiculous : but then I'm Me, born to be so. Only this minute have I perceived quite how ridiculous : I gave you a reason in my first letter, and I started this later letter by saying that that reason was the dominant : now I perceive that my one fundamental reason was obscurely the motor cause and simply flung out the Rank idea (true in itself) as a God-nose-y cover for its nakedness. All which makes me more and more ridiculous and less and less Academisable. I'm in fact the least coherent being I have known in all my life : Ireland, as I under- or misunder-stand its rights and needs, is absolutely the one only enduring unification of my mind, except indeed—another example of my incoherence here—except the Hindu or Buddhist Ahimsa as the sole basis and law of morals. As long as I remember I have had no deep care for anything in all the world of mind and matter but those two things : even as a devout Catholic kid I felt Ahimsa, without naming it, as enveloping and transcending all the dogmas, lessons and practices; and so in all the rest, in all of this world, I cared for the dream of an Ireland free and expressive. I'm suddenly tired—not well—hope to write soon. A thousand kindnesses.

S. M. K.

84

To MARGARET NUNN

RESKADINNICK,
CAMBORNE,
CORNWALL [*April* 7, 1933].

MY DEAR X.—Ridiculous procedure : I'm answering your letter without having read it : I muddled the envelope, gladly recognised, away in my kitchen while teamaking, went back to bed to sip my tea, horribly forgetting the letter. In an hour, when the world's warm, I'll get up the courage, and myself, to recover it. The odd thing—not so odd in this rum and inexplicable world—is that of late I have been often thinking of you, wondering where you were living your young life, faring how, stepping up perhaps in your profession and dismissing your old friends. The world, rum and inexplicable, is full of such echoes from mind to mind : you were, without doubt, slowly elaborating your letter to me, and I got the whiff of it over the thousands of miles, or inches, that separate Midlands from Lands Ends.

I mocycled the other day to that same, the End of the Land—a lovely day, here at R. all gay and summery, bees and butterflies being and flying over the flowers ; there an awesome bleak desolation—they tell me that later in the season it turns its bleak horror into a comfortable grandeur, but I was glad to leave it and get into smug spring countryside. I often think I have here the smuggest warmest spot in the British Island (not -s'you, now : you're only one Island now, since we have shook you off as the dust from the soles of our brogues) : when I leave my fields in a shirt I do be pining on the road for an electrically warmed suit with a kettle of hot tea on the floor of the pram or tank of the mocycle : there bes a wind outside, not strong but stingy (no : stingsome, having a sting), and I never did like stingy winds. Often I return and plant my little place—shrubs and a few Woolworth seeds—in 50 years it'll look rich : already it is the prettiest little corner I ever inhabited. Had I not made a vow never, with the help of God, to earn another penny, I'd like to spend a few hundred pounds on titivating it : it could be made into a pocket edition of heaven. I have a field beyond my orchard which I'd like to plant entirely with Magnolias and make a tropical forest of it : do you know the Magnolia? At Falmouth there are scores—each 3 miles high and covered with flaming scarlet blossoms each the size of a cabbage or a small fat baby ; gorgeous the sight ; I think there should be a law making it a mortal sin, punishable by death, not to plant Magnolias. It's like the guitar—I hope to read about your guitarplaying when the world will be warm—not to plant Magnolias, not to play the Guitar, let no such thing be heard of.

I often wonder, talking of guitars, what you think of your Ramsay now.* * * * But that's a foolish moment : let's leave him to his conscience ; he had one once : and let's get back to serious and pleasant things : I'm going ahead like old boots with the guitar : yesterday, playing to the thrushes and blackbirds as evening fell mild and moony, seated at the table I have between my grianan [1] and orchard, I noticed with joy and pride that I have gotten up to page 35 of my tutor—pretty good going in only ten years. I can play 3 pieces, not of course by heart, one with 2 sharps and 3 notes at a whack (this however has a disconcerting flat in it which rather upsets one, but

[1] Irish, " sun-parlour."

in a few years I'll have mastered that and go on to fresh triumphs). Funny how the sounds of the guitar pierce my soul ; I could never give it up : I hope this is true of you too ? I often get good guitar on the wireless—Paris, Toulouse and once I heard from I dono where a guitar band (Argentine) whose velvety richness with passion and plaintiveness brought tears to my aged eyes : I often wish I lived in a civilised land where everyone plays the guitar from the cradle to the grave. Which reminds me, I know not why, that the other day I heard a thing I often dreamed of—and it was as good as my dream—violin with, don't scream, with harmonium. The double continuity made a perfect thing—the piano trotting under the continuous violin always enfuriated me : but indeed I loathe the piano : how much better the harps and clavichord : progress is often ruin. . . .

Two hours have passed, and I got up, and your letter—very gorgeous—I ought to have typed this to be in the fashion, but I don't love the typer, mine never did know how to spell tho' it has written 5 vols. of stuff full of big words. But I think everyone should type letters—almost no one but me writes a readable hand—just sticking a few illegible words in handwriting at the end to give the personal touch.

My dear Xy ; why not write to Dr. Bertwistle, Preston Rd., Nr. Harrow, asking him to let you know if he hears (he is sure to soon or late) of some desirable jobplace ? He is the kindliest of men ; he is an authority ; he likes you (who could fail to ?), you have experience, are in a jobplace, not simply pining for one : soon or late he'd fix you directly or indirectly. Is there no professional journal advertising " Wanted charming young lady to radiologicalize millionaires : with knowledge of guitar preferred " ? or " Charming young lady, with knowledge of guitar, immense experience in Radiologicality, desires meet diseased millionaire with no family and capable of making legal will " ? I saw in some paper the other day an advertisement which made me think of you : some nursing home asking for qualified Radiologist—probably in the " Irish Press ", tho'. You might, I'd think, easily —no, but actually—get a travelling job—aren't there ships with Radioists on them ? But I don't know anything —I ramble—I err—forgive my nonsense—only don't lose heart, you are very young and very charming and very intelligent and all will be splendid yet. Probably you will get fixed in some London hospital where you'd be able for many hours a week to see life, make friends, go to shows, hear music, feel not stranded but swimming.

You write wisely about disarmament and such things : seems to me quite hopeless : I was struck by a phrase wirelessly heard the other day, " this period of worldwide insanity " : but what is good is that while all the statesmen of all the world seem mad, the plain people of all the world go on getting day by day in every way saner and more sane. I greatly honour the plain people : the more I look into their minds and lives the more I honour them : their one fault is their tendency to make the best of things, instead of making things over for the best : their contentment or resignation is of the animal world—sheep being driven, where they should be wolves pouncing. But I do think they won't go to war again in our time, i.e. for the next 50 years. Probably the statesmen know this, even hope for this, and keep their silly Geneva business going as a help towards keeping this on as a living force—Geneva echoes thro' the world as a perpetual reminder that war is a mad horror ; its futile planning serves to focus the plain man's will. That is not clear ; but meditate it for a few months and you'll make it out—a thing I'm too lazy to do.

Listen, Excellence, I'm getting tired—being old—also the day has progressed, the sun is hot, tho' it is only 9¼ I see : I'm going to plant some fuchsias ; in other words I dry up, only imploring from the powers every joy to you, and not merely imploring but assuring you ; you have everything in your favour ; you'll have a happy career and be a gain to the world and a joy to your little self—this I swear—

S. M. K.

85

TO MARGARET NUNN

[RESKADINNICK, *April* 22, 1933.]

DEAR MISS X.—You write a good letter : it's almost friendly. I enclose one that came with yours and might interest you, only you must—m u s t—RETURN IT. Pity : I didn't know you had a low taste for harmoniums—I bought a beauty £15 'tother day and gave it away very soon to make room in my little place for a teapot and Buddha : you could have had it—but probably the carriage would be more than the cost.

I'd not " ask for a job " at all—I'd ask does he with all his large contacts " know of a job." But give all your qualifications (plus a little).

Why, my dear Miss Nunn, I'd be more than delighted if you ramshackled down here. Cornwall is really hideous, and full to the brim, and to the overrunning, of spots of a most rare loveliness. I'm not one of the last, but neither of the first : I'm within easy motoring reach of chops and steaks and slices and peelings of Heaven, and I'm pleasant where I am, looking over far fields and my own orchard, and having a lovely moon perched day and night just in the line of my pillowed head. Come in May, please, but come also when the magnolias I'm to plant in October will be grown and flaming, making a red road to hell of my placeen. I'm assured that they'll be in full glory of mass and height in only 50 years.

I notice a guilty silence re guitar : Miss Nunn, is it possible that . . . but I daren't write it : no, no, not never.

Space for meditation

. . . . . .

. . . . . .

x.—this isn't a letter : only a welcome—with huge delight at the prospect. I'll dig you up soon and send you an advt. book on Cornwall—hoping to confirm you : young people do be so fickle : they take up the guitar and drop it ; they propose Cornwall and shirk it ; they promise visits and then put their fingers to their nose and spread their thumbs—or whatever you do to express contempt—so long since I felt contempt for anyone that I forget the technique.

A blessing on you,

S. M. K.

86

To MARGARET NUNN

RESKADINNICK,
CAMBORNE,
CORNWALL, *Aug.* [11*th*] 1933.

DEAR MISS NUNN,—Dear Mr. MacKenna wishes to thank you for your again letter, your fidelity, and to assure you that he appreciates all and will write as soon as the gods give him back a pennyworth of brains and the same of energy. For the present the poor little old lad just drags about like a wounded worm, paying huge prices for villagers to clean his 3 months overgrown garden,[1] buy him butter and tea, and mail his very few letters for him. But worms will turn, and he hopes to before many years are over, and he to be young and lovely again, spinning down the roads and especially up them (since C. is all one uphill like a church steeple) and in general behaving young and silly, which is much better than the Yoga-stance of the nonce (what is a nonce ? How many nonces in a day ? in a week ? in a month ? in a year ?).

Dear Mr. M. K. wishes he'd hear of dear Miss Nunn getting her deserts—tho' he wouldn't like his own—and becoming rich and illustrious.

[1] He had just returned from a long illness in hospital.

He begs forgiveness and promises that as soon as strength and life return he'll write—for the moment, all correspondents must suspend sentence on him, striving to believe in his good faith and good wishes.

S. M. K.

87

To LIAM O'RINN

[RESKADINNICK] *August*, 1933.

D.L.—I'll hold back the Album till you return, full of wine and health and French and hopefulness and ideas, a pilgrim seeking strange strondes and ferne hollows couth in dam queer londes. Have you ever Chaucerised? Much of him would go lovely into Gaelic : not that I want it done. I'm thinking your French tour will be mighty good for your Irish and therefore for Ireland—a part of whom must read you and be modified by you. I hope you won't be thinking directly of Irish : put it away : let the French soak in ; that's your service to Ireland. Not that anyone in his senses wants to make French the Human Standard—but that French is the easy way to that *Europachas*,[1] to use your good word * * * *

A trait in nearly all Gaelic writers :—that their idea of what is in English impressive is just the thing which every good writer of English avoids like poison unless he means to be funny or, the same thing tother way round, to represent the funny speech of the half educated.

In other words, " Epic Struggle " [2] is just the sortathing no one but an orator at the Christian Draper's-assistants' Debating Society—Tea 6d.—would permit himself to use. It is—on a higher, no really a lower, level—the same as that most curious phenomenon of the Gaelic taste for English slang : i.e. just when the English lords are giving up a form of slang we adopt it, saying " This precisely is

[1] Irish, " Europeanism."

[2] A Gaelic writer had adorned his prose with a literal translation of this cliché.

what we need if Irish is to be quite too-too and really up to date and definitely the thing." " Epic struggle " was once an invention and a good one, a little triumph : when it is so soiled that no one would use it even for purposes I leave to your imagination, then we stick it on a stick and wave it in the air and ask the world to admire us—exactly like the negro chiefs, real or imaginary, who pick up, and wear as a crown, a European p— p— with a hole in it. * * * *

I don't greatly care for the idea of translating (modernising) old Irish stuff : probably I haven't thought enough about it to be right in saying even that much. But I have always been a huge admirer, passionate, of the wonderful phrasing of the Bards—there's a terseness and a *clash* about them that we sorely need in the literary Irish of to-day, which has no clash but is Melted Butter—that beastly ceól na cainte,[1] you know,—no surprise, but a baby flow of the déjà dit and toujours à dire. I reflect nearly every day as I read Irish that long ago (when Japan was a joke) I began a Freeman article " The little yellow men are rejoicing " ; and Brayden served it up " In view of the latest Reuter despatches from Tokyo referring to the celebrations inaugurating the new régime it would appear that the little yellow men etc." All the little sparkle and strangeness gone—all is melted butter—all squash and slob . . . as level and as greasy as a flow of milk on a satinwood table-top. Beasts. A boy here—quite incult, Stanley—does better. " I heard her head strike on the banisters " (ambulance men were carrying her from home to hospital) " and I was so-rry : and I heard the men say ' O she's dead ', and her mother screamed, and I was so-rry ". I wept when he told me this ; I never weep or thrill over anything in Irish—it would all be laid out so flat and prim, like a man explaining his joke before he makes it and while he's making it and when he has made it : you vomit. * * * *

S. M. K.

[1] " music of the common speech," a stock phrase in Gaelic League circles.

88

To GRACE TURNBULL

RESKADINNICK,
CAMBORNE,
CORNWALL, *August* '33.

DEAR LADY,—I find nothing whatever to suggest in the way of modification of your proposals.[1] As I have said a hundred times, I have utterly given up Plotinus : once you have Sir E. Debenham's permission you have all from this side ; the rest is your own judgement, taste, fancy.

You'll inevitably notice places where all my agony couldn't eliminate the signs of translation : if you, coming fresh to the matter, can clear away these foulnesses, it'd be a gain (always understanding that you explain in general terms what you're doing and clear me—of your guilt as of your merit.)

Regarding title, I like none of those suggested. Were I doing the thing I'd spend a few years searching for some not-ignoble equivalent of "The Gist of Plotinus"—something suggesting that you had Beefoed or Bovrilised Plotinus (do you have those bottled beeves in America ?).

Perhaps more attractive would be to postpone Plotinus ? "The Values of Life : Plotinus Beefoed." (By the way in subtitle I'd just as soon you didn't say "from the Greek"—sounds to me sort of amateurish, or like a man saying on his visiting card that he never steals the spoons : it would to me mean, really, that Plotinus didn't write in Greek but in Arabic or in Irish perhaps, and I had found it better to translate a translation.)

This is a very wandering letter : I'm just after a grave operation and still very weak and can't concentrate : I go to one point on which of course you'll exercise your freedom but perhaps not refuse to consider a point of view. It's this Intellectual Principle[2] business. Intellectual

[1] This American lady wished to make a popular anthology of passages from Plotinus in MacKenna's English version.

[2] The term by which MacKenna usually rendered Plotinus's νοῦς.

Principle is a horrid word ; but so to me would be Intellect or, still worse, Intelligence. But to my mind (and I quarrelled violently with Dean Inge and others on the point) " Divine Mind," while not ugly or mean, is an abominable falsification.

Plotinus sometimes (rarely) uses the words *ὁ θεῖος νοῦς* (literally Divine Mind), but never except where the " Divine " is a sort of compliment as if one, in Christian writing, spoke of " the Paternal God " or " the Adorable God," " the Loving God," and the like. Where there's no question of rapturous praise the word is *νοῦς* stark: *νοῦς* is the first knowable, at once Intelligent and Intelligible : it is Intelligible because it is the source and counterpart of the Human Intellect : to speak of " Divine Mind " does fatally falsely and sinfully, criminally, hangably, cover up this most essential doctrine, separating God and Man where Plotinus is precisely toiling like 10 devils to make them all but identical.

" Mind " (capitalised) if you will : but not " D. M." (unless you will).

" Spirit " Inge used : I think this even more hangable. The French can use " Esprit " because of the double sense of *esprit* : so the German " Geist " : the English " Spirit " brings in Holy Ghost associations, the last word —to me—in criminal falsification.

I believe—but vaguely—that if I were doing the whole thing again I'd labour over " *Mind* " stark and simple ; in fact without looking at Greek or English I can't imagine the difficulty or understand why I didn't plump for it.

Excuse me : I'm ill : I stop : if I think of anything else to say I'll write again—I'd like to know you get this.

All good wishes : respectfully

S. M. K.

I open to add—another incoherence—that I now remember the difficulty I had with stark " Mind " : the only related adjective is " mental," utterly unsuitable mostly: whereas "intellectual" had all the relations and implications.

Re Inge's "Spirit": my main objection was not that mentioned, but that Spirit conceals and misleads—conceals the teaching that the Good of Man is noetic, an affair of Intellectual Perception and Intellectual Act thereby; misleads, proportionately (and gravely), by implying "salvation" rather than "rectification" or "orientation"—a sort of dreamy merging, "Spirit with Spirit shall meet," rather than an active ratiocination in the first and most of the stages, though coming finally to a perception that somehow transcends even our highest philosophical verification of truth—the other word, "Spirit," seems to me to throw the door wide open to a whole system of belief and of action utterly contrary to all Plotinus means and wishes.

Perhaps I may ask you to add to your remarks re your changes that "the translator"—that's me—"wishes, for conscience' sake, to make it clear that he holds firmly to his translations of *νοῦς* and of *νοητά*": something like that: you'll find a neat way: essentially:—those that get Debenham's permission can do what they like with the stuff, but they must distinctly clear me on this one absolutely cardinal point.

Once more excuse my incoherence and slovenliness: I'm permanently tired, but also actually ill—convalescent, which nurses tell me is generally worse.

Once more good wishes,

S. M. K.

One more effort:—The Good—"salvation"—is attained by way of philosophy, not by way of sanctity, except in that sanctity, or rather morality, is the condition of sound philosophy and is also indicated by philosophic thinking as the only wise worthy way. This is to my mind separated by mountains and oceans and Milky Ways from all that is suggested by the Divine-Minders and Spiriters.

89

To GRACE TURNBULL

RESKADINNICK,
CAMBORNE,
CORNWALL,
[*about September*, 1933.]

A CHARA,—Perhaps out of contrariety, I'm not disposed to blaspheme " Essence of Plotinus." [1] It has the obvious disadvantage of using à propos of a philosopher a philosophic term in an unphilosophical sense. But it does say the thing : Plotinus potted for the Potty (Potty is English if not American for the less intelligent of the brethren): failing a better I'd say 'tis good. Should you write again and get no answer, the reason will be that I'm too ill or too dead : an operation a month ago has proven a failure and may be a prelude to a "Hence with Life's Pale Lure."

I don't like Intellectual as adjective of Mind since it isn't : it doesn't connect the two peremptorily. But you're free as long as I'm cleared.

You think too little of America or too highly of Europe : I suppose not one per million of Europeans has ever heard of Plotinus : people seem somehow to be able to live without him—just as there are who don't play the guitar or keep a Buddha in every room : " a queer world, my masters."

A blessing on your work.

S. M. K.

90

To MARGARET NUNN

RESKADINNICK,
CAMBORNE,
CORNWALL, *September*, 1933.

DEAR X.—A line—

I'm not writing because I'm ill again—operation a failure, a mistake—I'll not go under another but be tran-

[1] This was the title eventually adopted.

quilly ill either here or, if things worsen, at a nursing home.

I'd not like you to think I of malice failed to write.

All joy to you.

S. M. K.

91

To MARGARET NUNN

[*September*, 1933.]

Stephen MacKenna, Reskadinnick, Camborne, Cornwall, is very thankful for Miss Nunn's friendly note, hopes she's playing the guitar and otherwise doing well—Mr. MK. will write as soon as he'll be right enough : for the moment he's feeling and looking like the devil.

92

To VICTOR KRAMINSKY

RESKADINNICK,
CAMBORNE,
CORNWALL,
[*late Summer or Autumn*, 1933].

OGÁNAÍ UASAIL, DEAGH-CHROÍ,[1]—Aren't you the good soul—with all your concern and kindly offers ! But there's nothing to be done. If you saw me you'd say, cry, roar " fraud." I look quite young and lovely and suffer only intermittently ; but the deepseated trouble is there au fort intérieur, rongeing me beyond cure. An operation, which with three months' treatment in hospitals and nursing homes cost me exactly one year's income and much misery, has left me as I was : je me résigne and j'attends and that's all. Sometimes I can do more : a few miles on my pram to do my shopping and take the air. I learn to potter about my garden and orchard and to plan and make improvements in my pretty little house : I

[1] Irish, " Noble, goodhearted youth."

listen to curious things over Radio from London, Paris and Dublin : I read much Irish and a little French, and I write Irish with the idea, if I live and keep any courage and energy, of bringing out a slim vol. of essays—" I says "—which I think may be suggestive to my Betters in Irish Letters. I play the guitar—or with it—and love it and pity those that (1) don't know it or (2) having known it backslide (I have heard this incredibility : there are such : for this is a rum world, all sorts of rumosities lurking in it and popping out where one least expex um. Having preacht to others one may become a Castaway : have you noticed das selbe, mein lieber Freund ?).

Ni (however you spell it) chevo [1] is the final wisdom, and I'm fast becoming wise : in fact I nietchevo like anything and am not unhappy. Before I was quite resigned I said to the doctor " But Docky dear " says I " I can't work." He gave me devastating, out of the simple kindness of him, comfort : says he " Dearest of patients you have DONE your work." Devastating comfort : but after times and a time behold you it did comfort me. My work isn't much, but it stands done : now on milk and eggs and with music and Irish I can idle and wait, in peace of conscience.

I wish, only, that 2 people lived in some reasonable place—yourself and Jamesy—that I might see and hear you and with simple inefficiency play the guitar with yez.

Good soul you.

S. M. K.

All my homages to Madame and little Monsieur K. and, at your expense, one bonbon (but one very bon) to each.

93

To MARGARET NUNN

Dear Mr. MacKenna, Reskadinnick, Camborne, Cornwall, mid. Oct. '33, hopes dear Miss Nunn will understand

[1] Russ. *nichego* (pronounced " nietchevo "), " it doesn't matter."

and believe that he isn't in the least thinking to hurry worry scurry or blurry her but writes purely out of his beautiful character with no ulterior motive, simply desiring to wish her well out of her grecian misfortunes,[1] in fact to offer her merely his sympathy and to perhaps give her one moment's mild pleasure in the thought that she does be thought of even in places far from Harts Well Stoke on Trent which isn't for all its rather queer and possibly rather pretty name half so jolly a place as Reskadinnick where at the present moment the sun shines and the blue sky gleams with that Cornwall gleam of innocent delicacy not to be met in many other places in a world which holds many lovely things on soil and in sky tho' indeed he finds it hard to believe that manywhere else there is so much joyous beauty as he at this very hour, of a Sunday morning, gazes out upon from his little bed wherein he has to lie much, the only thing he's capable of, because all the science of all the doctors hasn't been able to put him right and he often wishes they had put him quite wrong on that great opportunity when they had him completely in hand with his poor wits away and he quite content to be away with them, or without them since they never did him much good but enchained him to a dreary labour for which they were really not competent, thus sapping his youthful vigour and bringing his greying hairs in sorrow or rather in fatigue to where grey hairs go, a thing of which no one is sure tho' lots of people talk as if they knew all about it which is why he preaches, to no congregation, his own discovery of the only true Tao which is Chinese for Path and the dear knows a clear Path is the main thing man wants here below or above whichever you like to call it, for as some sage said the Above is the Below and the Below is the Above and the Whence is the Whither, tho' he wasn't very clear as to where either the Whence or the Whither was so that in the long run it would seem that the best one can do is to have honestly,

[1] Miss Nunn had diphtheria.

and give generously, the best time one can with one eye open on the Infinities and Sublimities and another peering sidewise at one's guitar and another still on all the beauties of the wonderful world which one strives to make more lovely still by such harmless devices as landscaping one's garden and opening a large window in one's dark middle room and making one's kitchen like a Dutch picture by prettily setting forth one's crockery with a Lord Buddha peeping out here and there, lest at any spot within or without the eye should fail of that image of noble thoughtfulness and benevolence, the two most beautiful and valuable things in all this quaint and incomprehensible world which however unfathomable must be in the end destined to good, fashioned for and out of good, since all its framework, and much of its inside too, is of so miraculous a loveliness, friendly and one must think well-wishing just as dear Mr. MacKenna is to dear Miss Nunn and would like to think she is to he now and for ever more Amen.

S. M. K.

94

To OCTAVIAN MACKENNA

RESKADINNICK,
CAMBORNE,
CORNWALL, 3*rd Nov.* '33.

MY DEAR TAVE,—Will you kindly send a line to Bob to tell him, after absorbing it for yourself, that any time from about this day week all communication—papers etc.—will be suspended. Getting rapidly worse, I'm going to London for specialist treatment (not an operation : I'll never take another). How long I'll be away I don't know. If the treatment seems to promise results, perhaps a month or more : if not I'll come back and die cheaply here. The local surgeon, who operated unsuccessfully, says I might well live long ; but in increasing misery, of necessity : I'd greatly prefer the death for which I was quite prepared at the time of the operation. You, I suddenly remember, think that morbid : me, not : to me it's a simple matter of fact, of values. I've got to die sometime ; the little work I could by temperament and ability do, is done : I necessarily slide downwards, and I have more than begun to slide ; a short slide and easy charms me more than a long and painful : et voilà tout ! To me that's as simple, as non-morbid, a statement as that Health and Painlessness are better than Pains and Putridities—or that Deep Sleep is preferable to grinding at an uninteresting mill. Of course if I could have health and no money-worry and power to work—to complete a book in Irish I have been tinkering at : Horace's Satires I've been translating—then I'd be glad to live : if then I didn't, I'd call me morbid. As things are, I call me rational. (When no one else praises me, I play fair and praise myself.)

You notice I'm not saying any good-bye : I did before the operation I suppose—or praps I didn't, but wrote only after ? Anyhow I'm not " in danger " now, as I of course was then : I simply announce breach of communication, lest yous worry or wonder.

So all cordial good wishes to all

S. M. K.

95

To GRACE TURNBULL

RESKADINNICK,
CAMBORNE,
CORNWALL, ENGLAND,
Nov. '33 (I do date my letters).

DEAR LADY,—I wouldn't worry you again but that you are one of the millions who think I'm or ought to be the real S. M. K. : that has embittered all my life—not in any disrespect to the Real S. M., but simply because it's horribly inconvenient—to both of us.

If I were not on my deathbed I could write you an

amusing book on 30 years of this confusion—the Real S. M. accused of my indiscretions (I'm, or have been, publicly and to the sound of trumpets a mad and murderous Irish Republican and he lives among English Duchesses [1]). I and my wife once took a furnished flat in London which we didn't know he had just left, and I opened in all innocence love letters to him from Countesses and Queens : my wife once in Vienna nearly got deported as an immoral person for posing as the wife of " the writer " S. M., and he known not to be married, and so on—an infinite budget of funny inconveniences. He's a good fellow, and has always forgiven me in lovely letters when I have had to write him excusing myself for innocently spattering him with mud. But I'm not a good fellow, and don't forgive him : for he has two sins : first he's called S. M., and secondly he misspells our lovely and honourable name, degrading it to a Kaffir click—McK (! !), the noble Mac-ness and Enna-ness quite concealed—Mac in Irish meaning Son, and Enna being a very great Chieftain or Duke or Toff of some kind in Ireland 2000 (2 thous-and) years ago (the k is adventitious—to prevent the ignorant English calling us Masennas—Irish is an intelligent language and has no K : we are in Irish MacEnnas). All which doesn't matter, except that it infuriates me, this perpetual confusion. One of the joys of dying to me will be the end of that.

As for my death, the date isn't fixed yet : I'm leaving for London in a week to be specialised : local opinion is that I'm hopeless. I shall know in a month or so.

A blessing on you and your work

STIOFÁN MAC ENNA

(or STEPHEN MACKENNA or MACKENNA).

P.S. One more serious word : though I'm too ill to

[1] Mr. McKenna writes : " I do not live and have never lived among English duchesses. And I have never received love letters from countesses or queens ; this may be because my namesake had the good fortune to intercept them."

phrase my feeling with any discrimination : my conscience won't allow me to pass as a Plotinian : I loved the work (except for the awful strain of it) but I was never convinced by the philosophy or the ethic of it : I'm a secularist agnostic : I don't know anything about the Soul or the Divine or Immortality or anything of that order, and I do believe in this life : I hate those who hate the world : had I children I'd try to lead them to love beauty, nobility, even what I vaguely call Spirituality ; but I'd want them to get and give all the good of the world, all the honourable or not dishonourable pleasure of it—of course I'd want them to think and work out what is the real pleasure, what is the false, deceptive—but to *them*, to themselves, not by any law of Moses or Plotinus or Daddy Stephen MackEnna. Plotinus and all the Mystics and Gospels of all the creeds are to my mind valuable as corrective, as poetry, as suggestion, as windows opening on to vistas of the possible : as law, as dogma, *wicked*.

96

TO MARGARET NUNN

STN. MACKENNA,
RESKADINNICK,
CAMBORNE, CORNWALL,
Earlysh Nov. 33.

PEGGY NUNN,—Above's[1] delighted to hear you to be young and lovely again, the way you ought to be. He's not. Evil men with knives and scissors are going to be at him again between 23 and 30 November, which he doesn't like. * * * *

You give a ghastly picture of your place : I like my own better : it's improving slowly, but often I stop in mid toil and think how it'll soon be probably in other hands

[1] MacKenna habitually wrote his name as well as his address at the head of his letters.

and all my work undone—my winter garden turned into cabbages and spuds (and very nice too), my shelves and other little inside tricks all pulled away. One thing is a permanent addition to the liveinableness of the world, my gorgeous new window in that dark middle room securing light and a green vista, a green thought in a green shade. I'd like to live to the spring also to see will a new hedge I have raised and planted come out as it should. Also I'd like to play the guitar a little better if possible (you've heard of the guitar ?).

Well—Here's wishing you health and wealth and joy for evermore óm chroí amách.[1]

S. M. K.

97

To MARGARET NUNN

[RESKADINNICK,
Nov. 17, 1933.]

A thousand thanks : I think I'd recognise your friend at sight from your double portrait : but you didn't tell me where the original lives or how. Well, we can't help that now : since I go very soon to my unknown destination whither, as I hope and believe I told you, no letters will travel from here.

Here's a pretty thing : an old servant writes to me 3 times a year : in my last answer I warned her I might not answer her next, me going to be operated. To-day she writes again and wants to know, " Will you excuse me, you being a great gentleman and me a miserable maid " ; this is the preface to the fact that she has only been able to save £20 in her, I guess 50 years of, life : but operations and illnesses are very expensive, and she knows I never could manage money, and if it would be of any use she'd take it out and send it in English notes and no one would ever hear a word of it. Now isn't that lovely ? Shows you

[1] Irish, " from my heart."

there must be some good in me too, to inspire that splendid devotion : you'll excuse me mentioning it, but as people are apt to overlook my merits—sort of find it hard to uncover them—I feel it right to quote the evidence that they really are there.

If I come out young and lovely as you assure me you are, I'll of course write : if I don't I won't, but you'll know I wish you well if there's any wishing where I'll be.

So for the present at least goodbye X—

From your devoted friend

S.

98

To T. COBURN [1]

WARD 2,
ROYAL NORTHERN HOSPITAL,
HOLLOWAY ROAD,
LONDON, N. [? *December* 1933.]

DEAR MR. COBURN,—After one operation : a second is being continuously postponed—moon in wrong quarter, Saturn adverse, etc. This is only to wish you well and to ask you to let me know in time should any move of yours upset the present ideal arrangement by which I can wash my mind of all concern over my vacant shack and its mingled junk.

But do not on any account send me anything that may come, books, papers, crocks of gold, guitars or anything whatever. All papers, save the French Horrible which I hope you may read, should be burned as with fire, and all letters not obviously advertisement be kept in huge coffers for my return in the spring if so it be written in the stars. Many a dreary day and miserable night I have thought of the orchard, the birds, a spray of red rose berries against the blue Cornish sky. I hope you may sometimes have found pleasure in my grianan and the

[1] MacKenna's neighbour and landlord at Reskadinnick.

books not only there but all over the place. The Upper Chambers in their utter messiness have some buried treasure. I confess I'd like to know that Boy Arthur is doing well and my pretty baby Theodore and good Scout Stanley.

Not one moment of blue sky yet : sun sometimes, shining prettily on snow on roofs, but never once a gleam of blue : a red rose berry spray flung against a Cornish sky—that with health and wealth and virtue and a guitar and a few thousand books—what more does man want here below ?

Be good and happy

S. M. K.

99

To MARGARET NUNN

[ROYAL NORTHERN HOSPITAL,
March 3, 1934.]

DEAR PEGGY,—I cannot resist : tho' I meant to see no one, not never no more. But you mustn't bring me anything whatever : I abhor grapes, am worried by flowers, can't read magazines.

I'm greatly touched by your goodness, Peggy. Probably you could come any hour, simply arranging things over telephone with the Sister—you know the ropes.

But
Regular Visiting Fixtures :
Sunday 2–3½.
Tuesd. and Frid. 5–6.

I wept when I got you—

S. M. K.

What a howling swell of an address you have acquired—go vfoiri dia orainn.[1]

[1] Irish, " God save us."

INDEX

[All numerals refer to pages]

9 781597 313186

Made in United States
North Haven, CT
01 July 2022